Applied Motor Learning in Physical Education and Sports

"*Applied Motor Learning in Physical Education and Sports* provides valuable information about integrating sport science principles to practice for teaching and learning motor skills. I believe that physical educators, coaches, and practitioners can largely benefit from this applied book that is rarely found in the market. I highly recommend this book to any professionals who learn or teach motor skills. You will find this book informative and valuable with an easy-to-understand approach to effectively illustrate motor learning concepts. As my consultant, Dr. Wang's approaches, I find, are very effective and useful in motor skill training."

–*Anson Dorrance, Head Women's Varsity Soccer Coach at the University of North Carolina, 22-Time National Champions; former U.S. Women's National Soccer Coach (1986-1994), 1991 Women's World Champions*

"Dr. Wang provided effective psychological and technical consultations to me and helped me eliminate competitive anxiety and keep concentrated for achieving the Olympic gold medal at the 2006 Winter Olympic Games in Italy. I am truly thankful for Dr. Wang's consultations. Dr. Wang's new applied motor learning book will help coaches and athletes understand the important scientific principles related to sport skill training."

–*Han Xiao Peng, Chinese Free-Style Skiing Aero-Jump Olympic Athlete who won the Olympic gold medal at the 2006 Winter Olympic Games in Italy*

"This is the book coaches and PE teachers have been waiting for. Dr. Wang, a former elite soccer player and coach, and Dr. Chen show coaches how to take motor learning principles and integrate them into their practice sessions. In their treatment of skill learning, the authors not only show coaches how to break motor skills down into their component parts but they also demonstrate how to enhance learning by taking skills from practice sessions and putting them into actual competition. *Applied Motor Learning* is a welcomed addition to the motor learning literature because of its theoretical and practical orientations. It is a new approach to the study of one of the most important aspects of teaching/coaching."

–*William F. Straub, PhD, FACSM, Certified Sport Psychology Consultant for Association of Applied Sport Psychology; former professor, dean, and professional athlete and coach*

"The information compiled by Dr. Wang and Dr. Chen is extremely valuable. As a physical educator, I especially enjoyed the concepts of the application of practice in various settings and how that can be transferred to the game or competition setting. *Applied Motor Learning* is easy to follow and enjoyable to read. I highly recommend this for those looking to maximize the efficiency of practice to game transfer."

–*R. David Worrall, Elementary Physical Educator, Former GAHPERD State President, and former GAHPERD Elementary Physical Education Teacher of the Year*

Applied Motor Learning in Physical Education and Sports

Jin Wang, PhD
Kennesaw State University

Shihui Chen, PhD, CAPE
Hong Kong Institute of Education

FiT Publishing
A DIVISION OF THE INTERNATIONAL CENTER FOR PERFORMANCE EXCELLENCE

262 Coliseum, WVU-CPASS
PO Box 6116
Morgantown, WV 26506-6116

Library of Congress Card Catalog Number: 2014930875

ISBN: 978-1-935412-52-6

Cover Design: 40 West Studios
Cover Photo: Dreamstime.com
Typesetter: 40 West Studios
Production Editor: Rachel Tibbs
Copyeditor: Mark Slider
Proofreader: Geoffrey Fuller
Indexer: Geoffrey Fuller
Printed by: Data Reproductions Corp.

10 9 8 7 6 5 4 3 2 1

FiT Publishing
A Division of the International Center for Performance Excellence
West Virginia University
262 Coliseum, WVU-CPASS
PO Box 6116
Morgantown, WV 26506-6116

800.477.4348 (toll free)
304.293.6888 (phone)
304.293.6658 (fax)
Email: fitcustomerservice@mail.wvu.edu
Website: www.fitpublishing.com

Contents

Preface

Motor learning is an academic discipline of kinesiology involving scientific principles of learning human motor skills. The scope of motor learning is broad and includes physical education, exercise science, physical therapy, occupational therapy, sports skill training, military training, and any professions that require the engagement of human movements or human motor skills. Motor learning is also the study of how the human brain works together with the muscular system to achieve coordinated movements. Because open and tangible analysis of the complex human brain is not possible, we commonly rely on the use of motor learning models through experimental studies to validate theoretical hypotheses to determine how learning occurs in a learner's brain. Motor learning concepts in general are abstract, theoretical, and dry in nature. Without effective practical examples to illustrate the theoretical concepts, student learning could be compromised. This is why many undergraduate students find understanding motor learning concepts, and applying the learned knowledge to real-life situations, to be a significant challenge. The applied knowledge of motor learning is very essential because it contributes to students' success in their future education and coaching professions.

The major strength of this applied motor learning book is that it is designed to make a strong bridge between theory and practice. All theories and concepts introduced in this book connect to real-life situations in various related professions. Each chapter includes the following components: (1) an introduction to the imperative theoretical models of motor learning; (2) case studies and life examples to illustrate the learned theoretical concepts that can be effectively applied to practical teaching, coaching, or motor learning settings; (3) project topics that give students opportunities to integrate theory with practice; and (4) clear illustrations, diagrams, and key components of concepts depicting the main ideas. This straightforward and easy-to-understand writing format allows students to effectively grasp the theoretical concepts of motor learning. We hope that our new book, *Applied Motor Learning in Physical Education and Sports,* becomes a great resource for undergraduate students, PE teachers, coaches, athletes, and practitioners who can apply the learned knowledge to physical education, sports, and movement-related professions.

Basic Concepts of Applied Motor Learning and Performance

OBJECTIVES

- Define motor learning and its relationship to other related disciplines
- Define motor control, motor development, motor behaviors, and motor performance
- Understand how learned motor learning principles can be applied to various professions such as physical education, exercise and sports science, sports coaching, physical therapy, the military, police and special forces, ballet and other dance forms, recreational activities, etc.
- Understand the importance of using new technology or training methods for the enhancement of the motor learning process
- Understand the factors contributing to motor learning performance
- Understand the importance of research methods and know the nature of experimental and descriptive research methods
- Understand the characteristics of this applied motor learning and performance textbook
- Understand some of the important terminology used in research

INTRODUCTION

At the 2012 London Olympic Games, Ms. Gabby Douglas won an individual all-around Olympic gold medal, Michael Jordon, a basketball legend, enthralls us with his skills, and Bruce Lee's lightning-quick actions knocking down multiple opponents within a second (Picture 1, 2, and 3) have stunned the sports world. How can these athletes perform such fascinating movements so flawlessly? What kinds of learning processes brought these athletes to such levels? Is any human being capable of performing such incredible movements with the proper training?

From a motor learning perspective, the majority of human movements are learned skills (Enoka, 2009; Payne & Isaacs, 2008). The human body has a total of about 656 skeletal muscles and these muscles must be coordinated with each other to produce designated movements. All human actions or movements are the result of a neuromuscular integrated brain and body controlled process (Voight, Hoogenboom & Preventice, 2007). In other words, the nervous and skeletal muscle systems work together to perform the designated and coordinated human movements. According to Lundy-Ekman (2007) and Bear, Connors, and Paradiso (1996), there are billions of nerve cells coordinated and working together from various regions of the human brain. Certainly, it is a tremendous challenge for a novice to learn the fundamental motor skills required to eventually become an elite athlete who can execute extraordinary coordinated movements precisely and perfectly. When performing certain motor skills such as those required for football, gymnastics, free-style aerial skiing, ultimate fighting, martial arts, combat sports, etc., any slight deviation from the planned movements can result either in failure to perform the designated motor skills successfully or in injury, possibly fatal. Without proper training, it is almost impossible for any human being to engage

in those coordinated movements. For example, kicking a ball, throwing a rock, or shooting a basketball are considered to be easy motor tasks to execute. But, without learning, children cannot even perform these simple motor tasks properly. Consequently, motor learning is essential for the majority of human movements, especially for many movement-related professions.

Motor learning refers to the relatively permanent gains in motor skill capability associated with practice or experience (Schimidt & Lee, 2005). Motor learning is an essential subject for many different professions. Especially, students who major in physical education/kinesiology, exercise or sports science, coaching education, physical therapy or the pedagogy of movement, as well as people in the military, the police and special forces, etc. should have a concrete understanding of the proper motor learning processes related to particular motor skills. In sum, *motor learning* is a multifaceted set of internal processes that effect relatively permanent change in human performance through practice, provided the change of motor skills cannot be attributed to a human's maturation, temporary state, or instinct (Kluka, 1999). In other words, the main objective of motor learning is to make a permanent change in the neurological functions which happen in the brain (see Figure 1.1).

In our society, people attempt to learn many different motor skills for a variety of purposes. Some skills are very complex and difficult to perform while others are easily learned. Sport scientists are always searching for the most effective training approaches to help learners efficiently master the required motor skills in the minimal time. The following are the five characteristics of the motor learning process (Figure 1.2; Schmidt & Wrisberg, 2008).

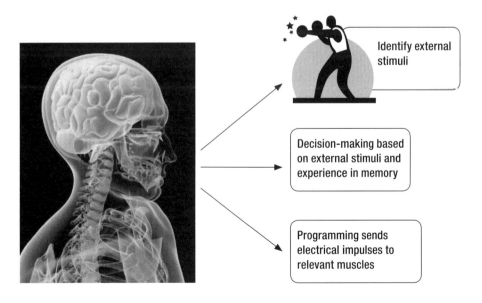

FIGURE 1.1. Brain's three stages of information processing in responding to the above attack.

1) Motor learning is an internal process that cannot be observed from an external perspective. This means that how much an athlete has learned is an unknown factor from an outsider's perspective because motor learning takes place inside the learner's brain and the muscular movements are only a reflection of brain activities. Observing motor performance provides only an indirect assessment of the learning progress of a learner.

2) Motor learning is a set of processes for the purpose of reaching specific learning objectives. Obviously, different types of learning will produce different results and sports scientists continuously search for the best motor learning processes for particular motor skills based on individual differences.

3) The goal of motor learning is to form the designated motor behavioral habits through proper training.

4) Once a motor skill is learned, it becomes relatively permanent and will not be easily forgotten. For example, once an individual has learned how to ride a bike, he/she will never forget how to do it (Schmidt & Wrisberg, 2008).

5) According to Wang & Yang (2012), motor learning is not value free and it can be negative to form a bad habit that is extremely hard to be changed once it is formed.

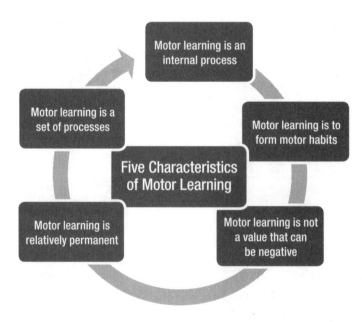

FIGURE 1.2. Five characteristics of motor learning.

From the perspective of the discipline of kinesiology, several other academic disciplines are related to motor learning, namely motor behavior, motor control, motor development, and motor performance. At the graduate level, kinesiology departments usually offer these courses separately, even though these disciplines are interrelated. However, at the undergraduate level, many schools only offer motor learning and motor development. To provide a comprehensive understanding of motor learning and its related disciplines, an introduction to the concepts of the various disciplines has been described as follows.

Motor behavior can be considered the study of executed human performances and postures that are the result of integrated internal process that lead to a relatively permanent change in performance (Figure 1.3; Kluka, 1999).

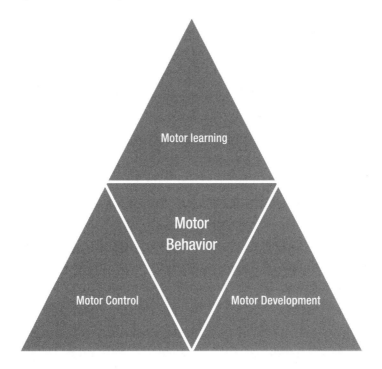

FIGURE 1.3. Motor behavior's relationship with the related subjects.

Motor control is the study of postures and movements and the mechanisms that underlie them (Rose & Christina, 2006). Also, motor control can be defined as the study of how an individual can execute designated motor skills through the neuromuscular control process in response to external environmental demands (Haywood & Getchell, 2009; Latash & Lestienne, 2006). For example, a race car driver's brain activities include quickly processing external information (seeing the opponents' cars) to find an open space through which to get ahead of the others and achieve success. Specifically, motor control deals with issues such as information processing, attention and interferences, the mechanism of

TABLE 1.1. Three components of motor control areas of human movements

Motor Control

Neuromuscular control mechanism of responding to external stimuli	Neuromuscular mechanism of decision-making in advance for taking actions	Unconscious control mechanism for controlling reflex movements

muscular coordination, sensory contributions to motor performance, and production of movements through neuromuscular systems (Table 1.1).

In sum, if researchers could understand the control mechanisms of the human brain for producing coordinated muscular movements, a motor learning process could be scientifically designed according to the characteristics of the neuromuscular control systems. For example, the neuromuscular control mechanism of high jumping is quite different from that of boxing because the action of high jumping can be planned in advance, while a boxer's action must rely on immediate external stimuli (opponent's actions). Needless to say, the advanced planning and consistency of movement control should be the high jumper's main concern in training; conversely, for boxing, speed, timing, and accuracy of response to an opponent's attack should be emphasized in training. More specifically, extero- and proprio-sensory information recognition, speed of decision-making, and programming of an action should be carefully examined to achieve the designated goals of boxing. Hence, motor control mechanisms for high jumping and boxing are vastly different. The human brain is a control center for carrying out movements and motor control studies how the brain controls coordinated movements in response to varied external environmental demands.

Motor development refers to the continuous, age-related process of change in movement, as well as the interacting constraints (or factors) in the individual, environment, and task that drive these changes (Haywood & Getchell, 2009). From a comprehensive perspective, motor development not only deals with the growth and developmental process of human movements, it also studies how the learning process affects the developmental process. Specifically, such study addresses both the process of change and the resultant movement outcome. With a complete understanding of the normal growth and developmental process as it relates to the motor learning process, teachers and practitioners can teach motor skills effectively to populations ranging from preschoolers to older adults.

Motor performance is an end result or outcome of executing a motor skill that can be observed from an external perspective. For example, coaches can see how a tennis player actually plays a game and how he/she performs during practice or competition. A tennis player's motor skills for performing a forehand or backhand stroke or for serving can be purposefully observed or assessed by instructors. Practically speaking, since motor

TABLE 1.2. Three components contribute to motor performance

Factor Contribute to Motor Performance

Learner's Characteristics (age, gender, experience, cognitive ability, genetic traits, psychological characteristics, etc.	Instructor's Competence (sports science background, athletic experience, knowledge of sport, administration and communication skill, human relation skills, etc.)	Learning Environment and Conditions (Undistractive learning environment, facility and equipment, sports field and settings, organization of training)

learning takes place in an internal fashion in a learner's brain, one of the effective ways for an instructor to understand how much a student has learned is to observe his/her performance, which indirectly reflects the student's learning progress (Table 1.2.). In addition, other approaches such as asking students to explain the proper motor skill structures or to distinguish between correct or incorrect motor skill demonstrations can be used to test the extent of their understanding of motor skill concepts.

APPLICATIONS OF MOTOR LEARNING TO RELATED PROFESSIONS

Motor learning is a subject with broad implications from which people teaching in many fields can benefit, ranging from the elementary school to the Olympic level, from recreational sports to the military, from non-competitive to combat institutions, from individual to team sports, etc. The emphasis in teaching can be quite varied and is based on the purpose of the motor learning, the particular motor skills required, and the needs of the learners. For example, at the elementary school level youngsters are taught basic motor skills such as kicking, throwing, jumping, running, catching, or climbing and these learned skills can then be transferred to various sports-related movements in the future. At the Olympic level, the purpose of motor learning is to achieve peak performance in competition. The following sections illustrate certain professions in which motor learning is an essential component.

In the area of physical education, from elementary school to the college level, students learn the different motor skills of various sports to keep fit, have fun, and develop a healthy lifestyle (NASPE, 2004). Learning proper motor skills is one of the most important objectives of physical education programs in school settings. With limited time available for physical education classes, teachers would be wise to teach students the proper motor skills for exercise and sports. According to Harter's perceived competence motivation theory (Harter, 1978; Harter, 1981), when an individual perceives himself/herself to be good at doing something, his/her motivation to engage in this activity is enhanced as well. The more successful the students are at mastering motor skills, the more likely they are to keep

COURTESY OF BIGSTOCKPHOTO.COM

playing sports as their life-long leisure activities. In other words, the effective teaching of motor skills to students in school settings will directly impact their future lifestyles and exercise habits. Thus, school physical education teachers should understand motor learning principles in order to teach students the correct motor skills.

With a thorough knowledge of motor learning, exercise and sports science professionals can effectively help their clients design training programs that incorporate the ideal movement activities required for the particular situation. One of the major responsibilities of these specialists is to engage the athletes, who play different sports, in strength and conditioning training; with an understanding of motor learning principles, they can properly design appropriate training programs for these athletes.

Likewise, an understanding of particular motor skills in relation to fitness benefits enables exercise science practitioners to design training programs that are enjoyable and help clients achieve their personal training goals. Participants in certain sports, such as football, soccer, ice hockey, boxing, martial arts, gymnastics, etc., are vulnerable to injuries. Using their knowledge of the structure of various motor skills, sports scientists can effectively advise these athletes on ways to avoid injury. In so many practical settings, exercise programs have direct correlations with the particular sports skill training chosen. Therefore, it would be very advantageous for exercise science specialists to know the motor learning principles for their teaching or consultation activities.

In the coaching arena, one of the major responsibilities of coaches is to enhance athletes' technical skills since their performance is mainly determined by these skills, along with their physical ability and psychological well-being. Athletes' technical abilities play a crucial role in whether they win or lose in competitions. Not only should a coach teach proper technical skills, he/she should also be continuously developing creative new training methods to give the athletes an extra advantage in competition. This is because today's superior technical routines could be out of date in a few years. History has repeatedly shown that the human limits of performance of motor skills are constantly being surpassed. For example, today's gymnastic routines could have been perceived to be impossible to execute in the past. Likewise, the 10 seconds of 100-meter race records have been repeatedly broken in the recent Olympic Games. Due to the efforts of sports scientists and coaches, the level of technical training is now so far ahead that motor skills which once seemed impossible to learn have now become attainable. These accomplishments can, in part, be attributed to the advancement of our knowledge in the area of motor learning and its relationship to human movement potentials. Motor skill learning in the coaching arena has always been one of the most important factors of training for achieving peak performance in competition.

When injuries occur, physical therapists assist patients to recover through the appropriate rehabilitation processes. By assessing whether patients are capable of performing certain movements or motor skills, they are able to determine the most effective treatment methods. Sports injuries are sometimes unavoidable; millions of athletes from amateurs to professionals are injured while participating in sports activities. For many athletes, a speedy recovery from an injury is crucial for regaining their physical condition, maintaining skill routines, regaining self-confidence, and achieving peak performance. Hence physical therapists' knowledge of motor learning plays a vital role in enabling them to properly evaluate the degree of injury, design rehabilitation strategies, and assess the recovery progress. Based on their evaluation, they can provide accurate recommendations as to whether an athlete is capable of resuming certain technical training after an injury. When physical therapists understand the structures of the various motor skills and potential volatile factors related to the injury, they can develop effective treatment strategies to aid their patients' recovery and provide them with valuable advice on how to avoid injuries in the future with the correct movements.

Motor learning principles can be also used widely in military settings because soldiers must engage in combat with the enemy, either with bare bands or weapons, under severe or critical conditions; many times, any slight delay in their actions in battle could cost them their lives. Thus, soldiers' efficient, forceful, and timely reaction to the enemy's attacks and their swift fighting abilities play a significant role not only in winning battles but also in saving their lives. Military, special forces and ground soldiers, as well as police officers, are required to learn various motor skills to carry out their job responsibilities. With knowledge of motor learning principles, the professionals who train them can purposefully develop appropriate training regimes to fit the needs of their job requirements.

Ballet and other forms of dance involve artistic, beautiful, and swift kinematic movements that usually take years to perfect. In fact, many dancing movements are very difficult to learn and master. Dancing instructors should learn human anatomy and motor learning concepts in order to understand the relationship between a dancer's anatomical capability and the performance of these movements. By using scientific principles, dancers can speed up their learning progress, especially for difficult and challenging movements that require perfect coordination among different dancers, split-second timing of the jumps and turns, and excellent body kinematics of the movements. Since dancing movements are considered to be process-oriented motor skills, dancers are unable to observe their own movements during practice or performance so they must rely on their instructors' accurate feedback to find out how well they are progressing. Without this external feedback, learning cannot occur. Consequently, if the instructor cannot grasp the key structures of certain motor skill routines, learning progress will be significantly compromised. Dancing instructors should understand more clearly the critical components of dancing routines and properly teach the skill transitions accordingly. In fact, dancing is great exercise for youngsters and adults; many people truly enjoy dancing for pleasure, competition, or exercise.

> **Kinematic movement – refers to a technique, body posture, movement pattern, process of movement, or structure of movement, which can be only evaluated by subjective approaches.**

In addition to the aforementioned professionals, many amateur athletes regularly engage in different recreational sports or other physical activities in their spare time and they also would like to learn motor skills to enhance their enjoyment or for self-improvement and competition. Besides that, many of these amateur athletes serve as club coaches teaching sports skills to children, training them to improve their skills, and running competitions. In fact, there are thousands of sports clubs or sport organizations around the world providing opportunities for people of all ages (from the very young to older adults) to actively participate in sports activities. Having the necessary motor learning knowledge would be very beneficial for these athletes and coaches. The range of professions that involve motor skill related activities is much broader than we could possibly cover here.

UNDERSTANDING BASIC SCIENTIFIC METHODS IN THE MOTOR LEARNING PROCESS

Practitioners regularly have to face challenges and solve practical problems they may experience. Generally speaking, they gain their knowledge either through scientific approaches or from real-life experiences through trial and error approaches (Weinberg & Gould, 2011). Any knowledge they gain based on their experience must be validated through scientific methods and then the knowledge gained can become theory. If this knowledge is not validated through scientific methods, it is called empirical knowledge. The advantages of the empirical approach for gaining knowledge are that it is convenient, flexible, and case-oriented. The disadvantages are that the results may be biased, invalid, or unreliable.

Traditionally, sport scientists prefer to use reliable and consistent ways of finding relationships among different variables to gain knowledge and develop theories that describe, explain, and predict the phenomena. These scientific approaches reveal more objective, reliable, and valid research findings (Gay, Mills, & Airasian, 2011; Schloss & Smith, 1999). However, the disadvantages of using scientific methods are that the research is often lab-related and perhaps is difficult to apply to real-life situations, and that it is difficult to control so many variables. In addition, scientific research takes longer, costs more, and involves more people.

In the recent decades countless motor learning and control research studies have been conducted, including basic and applied research according to the purposes of the studies. Research studies require strict control of the different variables in order to increase their validity and reliability (Kothari, 2008). In reality, the more variables a researcher controls for the studies, the more difficult it is to make a bridge between theory and practice. In fact, motor learning researchers have validated many scientific phenomena and found the relationships among different variables, but often the research findings cannot be easily applied to practical settings due to gaps between the theory and the practice. Making connections between theory and practice requires professionals who have both practical and theoretical experience and thus can interpret research data and then integrate research findings with practical uses. A merger between theory and practice in the areas of motor learning and control should be advocated in our professions. Thus, the following section briefly introduces some useful research methods that can be applied to motor learning areas.

RESEARCH METHODS

Two types of research studies are commonly conducted, one of which is *basic research,* of which the goal is solely for the purpose of theory development and refinement (Gay, Mills, & Airasian, 2011). The objective of this type of research may not necessarily be to solve practical problems in the real world and instead, most closely resembles the laboratory conditions associated with scientific research. The second type is *applied research* that studies or solves specific real-life problems. In the area of motor learning and performance, sport scientists, students, and the various practitioners would from time to time like to run research studies to investigate certain phenomena that are of interest to them. To accomplish these goals, they must understand the research methods in order to conduct studies purposefully and scientifically, otherwise the research findings may not have the required validity or reliability. *Validity* means that the experiment really measures what it is supposed to measure; if we intend to measure height, we don't want a test that measures temperature. *Reliability* refers to the extent to which, when measuring the same variable(s), a test can be repeated and give consistent results. In addition, practitioners need a basic scientific background in order to comprehend what they read in sport science journals so that they can apply the concepts to their daily training or practice. Having a basic knowledge of research methods is also a necessary step for students to be able to efficiently read textbooks, science journals, newspapers, or any sport science related materials. Since scientific terminology is generally specialized, dry and abstract, understanding these materials can be very challenging without proper training.

> **Basic Research**
>
> **The purpose of basic research is to enrich knowledge, discover new phenomena, and develop new theories.**

> **Applied Research**
>
> **The purpose of applied research is to study or solve specific real-life problems.**

There are many different ways of conducting research studies depending on the topic, but in this short section we introduce just two basic research methods that are widely used in the areas of motor learning and performance: (1) experimental research, and (2) descriptive research. It would require taking several courses to develop a thorough understanding of these two research methods and become competent to undertake research studies properly and accurately. We therefore only provide a brief description of the basic elements of these research methods.

Experimental Research

The purpose of an *experimental study* is to find a relationship between cause and effect (Gay, Mills, & Airasian, 2011). Cause refers to the reason for the changes, and the effect is the result of the causes. For example, a basketball coach may be interested in knowing the effect of mental imagery on basketball free-shooting performance. The intent of this type of study is to reveal the *cause-effect relationship* of how mental imagery affects basketball free-shooting performance. If mental imagery training (cause) enhances the free-shooting performance (effect) of learning, the practitioner can claim that mental imagery has a positive relationship to free-shooting performance, or vice versa.

Conversely, a basketball coach may try to investigate the relationship between college players' GPA scores (independent variable) and players' athletic performance (dependent variable). This type of study is called a *correlation study* and it reveals whether there is a relationship between the independent and dependent variables; such a research finding only indicates a correlation, not necessarily a cause-effect relationship. Clearly, the main characteristic of the experimental study is to reveal causal relationship(s) between independent and dependent variables; one is the cause and the other is the effect. The descriptive study looks for a correlation between two or more variables, but such relationships are not necessarily cause-effect relationships.

In the motor learning process, instructors can conduct experimental studies to find the cause-effect relationship between two or more factors to accomplish training objectives. For example, a soccer coach could investigate whether different air pressures of the soccer ball affect the progress of soccer skill learning for a particular group of soccer learners. If more pressure in the ball helps kids learn dribbling skills more effectively, a positive cause-effect relationship has been found between the pressure of the ball and dribbling performance. Based on such a research finding, soccer instructors can use high-pressured balls to develop learners' dribbling skills more effectively. Similarly, a basketball coach might manipulate the ball-possession time before passing as a variable to find out whether there is a relationship between ball-possession time and performance of players. If the studies show that in practice players perform more effectively with a shorter ball-possession time before passing, then a positive cause-effect relationship has been established between ball-possession time before passing and performance. As a result, a basketball coach can manipulate the ball-possession time before passing as an essential variable for speeding up the pace of practice or scrimmage to achieve peak performance in competition. During the process of motor learning, instructors can manipulate many different independent variables (different training approaches) to reveal consequences (dependent variables, outcome of training or competition) found. Practitioners should think creatively when developing new training approaches or testing existing methods to see if the training approaches they design produce effective learning outcomes. In sum, the purpose of the experimental study is to reveal cause-effect relationships between independent and dependent variables.

> ## Experimental Research
>
> **is to find the relationship between cause and effect.**

To conduct a valid and reliable experimental research study, the researcher must select participants carefully because the method used in this kind of study is to compare two or more groups of participants and investigation must be well controlled, based on the nature of the study (Ross & Morrison, 2004). For example, control and experimental groups must be *compatible,* with similar characteristics such as age, experience, skill level, gender, type of sport they play, etc. The control of experimental conditions is vital for determining whether the results of the studies have the required validity and reliability. For instance, if an instructor is interested in finding out if a new training method has effective outcomes for basketball dribbling skills, he or she needs a control group that practices using the traditional dribbling training method and an experimental group that practices using the new method. However, if a different coach was assigned to train each group and the result revealed that the group with a new training method outperformed the control group during training, such a positive finding in favor of the new training method could not be attributed to that method because it could have been caused by the different coaches' competence levels. Thus, because of the lack of control (i.e., two independent variables: different coaches and different training methods), the researchers would be unable to verify which factors contribute to the learning outcomes and hence the validity and reliability of the research is compromised.

To accurately compare the outcome when testing two groups, the participants must be compatible. The size of the group is also an important variable to control, based on the study. If the sample size is too small, the result cannot represent a large population; if the sample size is too large, the power is too large, so the significant difference of the study could be hardly revealed.

Descriptive Research

Descriptive study involves collecting data in order to test hypotheses or answer questions concerning the current status of the subject of the study (Gay, 2009). A typical of descriptive study is a correlational study which is to determine whether or not a relationship exists between two or more quantifiable variables. The purpose of such a study is to find correlations between independent and dependent variables without manipulating any of the variables. The relationships found in such a study are not necessarily cause-effect relationships; instead they just indicate that a correlation has been established between the variables. For example, an ice-hockey coach might want to find out whether there is a relationship in the progress of learning between participants' body weight and puck handling speed, which is a crucial skill for competition. So the coach divides 90 players into three groups as follows: (1) the heaviest players; (2) the players with intermediate body weight; and (3) the players with the lowest body weight. If, after six months of training, the players with the lowest body weight demonstrate the most effective puck handling speed, the coach has found a correlation between the participants' body weight and puck handling speed for this particular population. This is not, however, a cause-effect relationship, as it only indicates a correlation between participants' body weight and learning outcome for puck handling speed.

Obviously, the coach cannot draw a conclusion that the superior learning progress of the lowest body weight group was caused purely by the lower body weight of the participants. This is because many other factors could contribute to the learning progress for that group. The concepts of correlation and causal relationship are similar in certain perspectives, but in terms of revealing the reason why something happens, they are quite different.

> **Descriptive Research**
>
> **is to find correlations between independent and dependent variables without manipulating any of the variables.**

Practitioners can conduct research studies in practical settings to help teachers and coaches accomplish their designated goals of training. The above topics are examples of some studies on motor learning and performance that can be conducted or are being undertaken by researchers or practitioners.

The above examples provide readers with a glimpse of research topics and they can use these as a reference to choose topics of research for accomplishing their goals of training. In sum, sound research methods can eliminate biases and objectively find correlations or cause-effect relationships which could help practitioners improve the effectiveness of their teaching of motor skills.

- Find the relationship between the amount of instruction by coaches during training and players' satisfaction with the training.
- Which training approaches can reduce reaction time for elite athletes?
- How can an instructor help novice learners quickly establish proper cognitive images of accurate motor skills?
- Which training approaches can help athletes minimize their fear of executing difficult movement routines for certain sports?
- Which training approaches are the best to develop soccer players' dribbling skills?
- Do male and female athletes learn motor skills with similar progress? If not, what factors account for the difference?
- What types of instructions produce optimal performance for novice learners?
- Does ball size affect baseball batters' learning progress?
- Does ball size affect children's ability to learn soccer motor skills?
- Does an over-sized and lighter ball promote soccer juggling learning progress?
- What are the differences in learning styles between male and female athletes?

- How does body weight affect youngsters' learning of motor skills?

- How does anxiety affect youngsters' learning of motor skills?

- How does intrinsic motivation affect young athletes' learning of motor skills?

In addition, in order to give readers a better understanding of scientific methods, a list of terms commonly used in research described as follows. It would be extremely beneficial for students and practitioners to become familiar with these terms before reading this textbook or conducting any applied research studies in the future.

KEY TERMS TO REMEMBER

- *Motor learning* refers to the relatively permanent gains in motor skill capability associated with practice or experience (Schmidt & Lee, 2005).

- *Motor control* is the study of postures and movements and the mechanisms that underlie them (Rose & Christina, 2006).

- *Motor behavior* refers to the study of motor learning, motor control, and motor development.

- *Motor development* refers to the continuous, age-related process of change in movement, as well as the interacting constraints in the individual, environment, and task that drive these changes (Haywood & Getchell, 2009).

- *Motor performance* is an end result or outcome of executing a motor skill.

- *Independent variable* is the cause of the change being studied and can be manipulated in order to see the result of the study.

- *Dependent variable* is the result of the study caused by the independent variable.

- *Validity* refers to whether the experiment really measures what it is supposed to measure.

- *Reliability* refers to the extent to which, when measuring the same variable(s), a test can be repeated and give consistent results.

- *Control group* refers to a group in an experimental study that is not being manipulated and serves as a standard for comparison against a group that is being manipulated.

- *Experimental group* is the group that is being manipulated by being exposed to an independent variable as the cause of the change.

- *Correlation* is the relationship(s) between two or more variables.

- *Causal relationship* is the relationship that reflects the cause (independent variable) and effect (dependent variable).

- *Experimental study* is to find the causal relationship by manipulating an independent variable to see the change of the dependent variable.

- *Descriptive study* is to find correlations between independent and dependent variables which may not be cause-effect relationships.

- *Participants* are the people who participate in the study.

- *T-test* is a statistical test, which reveals if there is(are) significant relationship(s) between two or more variables.

- *One Way ANOVA* is statistical comparison(s) between two or more groups with only one independent variable.

- *Two Way ANOVA* is statistical comparison(s) between two or more groups with at least two or more independent variables.

- *Linear relationship* indicates a strong correlation either in a positive or negative way with a linear pattern.

- *Sample size* refers to the number of participants who are involved in the research study.

STUDENT ASSIGNMENTS FOR CONNECTING THEORY TO PRACTICE

- Distinguish the concepts of motor learning, motor development, motor control, and motor performance.

- Each student conducts a Web search to find one or two new technologies used for motor skill training and explains why these new technologies can enhance learning progress of motor skills.

- Interview a coach, teacher, or practitioner to find out the key elements of effective ways of teaching motor skills as well as the major challenges of teaching.

- Interview a successful coach to reveal how he/she gained coaching knowledge (from his/her previous coaches, books, school, or others).

- Write a narrative of your own experience of learning motor skills. Explain your rewarding and challenging aspects of the motor learning process in the past.

- Compare the job responsibilities of physical education teachers at the pre-school, elementary school, middle & high school, and college & university levels.

- Elaborate on your goals for the future career you would like to pursue.

- Describe the major differences between descriptive and experimental study.

- Design a study comparing two different training methods to see which one is more effective. Please integrate the above research method information to design your study.

- Visit a high school or college to observe how coaches run practice to engage in motor skill training.

- Visit a high school or college to observe how physical education teachers engage in teaching activities.

REFERENCES

Bear, M. F., Connors, B. W., & Paradiso, M. A. (1996). *Neuroscience: Exploring the brain*. Philadelphia, PA: Lippincott Williams & Williams.

Enoka, R. (2009). *Neuromechanics of human movement*. Champiagn, IL: Human Kinetics.

Gay, L. R., Mills, G. E., and Airasian, P. W. (2011). *Educational research: Competency for analysis & application*. Columbus, OH: Charles E. Merrill Publishing Co.

Harter, S. (1978). Effectance motivation reconsidered: Toward a developmental model. *Human Development, 21,* 34–64.

Harter, S. (1981). A model of intrinsic mastery motivation in children: Individual differences and developmental change. In A. Collins (Ed.), *Minnesota symposium on child psychology* (pp. 215–255). Hulsdale, NJ: Eribaum.

Haywood, K. M., & Getchell, N. (2009). *Life span motor development*. Champaign, IL: Human Kinetics.

Kluka, D. A. (1999). *Motor behavior from learning to performance*. Englewood, CO: Morton Publishing Company.

Kothari C. R. (2008). *Research methodology: Methods and techniques* (2nd ed.). New Delhi, India: New Age International.

Latash, M. L., & Lestienne, F. (2006). *Motor control and learning*. Boston, MA: Springer Science+Business Media, Inc.

Lundy-Ekman, L. (2007). *Neuroscience: Fundamentals for rehabilitation*. St. Louis, MO: Saunders Elsevier.

NASPE. (2004). National physical education standards. Retrieved from http://wheresmype.org/downloads/NASPE%20Standards%202004.pdf

Payne, V. G., & Isaacs, L. D. (2008). *Human motor development*. Boston, MA: McGraw-Hill.

Rose, D. J., & Christina, R. W. (2006). *A multilevel approach to the study of motor control and learning*. San Francisco, CA: Pearson Benjamin Cummings.

Ross, S. M., & Morrison, G. R. (2004). Experimental research methods. In D. H. Jonassen (Ed.), *Handbook of research on educational communications and technology* (2nd ed.; pp. 1021–1044). Hillsdale, NJ: Lawrence Erlbaum Associates.

Schloss, P. J., & Smith, M. A. (1999). *Conducting research*. Columbus, OH: Merrill.

Schmidt, R., & Lee, T. (2005). *Motor control and learning: A behavioral emphasis* (3rd ed.). Champaign, IL: Human Kinetics.

Schmidt, R. A., & Wrisberg, C. A. (2008). *Motor learning and performance: A situation-based learning approach* (4th ed.). Champion, IL: Human Kinetics.

Voight, M. L., Hoogenboom, B. J., & Preventice, W. E. (2007). *Musculoskeletal interventions techniques for therapeutic exercise*. Dubuque, IA: McGraw-Hill Company.

Wang, J. (2012). Connecting theory to practice: Effective ways of teaching motor learning course for undergraduate physical education students. *International Journal of Physical Education, Fitness and Sports, 1,* 1-13.

Wang, J., & Yang, G. B. (2013). *Transfer of learning: Key component of effective sport skill training*. Presented at AAHPERD Convention, Charlotte, NC.

Wenberg, R. S., & Gould, G. (2011). *Foundations of sport and exercise psychology*. Champiagn, IL: Human Kinetics.

Classifications of Motor Skills in Relation to the Motor Skill Learning Process

OBJECTIVES

- Understand the rationale for classifying motor skills into different categories based on the characteristics of each category
- Understand the nature and characteristics of open motor skills and closed motor skills of one-dimensional classification
- Understand the training implication for open motor skills and closed motor skill development
- Understand the nature and characteristics of muscular or cognitive oriented motor skills of one-dimensional classification
- Understand the training implication for muscular or cognitive oriented motor skill development
- Understand the nature and characteristics of cognitive and muscular combined motor skills
- Understand the training implication for cognitive and muscular combined motor skills
- Understand the nature and characteristics of discrete, series, and continuous motor skills of one-dimensional classification

- Understand the training implication for discrete, series, and continuous motor skills
- Understand the nature and characteristics of process and outcome oriented motor skills of one-dimensional classification
- Understand the training implication for process and outcome oriented motor skills
- Understand Gentile's taxonomy of two-dimensional motor skill classification and its implications for practitioners
- Understand alternative classifications of motor skills based on different perspectives
- Understand learners' required physical talents in relation to skill classifications
- Understand the motor skill learning process based on individual differences

INTRODUCTION

Motor performance is determined by many different factors such as learners' physical talent, motor skills, genetic make-up, psychological well-being, etc. Among these factors, motor skill is a critical element contributing to motor performance so coaches and practitioners spend a great deal of time trying to help athletes or students to develop their skills to achieve success in competition. To help learners reach the designated goals of learning, practitioners should devise structured training programs based on the characteristics of the particular motor skills and on the learners' individual differences. To this end, motor learning experts have classified motor skills according to their common characteristics and their unique structures (Magill, 2011; Schmidt & Lee, 2005; Schmidt & Wrisberg, 2008). The classification of motor skills provides practitioners with useful guidelines for designing motor skill training. In addition, the skill classification approach helps learners pay attention to the key elements of the learning processes to maximize their learning progress. Clearly, people have varying motivations for learning motor skills, but whatever the reasons, the skills should be taught as effectively as possible.

Since the 1960s, motor skills have been divided into various categories based on different perspectives. The two main classifications are the *one-dimensional classification of motor skills* in which skill is based on a single perspective to classify motor skills into various orientations, and the *two-dimensional classification of motor skills* in which the skills are based on two distinctive perspectives (Edwards, 2010; Magill, 2011). These two major classifications are described below.

ONE-DIMENSIONAL CLASSIFICATIONS OF MOTOR SKILLS

The first classification of motor skills was undertaken by Knapp (1963) who divided them into open and closed motor skills. According to Knapp (1963), motor skills are executed under two different types of environmental conditions: open motor skills are performed under unpredictable conditions and closed motor skills are performed under stable and unchanging conditions. This classification is solely based on the predictability of the environment. Due to their abstract nature, the terms open and closed are somewhat confusing for many practitioners, so Wang (2009) renamed them as reaction-time based and non-reaction-time based motor skills, respectively.

Open Motor Skills (Reaction-time Based Motor Skills)

Reaction-time (RT) based motor skills are those skills whose execution relies on unpredictable external stimuli and in which reaction time (RT) plays a significant role. RT-based motor skills are required in, among others, sports such as soccer, basketball, football, hockey, team handball, etc. The athletes' actions depend on immediate external unpredictable stimuli (where opponents are, where teammates are, where the ball is coming from, where there is open space, etc.) For example, athletes involved in combat sports must respond to unpredictable external stimuli because they cannot plan their actions in advance. Thus, RT is a critical factor in determining success when executing these kinds of motor skills. RT-based motor skills also require athletes to be able to move fast so that they can act quickly in fast-paced competition (Wang, 2009).

The classification of motor skills provides practitioners with necessary information on the fundamental structure and characteristics of particular motor skill categories so that the appropriate training can be applied to the learning process for maximizing learning outcomes. Before teaching RT-based motor skills, practitioners should understand the criteria for effective execution of these types of motor skills. The following four criteria should be used to measure the efficiency of RT-based motor skills: (1) perform motor skills with maximum consistency; (2) utilize the least energy expenditure to execute an action; and (3) complete a motor skill within a minimal time (Guthrie, 1952); (4) use the smallest space to complete and action (See Figure 2.1). Even though many different

COURTESY OF BIGSTOCKPHOTO.COM

Fighting for the ball is an RT-based skill.

Characteristics of Reaction-Time Based Motor Skills

- Quick Reaction Time
- Pay attention to external stimuli
- Quick Movement time
- Quick decision-making ability

types of RT-based motor skills are performed in different sports or movement settings such as basketball, volleyball, soccer, tennis, ice hockey, team handball, martial arts, or combat fighting, the above four criteria should be used to serve as universal standards or expectations for developing effective RT-based motor skills. These four criteria represent the core elements for successfully executing RT-based motor skills under unpredictable environments in competitive situations (Figure 2.1).

Training Emphasis for Open Motor Skills (RT-based Motor Skills)

Once the criteria for mastering RT-based motor skills have been identified, the next step is to determine how to achieve the objectives of training in order to maximize performance of the skills. Even though practitioners could use so many different approaches to design training for accomplishing a variety of objectives of training, to effectively develop learners' RT-based motor skills, the critical components must be captured and emphasized in order to maximize training outcomes efficiently. Based on the results of successful empirical experiments in motor skill training, practitioners should emphasize the following five pivotal aspects of training: (1) reduce learners' RT when responding to external stimuli under unpredictable conditions. Any delayed reaction to external stimuli will result in failure to reach the external environmental demands (Roitman & Shadlen, 2002); (2) develop learners' explosive ability to meet the demands of sudden changes of acceleration and deceleration of movements in competitive environments; (3) develop learners' transition

FIGURE 2.1. The criteria of evaluating efficient RT-based motor skills.

skills from one action to another by developing the skills for suddenly changing direction or speed within a minimal transition time (Wang, 2013). A smooth and minimal transition time should be one of the focal points of training; (4) maximize learners' adaptive skills to effectively respond to an ever-changing variety of unpredictable external stimuli (unpredictable game situations). Many times athletes have to act from off-balanced positions so they should develop their adaptability to as many difficult situations as possible to fit unpredictable environment demands; and (5) learners should be also encouraged to practice as many offensive skills as possible in order to lengthen their opponents' RT. The more offensive moves a learner can make, the longer the reaction time a defender requires (Wang, 2009) (Table 2.1).

TABLE 2.1. Training emphasis for RT-based motor skills

1	2	3	4	5
Reduce learner's RT in responding to external, unpredictable stimuli.	Develop learner's explosive ability to suddenly speed up.	Develop learner's transition skills for overcoming inertia to suddenly change speed and direction.	Develop learner's adaptive skills to encounter varied and unpredictable stimuli.	Learner should master a variety of offensive skills to increase unpredictability of attacks.

Practitioners should incorporate the above five key principles of training when developing their own training methods to accomplish the training objectives and maximize the outcome for those learning RT- based motor skills. In reality, there are many different methods of training, some of which are more effective than others, so practitioners should be creative and innovative to purposefully design the training approaches that best meet their own particular objectives. Training methods will not be covered in this chapter as practitioners are responsible for establishing their own programs for their particular needs.

Closed Motor Skills (Non-reaction-time Based Motor Skills)

Non-reaction-time (NRT) based motor skills are those skills which are executed under stable and unchanging environmental conditions where no response to external stimuli is required. These motor skills include, but are not limited to, high jumping, long jumping, shot put, javelin, diving, gymnastics, figure-skating, free-style skiing, tumbling, or rifle-shooting at a static target. The major characteristics of NRT-based motor skills are as follows: (1) learners can make decisions regarding the movement routines in advance before taking an action since competition conditions are predictable; that is, they do not need to respond to unpredictable external stimuli; (2) the structures of the motor skills are exactly the same during any competitions; and (3) the competition condition is stable and there are no defenders with whom to compete.

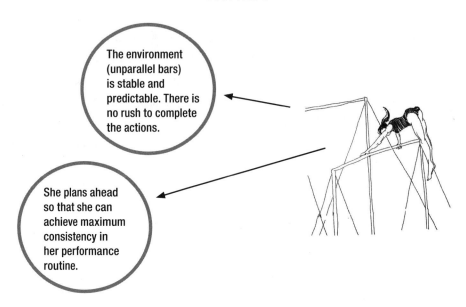

The environment (unparallel bars) is stable and predictable. There is no rush to complete the actions.

She plans ahead so that she can achieve maximum consistency in her performance routine.

FIGURE 2.2. The criteria of evaluating efficient NRT-based motor skills.

Characteristics of NRT-based Motor Skills

- **Advanced decision making**
- **Performing motor skills in a predictable environment**
- **Conditions of practice and competition are the same**
- **No requirements for making adjustments to motor skills in competition**

Training Emphasis for NRT-based Motor Skills

Obviously, the training emphasis for NRT-based motor skills should be vastly different from that for RT-based motor skills. The following are the critical aspects of training for NRT-based motor skills: (1) develop the learner's maximum consistency of performing motor skills under stable and unchanging conditions. For example, a long jumper needs to develop consistent movement patterns for the approach steps, take-off action, airborne style, and landing position in practice or competition (Taylor & Beith, 2010); (2) biomechanical principles should be applied to training for achieving maximum distance, fastest speed, perfect kinematics, etc. From the motor learning perspective, there are three distinctive goals in the performance of NRT-based motor skills: (a) achieve a maximum horizontal distance as in long jumping, disc-throwing, javelin, hammer-throwing, etc.,

(b) achieve a maximum vertical distance as in high jumping, vertical jumping, pole vaulting, etc., or (c) achieve pre-determined artistic and kinematic movements as in gymnastic routines, free-style aerial skiing, figure skating, etc. Each of the above varied motor skill categories requires the specific training principles to accomplish the objectives of learning. To achieve these goals, biomechanical principles should be explicitly implemented during the motor learning process. Ultimately, one of the major principles of training is to follow biomechanical laws to achieve training purposes. Practitioners should have a comprehensive understanding of how and which biomechanical principles impact on specific technical routines; (3) develop learners' ability to plan every technical detail in advance before an action is taken since the environment of skill executions can be clearly predicted. With advanced planning, athletes can develop the optimum physical strength and conditioning and mental preparedness to perform the technical routines perfectly; and (4) learners should know which major muscle groups are involved in the particular NRT-based motor skills so that specific training can be provided to develop muscular strength or power for performing these motor skills effectively (Table 2.2).

TABLE 2.2. Four components contribute to NRT-based motor performance

1	2	3	4
Develop maximum consistency performing skills	Properly apply biomechanical principles to specific motor skills	Make proper decisions in advance for the specific details of performing motor skills	Develop proper muscular sensations for executing motor skills effectively

Even though NRT-based motor skills are performed under stable and unchanging conditions, practitioners should not assume that these types of motor skills are easier to learn than RT-based motor skills. For example, hitting a golf ball to a designated place could be superficially perceived by some people as an easy task to accomplish, but, in reality, many golfers spend their lifetime practicing this skill with regrettable outcomes. Furthermore, not every athlete is capable of executing free-style aerial skiing routines even after years of training by the best Olympic coach because the athlete might not have the right genetic ability to swiftly master these types of motor skills. Therefore, the level of difficulty of performing certain motor skills should not be judged based on whether they are RT- or NRT-based skills since each of these two classifications has its own unique characteristics.

RT-based Motor Skills Under Predictable External Environments
Since RT and NRT based motor skills are performed under two extremely opposite situations, training focuses for both motor skills are truly different. However, there is another

category of motor skills that falls in between these two motor skills. Such a skill is referred to as an *RT-based motor skill under predictable environments,* which is the motor skill performed under predictable, stable, and unchanged environments, but requires performers to have very fast RT to successfully execute these motor skills. Any delay of reacting to these stable and predictable environments will fail to successfully complete the action. For example, the downhill mountain skiing, mountain biking, and mountain motor-biking are the examples of this set of motor skills performed under stable and predictable environments, but the athlete requires exceptionally fast RT in order to quickly make adjustments of his/her body to keep proper balance for completing skills successfully. This is because the shape, slope, and surface of the mountain are quite varied from place to place and without timely reaction to varied mountain environments and keeping a good balance of moving body parts, the athlete will easily fall down. Thus, although these motor skills are performed under stable and predictable environments, an athlete's RT becomes one of the major technical requirements of training for successfully performing this set of motor skills.

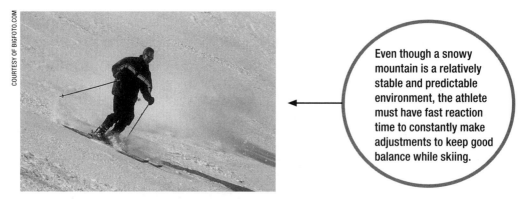

COURTESY OF BIGFOTO.COM

Even though a snowy mountain is a relatively stable and predictable environment, the athlete must have fast reaction time to constantly make adjustments to keep good balance while skiing.

FIGURE 2.3. Downhill skiing is the RT-based motor skill under predictable environment.

Classification based on muscular or cognitive orientation

The second classification of one-dimensional motor skills, introduced by Schmidt & Wrisberg, (2008), is related to how much muscular or cognitive effort an individual needs to exert to complete a particular motor skill.

Muscular-oriented Motor Skills

Motor skills that require a great deal of muscular exertion, such as weightlifting, high jumping, long jumping, gymnastics, and short distance racing, are referred to as *muscular-oriented motor skills* because the learners mainly use muscular movements to complete the actions, with only limited cognitive decision-making being required. Weightlifting is a typical example of a muscular oriented motor skill in which muscular effort is maximized and cognitive exertion minimized during the lifting process. The goal of weightlifting is simply to lift the maximum weight without requiring extensive cognitive decision-making or choice of actions.

> ## Characteristics of Muscular-oriented Motor Skills
>
> - **Muscular movement is maximized and cognitive effort is minimized**
> - **Usually large muscle groups are involved in these activities**
> - **Muscular strength, endurance, or power is fully utilized to carry out the actions**

Cognitive-oriented Motor Skills

Conversely, playing chess and race-car driving are considered to be more *cognitive-oriented motor skills*. Maximum cognitive effort and minimal muscular exertion are required during the performance of the motor skills for cognitive-oriented motor skills. With this type of skill, the cognitive process, rather than muscular movements, plays a crucial role in learning to accomplish the desired objectives.

> ## Characteristics of Cognitive-oriented Motor Skills
>
> - **Cognitive effort is maximized and muscular movement is minimized**
> - **Small muscular movements are involved in these activities**
> - **There are high cognitive demands when carrying out these motor skills**

Combination of Cognitive- and Muscular-oriented Motor Skills

Obviously, the above examples are the extremes that fall at opposite ends of the motor skill continuum. In practice many motor skills fall somewhere between these two extremes requiring the learners to exert both muscular and cognitive efforts almost equally to accomplish the performance goals (Moran, 2004). These motor skills include, but are not limited to, the sports skills of volleyball, soccer, basketball, tennis, ice hockey, team handball, and baseball. To successfully perform these types of motor skills, the cognitive process is as important as the muscular efforts (Figure 2.3). In reality there are many more motor skills that require a combination of cognitive and muscular exertions than purely one or the other.

FIGURE 2.3. Tennis skills are cognitive and muscular combined motor skills.

Training Emphasis for Both Cognitive- and Motor-oriented Skills

As already mentioned, the majority of motor skills require both cognitive decision-making and muscular-oriented skills. For example, to perform basketball skills, an athlete must decide where, when, and to whom he/she should pass a ball for the best play, or when, from where, and how he/she should shoot the ball for scoring. To perform these types of motor skills, not only does an athlete require muscular talents, but also he/she needs to have superb cognitive abilities to accomplish the goals of play. To successfully perform these types of motor skills, learners should develop their cognitive ability in six areas: (1) understand the nature of the motor skill used in competitive contexts, for example, how a particular motor skill is correctly integrated into strategies of play in order to fully use their strengths against the opponents' weaknesses; (2) understand the rules of competition and know how these rules can be used to their benefit, for example, in soccer, how to use the offside rule to gain advantages of play; (3) understand how to execute game strategies by using the learned motor skills that can be effectively used to fit the dynamics, trend, and flow of competition development even though such cognitive ability takes time to be developed; (4) understand self-protection strategies by using this motor skill while competing in contact sports since the aggressive behavior of opponents is almost unavoidable from time to time; (5) understand how to effectively use the learned motor skills to collaborate with teammates in competition; coordination among team players is a crucial element of teamwork; and (6) understand where, how, and when to effectively use the appropriate motor skills for the best outcomes. In sum, if the training only focuses on athletes' physical or technical skills and ignores cognitive development, the excellent skills learned may not be best utilized in competitive or required settings. The aforementioned six principles are the key components that should be emphasized in training for developing learners' cognitive ability.

Obviously, for training cognitive and muscular combined motor skills, development of learners' muscular aspects of athletic ability should be a vital component of the training regimen, since the brain only makes decisions that must be carried out by all the actions by muscle groups served as effectors. To achieve the expected outcomes of performing cognitive and muscular combined motor skills, the functions of muscular capability must be well developed to fit the specific environmental demands and requirements. The following training principles should be heavily emphasized: (1) develop learners' muscular power with maximum explosive ability since acceleration is a critical and fundamental ability for executing cognitive and muscular combined motor skills; (2) develop muscular strength as a foundation for enhancing muscular power since there is a linear relationship between muscular strength and power; (3) develop muscular endurance so that learners can sustain the activity over a long period for many sports such as basketball, soccer, ice hockey, tennis, etc; (4) understand how to efficiently use breathing to maximize the potential of muscular functions since the required energy supply systems largely rely on sufficient oxygen to synthesize ATP to muscles (Kilding, Brown, & McConnell, 2010). Proper breathing techniques can play a positive role of strengthening muscle functions; and (5) understand the ways in which to relax muscles, and know the relationship between mental effort and muscular exertion (Figure 2.5). Since motor skills are performed in many different situations, the above recommendations provide general guidelines for properly training muscle functions for a variety of settings. Ultimately, practitioners must design proper training based on particular learners, specific motor skills, and environmental demands.

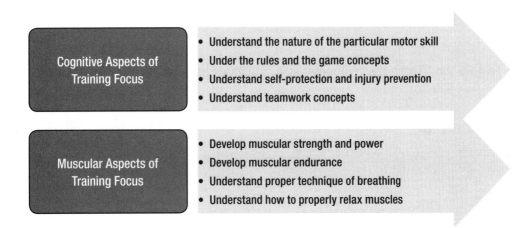

FIGURE 2.5. Training emphasis of cognitive- and muscular-oriented motor skills.

Classification Based on Task Orientations

The next one-dimensional classification of motor skills is based on task orientation and refers to discrete, series, and continuous motor skills (Magill, 2011). A *discrete motor skill* is a skill whose execution has a definite beginning and a definite ending. Motor skills of this type only require a very brief time to execute and include such skills as volleyball spiking, a soccer penalty shot, diving, disc throwing, javelin-throwing, high jumping, or long jumping. The *series skill* incorporates various discrete skills that are strung together; examples are floor movements, parallel or single bar routines in gymnastics, figure skating routines, diving, and pole-vaulting. The characteristics of series motor skills are: (1) the skills require a longer time to complete than discrete skills; (2) the components of a skill routine are distinctive from each other; and (3) there are various transitions from one discrete skill to another. The *continuous motor skill* has no definite beginning or ending and the process of performing it is continuous (Figure 2.4.). Examples of this type of skill are running, swimming, and riding a bicycle. The purpose of dividing these motor skills into different categories is to help coaches, teachers, and practitioners to understand their structures and characteristics in relation to the particular tasks. Once the unique structures of various motor skills are understood, appropriate and specific training can be implemented for maximum improvement of motor skill learning.

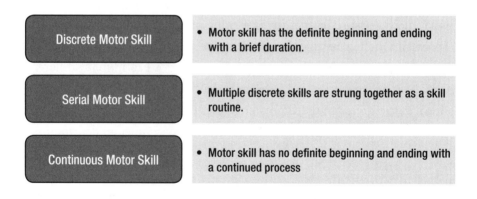

FIGURE 2.4. Three types of motor skill categories based on the task orientation.

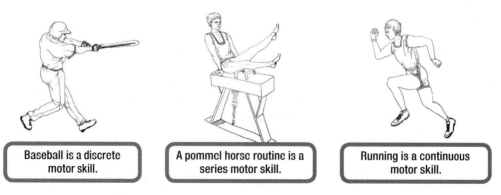

Baseball is a discrete motor skill.

A pommel horse routine is a series motor skill.

Running is a continuous motor skill.

Training Emphasis for Discrete Motor Skills

As already mentioned, discrete motor skills have a definite beginning and ending and are completed within a very brief time. Thus, muscular endurance need not be stressed; instead athletes should have a clear understanding of which key elements contribute to the success of performing the particular skill, and how they can effectively develop the ability to improve their skill level. For example, the discrete skill of baseball batting takes only half a second to complete, but many important elements should be taught for the correct implementation of the skill, such as: (a) choose a bat with the most suitable weight; (b) lengthen the radius of gyration during impact; and (c) increase angular velocity. These key elements need to be manipulated well to maximize baseball hitting performance. Yet, even though discrete motor skills are performed within a limited time, the different components of the skill should be smoothly transited to complete an entire action. Illustration 20 depicts the essential elements of performing discrete motor skills.

> **The Essential Elements of Performing Discrete Motor Skills**
>
> - **Understand the key components of discrete motor skills**
> - **Use part-practice to learn more difficult elements of the skill**
> - **Pay attention to the transitions of the skill process**
> - **Use proper demonstrations to illustrate accurate techniques**

Training Emphasis for Series Motor Skills

Since series motor skills are strung together by various discrete motor skills, the complexity and transition of this type of skill are far more challenging to learn. Many series motor skills take years and years to master. Thus, the capturing the key components of the particular skill structures for training becomes a crucial step to develop learners' ability of performing this type of motor skills. The following five pivotal areas of training for series motor skills should be emphasized, as follows:

1) Since a series motor skill routine comprises many discrete skills strung together, coaches or teachers should use part-practice to work on one section of a skill routine before transiting to the next discrete skill. Practicing all the components of the series motor skill together will result in distressing consequences due to the complexity and length of series skill structures.

2) Develop a comprehensive understanding of the relationships between the adjacent discrete skills of a series motor skill to develop proper training strategies based on the characteristics of discrete skills. For example, in a gymnastic vertical jump, a good approach run is crucial for gaining sufficient airtime after a jump to allow a learner to execute multiple summersaults, tilts, or rotates in the air before landing. Without sufficient height and airborne time after a jump, the learner has insufficient time to execute the required skill before landing. Thus, a thorough understanding of the relationship between approach running and vertical jumping, suitable training strategies for the two discrete skills, can be well developed.

3) Sufficient training and practice time should be allocated for the more difficult elements of certain discrete skills so that they can be perfected and eventually be incorporated into the complete routine. Once the more difficult discrete skills are mastered, the easier ones can be learned relatively quickly.

4) Emphasize development of swift transition techniques between two adjacent discrete skills. For example, in gymnastics, a proper landing technique of gymnastic floor movement routines has a ripple effect on the next discrete skill; the proper landing learned should be beneficial to the next discrete skill.

5) Since a series motor skill takes a relatively long time to complete, the athlete needs sufficient endurance to maintain the quality of the performance throughout the whole routine.

Training Emphasis for Continuous Motor Skills

Running, swimming, cycling, ice skating, or other repetitive types of motor skills are classified as continuous motor skills (Schmidt & Wrisberg, 2008). Some of these motor skills require speed and others might need endurance. Based on the different objectives of the continuous motor skill requirements, coaches and teachers should focus on not only biomechanical aspects of training, but, physiological training should be emphasized as well. Athletes should have a good grounding in proper breathing techniques, pacing, and psychological and energy-saving strategies to successfully perform continuous motor skills.

Classification Based on Process- or Outcome-oriented Motor Skills

Process-oriented Motor Skills

The last one-dimensional classification of motor skills is based on process- or outcome-oriented perspectives. The performance of *process-oriented motor skills* is based on performers' kinematics of skill executions and formats of body movements, such as angle of joints, speed of action, position of arms, trajectory of a jump, and position and posture of landing instead of relying on objective measurable outcomes. There are many motor skills that are considered to be process-oriented motor skills such as diving, gymnastics, figure skating, free-style skiing, tumbling, and synchronized swimming (Figure 2.6). The performance of these types of motor skills can be only evaluated from the referees' subjective perspective based on the criteria of body kinematics (Morrow, Jackson, Disch, & Mood, 2011). In other words, the performance of process-oriented motor skills cannot be objectively measured, and no instruments can be used to judge the level of the performance. Needless to say, this subjective evaluation process gives rise to differences among the judgments of the various referees and sometimes biased decisions occur. Taking an average score from multiple referees to make a final judgment is a common procedure in order to reduce referees' errors or biases when evaluating motor performance.

She is unable to see her own action during her performance.

Her performance requires her to be airborne off the single bar.

FIGURE 2.6. Gymnastic single-bar routine is a process-oriented motor skill.

Outcome-oriented Motor Skills

In contrast to process-oriented motor skills, the performance of *outcome-oriented motor skills* can be objectively judged based on the end results which can be measured by either instruments or scores. High jumping, long jumping, swimming, cycling, short and long distance races or car race, etc. are considered to be outcome-oriented motor skills because the performances of these motor skills can be objectively judged based on time, score, height, or distance.

Obviously, practitioners should design training programs that are appropriate to the characteristics of the motor skill and based on whether it is classified as a process- or outcome-oriented motor skill, to develop learners' technical abilities and help them to accomplish their goals. For example, if a coach is teaching diving skills, his/her main responsibility is to work on the learner's techniques, processes, posture, or kinematics of motor movements since these movement features are regarded as the criteria for judgment of motor performance in competition. Conversely, a high jumper needs to maximize his vertical distance of jumping because this is the sole criterion for measuring motor performance of high jumping. The different types of motor skills require varied coaching strategies and

FIGURE 2.7. High jumping represents an outcome-oriented skill.

methods. Hence, such motor skill classifications can greatly help coaches, teachers, and practitioners to understand what they should focus on for the specific motor skill training. The athlete's performance is based on referees' average score of their subjective judgments.

Training Emphasis for Process-oriented Motor Skills

As has been mentioned, process-oriented motor skills are those motor skills that rely on referees' subjective judgments for assessing athletes' kinematic or technical abilities rather than on the end results of performing. When executing these types of motor skills, athletes are unable to observe their own actions or skill routines. Thus to develop process-oriented motor skills, five training principles should be stressed, as follows: (1) practitioners should provide effective instructions or feedback to the learners to correct inaccurate mechanisms of the motor skill execution before and/or after an action. As this external instruction from practitioners is the only way learners can improve their motor skills through such an approach, and thus the quality of instructors' or coaches' tutelage ultimately determines the level of performance of process-oriented motor skills; (2) even though training should focus on the correct kinematics or format of learners' actions, it may also be necessary to train for speed, height, or distance of jumping, as these are often critical factors for successfully performing process-oriented motor skills. For example, to execute the multiple air-rotations or summersault actions required in gymnastic floor exercises, the athlete must jump with enough vertical distance to allow sufficient airborne time to complete these difficult high-level skill executions; (3) the teaching of process-oriented motor skills should be a gradual process from the simple to the complex because many of these skills, such as gymnastics, figure skating, and free-style aerial skiing, are extremely difficult to perform. Not only are they difficult to perform, but in addition, the skill routines consist of many complex discrete motor skills strung together with incredibly challenging transitions from one to another. Progressing too quickly when developing motor skills of this type could lead to injuries; (4) since the learners cannot observe themselves during the process of executing the motor skills, visual tools such as video-clips, movie, and live-demonstrations should be fully utilized to compare the correct and incorrect elements of skill executions in order that brain images of the accurate kinematic movements can be established (Wang & Griffin, 1998); and (5) mental imagery training should be incorporated to formalize and deepen the blueprints of brain memories of the kinematic patterns of the motor skills (Toga & Mazziotta, 2000). In sum, without the instructors' appropriate feedback and external instructions, learners will be unable to learn process-oriented motor skills.

Training Emphasis for Process-oriented Motor Skills

- **Provide effective external feedback**
- **Make progress with a gradual process**
- **Fully utilize visual tools to strengthen motor program**
- **Use mental imagery training**

Training Emphasis for Outcome-oriented Motor Skills

Of course, many motor skills are classified as outcome-oriented motor skills, as performance can be objectively evaluated either by instruments or win/loss records. Since there is a wide range of diverse outcome-oriented motor skills, it is difficult to identify the shared principles of training for these types of motor skills. Thus, to design proper training programs, practitioners must understand the key characteristics of the particular skill in order to match the training elements with the required criteria of peak performance. Any variables that can contribute to maximizing outcome should be incorporated. Innovative training programs are an essential part of the learning process.

TABLE 2.3. Classifications of motor skills

One-dimensional Classifications of Motor Skills

1. Classification based on environmental predictability

   (a) Reaction-time based motor skills. Examples: Soccer, basketball, tennis, ice hockey, boxing, wrestling, etc.

   (b) Non-reaction-time based motor skills. Examples: High jump, long jump, weight lifting, gymnastics, diving, etc.

2. Classification based on cognitive- or muscular-oriented motor skills

   (a) Cognitive maximized and muscular minimized motor skills. Examples: Car-racing, playing chess, shooting, etc.

TABLE 2.3. Classifications of motor skills (continued)

> (b) Muscular maximized and cognitive minimized motor skills. Examples: Weight lifting, high jump, long jump, running, swimming, javelin, etc.
>
> (c) Both cognitive and muscular combined motor skills. Examples: Soccer, basketball, volleyball, ice hockey, football, tennis, boxing, etc.
>
> 3. Classification based on task orientation
>
> (a) Discrete motor skills. Examples: Baseball batting, volleyball spiking, tennis serve, soccer penalty shot, etc.
>
> (b) Serial motor skills. Examples: Gymnastics routines, diving, pole vault, cheerleading, free-style skiing, etc.
>
> (c) Continuous motor skills. Examples: Running, swimming, cycling, etc.
>
> 4. Classification based on process- and outcome-oriented motor skills
>
> (a) Process-oriented motor skills. Examples: Diving, gymnastics, freestyle skiing, aerojumping, etc.
>
> (b) Outcome-oriented motor skills. Examples: Basketball, soccer, volleyball, track & field, swimming, tennis, baseball, football, etc.

TWO-DIMENSIONAL CLASSIFICATIONS OF MOTOR SKILLS

Following on from the one-dimensional classifications of motor skills just discussed, in the next section we will look at two-dimensional classifications of motor skills (Gentile, 2000). The first dimension is the action function which refers to body transport and object manipulation. Body transport means whether or not an individual is moving his/her body from one position to another during movement executions. Object manipulation refers to whether an individual manipulates an object while engaging in an activity. For example, a basketball player must move his/her body around and at the same time manipulate a basketball during dribbling. Thus, the skill of basketball dribbling meets the criteria of both action functions, body transport, and object manipulation. Obviously, many other sports motor skills also fall into this category, such as soccer dribbling, volleyball spiking, and team handball dribbling. The second dimension of Gentile's taxonomy of motor skills is the environmental context that refers to two elements, regulatory conditioning (stationary or in motion) and inter-trial variability (whether two trials are the same or different). For instance, if a soccer player engages in soccer dribbling two different times in a competition, presumably formats, kinematics, or methods of dribbling on these two occasions would not be the same. Thus, soccer dribbling in competition falls under the regulatory condition of motion with inter-trial variability, because dribbling is a dynamic process from one position to another and is performed differently on each occasion. Conversely, in high jumping there is body transport but no object manipulation, so the regulatory condition is motion without inter-trial variability.

According to Gentile's two-dimensional taxonomy classifications of motor skills (Gentile, 2000), we can divide all motor skills into 16 unique categories based on the two dimensions, action function and environmental context. The motor skills identified in these 16 sub-categories begin with the simplest and follow a logical progression to the most complex. These 16 sub-categories provide useful information to help practitioners evaluate the level of difficulty of a particular motor skill and also provide information about the different dimensions of varied motor skills. The matrix of Gentile's taxonomy classification of motor skills can also help physical therapists to evaluate patients' progress based on what motor skills they should be able to perform during the different stages of the rehabilitation process. In school settings, teachers can develop programs for teaching motor skills according to this two-dimensional framework and use it to monitor the students' motor learning progress. Obviously, the more dimensions that are involved in the execution of the motor skill, the more difficult it is to learn. Clearly, such classifications serve various roles in practical settings for motor skill learning processes.

OTHER CLASSIFICATIONS OF MOTOR SKILLS

Besides the above-mentioned classifications, there are several other ways of categorizing motor skills. For example, they can be classified according to particular purposes (Broer, 1966), such as providing support (sitting, standing, balancing), suspension (hanging, dangling), motion (running, skipping, hopping), moving external objects (throwing, hitting, pushing, pulling), or force reception (catching). The motor skills involved in sitting, standing, and balancing are performed with a supporting base to accomplish the goals and thus, bases of support and motion of actions should be accentuated in performing these motor skills. In contrast, running, skipping, and hopping are motor skills that characterize motion of action, so speed, direction, height, and rhythm of action should be part of the teaching emphasis. In addition, motor skills such as throwing, hitting, pushing, and pulling are characterized by using the hands to move external objects. Hand and finger dexterity and eye-hand coordination should be well developed.

Whiting (1969) classified the learning of motor skills through the use of an object, specifically a ball, as follows: (1) catching an object such as a basketball with the hands; (2) receiving a hockey ball from a teammate; (3) hitting a ball by using a golf club; (4) returning a tennis ball or ping pong ball. With this type of classification, the common features comprise using hand(s) to manipulate different objects and, generally speaking, the manipulation of two objects could be complex and challenging. The motor skills of precise eye-hand coordination, timing of action, and manipulation of hand movements and objects should be well developed and the specific teaching strategies should be structured accordingly. In the area of physical therapy, Logan and McKinney (1970) proposed a classification of motor skills based on the type of joint movements of the various body segments involved in performing motor skills, such as: flexion/extension, depression/elevation, circumduction, abduction/adduction, medial/lateral rotation, etc. During the rehabilitation process, physical therapy experts need to discover to what degree patients are capable of moving particular body parts in order to evaluate their recovery progress. The above classifications provide them with meaningful information for developing treatment strategies for their patients based on the tests of these human movements. Thus, physical therapists, occupational therapists, therapeutic recreation practitioners, medical doctors, or rehabilitative counselors could all benefit from using these classifications of motor skills in their practice of treating patients.

RELATIONSHIPS BETWEEN LEARNERS' PHYSICAL ABILITIES AND SKILL CLASSIFICATIONS

In this chapter we have extensively discussed the different ways of classifying motor skills, explaining the characteristics of each category and providing guidelines for training in relation to the various skill categories. However, in motor learning settings, especially at the elite level, practitioners are very interested in achieving peak performance in competition. Thus, the ways in which motor skill classifications provide a direction for training to maximize learning outcomes is a central issue of this chapter. Based on the analysis of motor performance structures, learners' motor performance can be attributed to factors such as their technical ability, genetic physical talents, psychological factors, and other preparations for competition. From the above, we can see that one critical factor determining motor performance is the learners' genetic make-up (Puthucheary et al., 2011; Roth, 2011). For example, high jumpers or long jumpers require fast-twitch dominant muscles in order to perform well and this type of muscle is genetically determined. For this reason practitioners should recruit learners who are genetically gifted for achieving peak performance in sports competition or competitive professions. With this concept in mind, this chapter has logically classified motor skills according to their unique characteristics. Practitioners can use these classifications as a guide when searching for athletes who are genetically predisposed to excel in certain types of sports. Even though we cannot promise such information with 100% accuracy, it is a great resource for coaches, teachers, instructors, and practitioners to accomplish their goals in the recruitment and training of athletes.

RELATIONSHIPS BETWEEN INDIVIDUAL DIFFERENCES AND MOTOR SKILL LEARNING

Classifications of motor skills provide practitioners with essential guidelines for designing effective training regimens. In addition, the motor skill learning process should be appropriate to the learners' characteristics and individual differences of age, physical makeup, experience, personality, psychological state, intellectual ability, etc. (Wrisberg, 2007).

Using a universal approach to training could significantly compromise the outcome of learning. For example, when teaching motor skills to early elementary school children, the patterns of the fundamental movement skills should be primarily emphasized, while elite athletes should be trained with the aid of cutting-edge technology that can make small but significant technical improvements. Also, professionals in different motor movement fields should structure the training according to the unique characteristics of the particular motor skill by stressing the appropriate components. For example, when teaching motor skills for leisure sports activities, precision of performance should not be a main focus; instead, it is more appropriate to structure the training so that the learning process is enjoyable. For teaching motor skills to college students majoring in physical education, cognitive under-standing of the skill structures and demonstrations of the motor skills should be the main focus rather than peak performance. This is because these college students will eventually become teachers, coaches, or practitioners and so their major concern should be that their students are able to comprehend how to perform and demonstrate motor skills. Once spe-cific learning objectives for particular learners have been identified, training approaches, evaluation methods, and teaching strategies can be purposefully designed to accomplish the objectives. In the ever-expanding motor learning field, new training methodologies, and new instruments or technology are continually being developed. Practitioners should keep up-to-date with the latest developments and incorporate them into their training programs. However, even though many motor learning principles have been developed for maximizing learning outcomes, ultimately, effective learning can only be achieved if the training is tailored to the individual learners' characteristics.

PRACTICAL IMPLICATIONS OF UNDERSTANDING MOTOR SKILL CLASSIFICATIONS

This chapter mainly discusses the various ways of classifying motor skills into different categories based on the unique characteristics of the specific motor skills. The critical question is why motor skills should be classified into different categories. From the techni-cal point of view, there are countless motor skills that are executed for various purposes. Some of these skills require perfect precision while others demand high-level cognitive ability, and still others require extreme muscular capability (McMorris et al., 2009; Reilly, 1997; Reilly & Williams, 2003). Some skills are more focused on the process of the execu-tion while for others the end result is more important (Jones, Hughes, & Kingston, 2008). Naturally, the motor learning process should consistently match with the unique charac-teristics of the motor skill so that the training design can be more fruitful. The classifica-tion of motor skills not only provides practitioners with useful guidelines for teaching the skills, but it can also effectively assist students or learners to understand the key compo-nents of the particular motor skills.

A thorough understanding of the characteristics of various motor skills could enable practitioners to develop new technologies to assist the motor learning process for maximizing learning outcomes. Nowadays, in the athletic arena, in addition to developing their physical, technical, and psychological talents, athletes also use new technology to gain every possible advantage for success. New training technologies are continuously being invented or developed, which not only help coaches to teach the motor skills more effectively, but also enhance the learners' performance. Examples of new technologies are: a projection machine for tennis training, an indoor virtual reality golf swing device, a soccer reaction time training light signal device, new brands of ice skates, sharkskin swimwear, a new aero-dynamic bicycle design, etc.

With an enhanced understanding of the classification of motor skills, practitioners and sport scientists are able to creatively develop new technologies or training methods. Since motor learning also involves a feedback procedure, the proper classification of motor skills into logical categories can help practitioners efficiently provide the right feedback to learners according to the particular motor skill being learned. For example, learners cannot see their own actions while performing process-oriented motor skills, so they must rely on instructors' extrinsic feedback to assist them in executing the skills with the correct kinematic form. Thus, timing, accuracy, frequency, and types of feedback play a significant role in determining the learners' progress. The implementation of extrinsic feedback to learners should be based not only on individual characteristics, but also, to a large degree, on the type of motor skill.

Key Terms to Remember

- *One-dimensional motor skills* are those in which skill is based on a single perspective to classify motor skills into various orientations.

- *Two-dimensional motor skills* are those in which the skills are based on two distinctive perspectives.

- *Reaction-time based motor skills* are those skills whose execution relies on unpredictable external stimuli and in which reaction time (RT) plays a significant role.

- *Non-RT-based motor skills* are those skills which are executed under stable and unchanging environmental conditions where no response to external stimuli is required.

- *Environment predictable and RT based motor skills* are those motor skills being performed under predictable environment with a demand of fast RT to effectively perform those skills.

- *Muscular-oriented motor skills* are those motor skills require large muscular movements to complete the actions, with only limited cognitive decision-making being required.

- *Cognitive-oriented motor skills* require maximum cognitive effort and minimal muscular exertion during the performance of the motor skills.

- *Cognitive and muscular combined motor skills* require a combination of cognitive and muscular exertions equally to complete motor skills.

- *Discrete motor skills* are those whose execution has a definite beginning and a definite ending.

- *Series motor skills* incorporate various discrete skills that are strung together.

- *Continuous motor skills* have no definite beginning or ending, and the process of performing them is continuous.

- *Process-oriented motor skills* are those motor skills in which performance is based on performers' kinematics of skill executions.

- *Outcome-oriented motor skills* are those motor skills in which performance can be objectively judged based on the end results measured by either instruments or scores.

Student Assignments for Connecting Theory to Practice

- Interview coaches for different types of sports and compare the differences of training emphasis.

- Interview a physical therapist to see what he/she knows about motor skills and how he/she treats patients during the rehabilitation process.

- Compare RT- and non-RT-based motor skill characteristics and explain the major differences of training emphasis.

- Explain the characteristics of process-oriented and outcome-oriented motor skills and describe the differences of training emphasis.

- Contrast and compare the differences of motor skills among discrete, series, and continuous skills. Explain the training focuses for each of three motor skills.

- Compare the differences and similarities between one-dimensional and two-dimensional classifications of motor skills.

- Give three examples for each of the following skills:
  1. Closed motor skill and open motor skill (three examples for each category)
  2. Discrete skill, serial skill, and continuous skill (three examples for each category)
  3. Motor control maximized motor skills, combination of decision making and motor control skills (three examples for each category)

- What are the practical reasons of classifying motor skills into open and closed motor skills and cognitive and muscular oriented motor skills? Please explain the implications of such classifications could help practitioners enhance the quality of teaching or coaching.

- According to motor learning perspective, please describe the criteria of peak performance of the best basketball skills.

REFERENCES

Broer, M. R. (1966). *Efficiency of human movement* (2nd ed.). Philadelphia, PA: W. B. Saunders.

Edwards, W. M. (2010). *Motor learning and control: From theory to practice.* Belmont, CA: Wadsworth.

Gentile, A. M. (2000). Skill acquisition: Action, movement, and neuromotor processes. In J. H. Carr & R. B. Shepherd (Eds.), *Movement science: Foundations for physical therapy in rehabilitation* (2nd ed.). Rockville, MD: Aspen.

Guthrie, E. R. (1952). *The psychology of learning.* New York, NY: Harper & Row.

Jones, R. L., Hughes, M. M., & Kingston, K. (Eds.). (2008). *An introduction to sports coaching: From science and theory to practice.* New York, NY: Routledge.

Kilding, A. E., Brown, S., & McConnell, A. K. (2010). Inspiratory muscle training improves 100 and 200m swimming performance. *European Journal of Applied Physiology, 108,* 505–511.

Knapp, B. (1963). *Skill in sport: The attainment of proficiency.* Croydon, UK: Routledge & Kegan Paul PLC.

Magill, R. A. (2011). *Motor learning and control: Concepts and applications.* New York, NY: McGraw-Hill.

McMorris, T., Tomporowski, P., & Audiffren, M. (Eds.). (2009). *Exercise and cognitive function.* Hoboken, NJ: Wiley-Blackwell.

Moran, A. P. (2004). *Sport and exercise psychology: A critical introduction.* London, UK: Routledge.

Morrow, J. R., Jackson, A., Disch, J., & Mood, D. (2011). *Measurement and evaluation in human performance.* Champaign, IL: Human Kinetics.

Logan, G. A., & McKinney, W. C. (1970). *Kinesiology* (Physical education series). Dubuque, IA: W. C. Brown.

Puthucheary, Z., Skipworth, J. A., Rawal, J., Loosemore, M., Someren, K., & Montgomery, H. E. (2011). Genetic influences in sport and physical performance. *Sports Medicine, 41,* 845.

Reilly, T. (1997). Energetics of high intensity exercise (soccer) with particular reference to fatigue. *Journal of Sports Sciences, 15,* 257–263.

Reilly, T., & Williams, A. M. (Eds.). (2003). *Science and soccer.* London, UK: Routledge.

Roitman, J., & Shadlen, M. (2002). Response of neurons in the lateral intraparietal area during a combined visual discrimination reaction time task. *The Journal of Neuroscience: The Official Journal of the Society for Neuroscience, 22,* 9475–9489.

Roth, S. M. (2011). Genes and talent selection. In C. Bouchard & E. P. Hoffman (Eds.), *Genetic and molecular aspects of sports performance* (pp. 362–372). Hoboken, NJ: John Wiley & Sons.

Schmidt, R. A., & Wrisberg, C. A. (2008). *Motor learning and performance: A situation-based learning approach* (4th ed.). Champaign, IL: Human Kinetics.

Schmidt, R. A., & Lee, T. (2005). *Motor control and learning: A behavioral emphasis.* Champaign, IL: Human Kinetics.

Smith, D., & Bar-Eli, M. (Eds.). (2007). *Essential readings in sport and exercise psychology.* Champaign, IL: Human Kinetics.

Taylor, M., & Beith, P. (2010). Fundamentals of the long jump: The need for a long-term unified training plan. *USA Track and Field Foundation.* Retrieved from http://www.usatffoundation.org/documents/LongJumpBrochure002.pdf

Toga, A. W., & Mazziotta, J. C. (Eds.). (2000). *Brain mapping: The systems*. San Diego, CA: Academic Press.

Wang, J. (2009). Reaction time training for elite athletes: A winning formula for champions. *International Journal of Sport Science, 3*, 67–78.

Wang, J., & Calloway, J. (2013). Speed training in soccer leading to peak performance. *Soccer Journal*.

Wang, J., & Griffin, M. (1998). Early correction of movement errors can help student performance. *Journal of Health, Physical Education, Recreation & Dance, 69*, 50–52.

Whiting, H. T. (1969). *Acquiring ball skills*. Philadelphia, PA: Lea & Febiger.

Wrisberg, C. A. (2007). *Sport skill instruction for coaches*. Champaign, IL: Human Kinetics.

Maximizing Motor Skill Learning Outcomes Based on Individual Differences

OBJECTIVES

- Understand how individual difference affects motor learning process
- Illustrate what types of individual differences need to be paid attention to during motor learning process
- Distinguish the concepts of motor skill, technique, motor ability, and capability
- Understand what types of human abilities exist
- Define what is the underlined ability and its relationships to potential motor performance
- Understand how to identify underlined abilities
- Understand various theories of motor ability
- Understand specific variables of individual differences and its relationships to motor performance
- Understand the learners' characteristics in relation to motor learning process

INTRODUCTION

The motor learning process is an imperative part of any sport skill training endeavor. One goal of training could be for recreational play, and another goal could be for high-level competition. Many athletes start training at a very young age in hopes they can compete at elite levels when they grow up. Olympic developmental teams are intentionally designed for such a purpose. The critical issue is that many children, for example, are trained together by the same coach, using the same training methods and same training environments over a long period of time, Eventually, some Olympic developmental athletes reach their goal of playing at Olympic or professional level while others may have good technical abilities, but cannot achieve their professional goals. Thus, the question is: What are the major reasons why certain athletes can reach the top level while others only maintain an average level, even though they are all trained by the same coach under the same training conditions? One of the main reasons for the differences between these two groups of athletes is their innate, or genetic, ability.

In fact, an individual's potential to learn a motor skill is determined by various factors such as genetic ability, the effect of the training regimen designed by the coach or instructor, learner's motivation, effort, cognitive ability, and many other elements. For example, learners' individual differences can be seen in many aspects, such as body size, muscle type, physiological make-up, age, gender, cultural background, attitude, motivation, learning style, personality, cognitive ability, athletic experience, etc. Some of these individual differences are genetically determined, and can be changed very little, while other factors can be modified with training. Therefore, individual differences are important and should be taken into account when teaching motor skills. For example, age difference should be taken into consideration when developing a teaching strategy because younger learners have a much shorter attention span, and less muscular strength and intellectual ability than older ones (Payne & Isaacs, 2008).

COURTESY OF BIGSTOCKPHOTO.COM

LEARNERS ARE DIFFERENT IN AGE, EXPERIENCES, GENDER, AND RACE

Moreover, motor learning process takes place in a variety of settings from physical education classes to athletic arenas, from recreational activities to military training, or from martial arts training to dancing practice. Obviously, the students in the different learning environments have varied training objectives, expectations, and training requirements. Therefore, individualized attention based on learners' needs and characteristics should be a crucial part of the motor learning process for achieving the designated objectives.

Individual differences can be attributed either to nature (genetic) or to nurture (training). Genetic differences consist of an individual's unique, stable traits that change very little with training. Conversely, non-genetic individual differences can be changed with training and experience. If practitioners want to help learners to reach the elite of sports competition, they need to understand the nature of individual differences, in order to recruit suitable athletes and provide them with appropriate training based on the particular needs. Lack of awareness of individual differences in the motor learning process could compromise learning outcomes (Schmidt & Wrisberg, 2008; Singer, 1975). Ideally, to achieve high levels of performance, there should be a good match between the genetic make-up of the athlete and the required motor skill criteria. For example, the genetic requirements for a high jumper are the proper height and body weight, fast-twitch dominated muscles, and extreme explosive ability. Thus, screening and recruiting are crucial steps for finding athletes with the required genes for a specific event who can be trained up to the elite level. Some athletes start training at the age of three with the dream of achieving Olympic medals in the future while other youngsters just play for fun. Therefore, knowing how to identify the required genetic traits for developing a particular sport talent is an essential part of determining the future performance potential of the learner (Bouchard & Hoffman, 2011). Finding suitable individuals for a particular sport should be the first step and designing appropriate training is the second step for cultivating elite athletes. From a motor learning perspective, it is important to address the following questions:

1) What percentage of performance potential is attributed to genetic factors vs. training?

2) Could an instructor help a learner achieve the elite performance level without the required genetics?

3) What is the correct motor learning process for achieving peak performance based on individual differences?

4) What are the relationships between skill, technique, and ability?

5) Which individual difference(s) should be given attention in the motor learning process?

In this chapter we will discuss in depth the elements of individual differences and their relationships to motor learning and performance.

THE CONCEPTS OF MOTOR SKILL, TECHNIQUE, MOTOR ABILITY, AND CAPABILITY

According to Schmidt and Wrisberg (2008), motor skill refers to a skill for which the primary determinant of success is the quality of the movement that the performer produces. Two elements are required to perform motor skills at the highest level: (1) the requisite genetic ability, and (2) the proper execution of the skill. Some people use the example of playing poker as an analogy for performing motor skills. An elite poker player not only needs good cards, but also excellent skills to determine when and how to play the cards in order to win games. In a sports setting, the cards represent an athlete's genetic ability and the ability to play cards represents the athlete's techniques. As already mentioned, motor ability is a learner's genetic trait, upon which training or practice would not have a large effect. For example, muscle type is considered to be a feature of ability; fast-twitch muscles can develop tension quickly, as opposed to slow-twitch muscles. Ability and technique are two very different concepts, but they are also intertwined. It is essential for us to have a comprehensive understanding of the two concepts in order to develop a clear perspective of the coaching and teaching of motor skills. Generally speaking, ability refers to athletes' genetic traits that are passed down from their parents. As mentioned above, these traits are stable and are difficult to change. Technique is the execution of human movements through proper training for accomplishing the designated objectives. Everyone can improve technique regardless of ability, so technique can be changed and developed through training.

Technique is a kinematic format, process, or body posture while motor skill is the end result, namely achieving the desired motor performance (Hall, 1999). Generally speaking, good techniques usually produce positive motor performance. However, motor skills also depend to a great extent on genetic ability. Bearing this in mind, a learner's strong technical ability may not correlate with his/her level of performance of a motor skill. Even if an athlete has beautiful techniques in non-competitive situations, this does not imply that this player can excel in competitive environments because in these situations players may require the techniques at a very fast speed and under high pressure. So mastering techniques only means that an athlete can execute the desired movement structures; it does not necessary imply that an athlete is capable of effectively performing the motor skills in a competitive and fast-paced environment (Wang, 2009). That is why many athletes who demonstrate great technical talents during practice are not necessarily capable of achieving peak performance in competition. For example, a soccer player might be able to dribble the ball beautifully with perfect coordination and precise timing in a non-competitive or slow-paced environment, but in competition, he/she may never get the ball due to his/her slow pace of dribbling. Thus, a player who has great soccer techniques may not have the required skills to achieve the goals of competition. Consequently, at the elite level of sport competition, an individual's ability commonly determines his/her performance potential, as ability is a stable, genetic factor that is necessary for peak performance.

On the other hand, learners must also learn the techniques, such as correct form, precise timing, and coordinated movements, to execute the motor skills. Obviously, Usain Bolt (Jamaica's 100M runner), the world's fastest short distance runner, would be unlikely to make it onto a low-level soccer team because he might not meet the technical requirements for playing soccer. Consistently, even though an athlete might have the best genes for a certain sport, without proper training and practice, his/her development of the motor skills required for that sport will be compromised. In sum, both genes and technical training play vital roles for elite performance.

The term *capability* refers to an individual's potential to perform a motor skill through practice and training (Wrisberg, 2007). In other words, capability is related to how much an athlete can improve through practice and training. Obviously, any improvement in performance will be influenced by many different factors such as training, genetic make-up, motivation, appropriate practice, use of scientific technology, etc. Ability and capability are two different and interrelated elements. Ability refers to one's genetic, determined, stable traits, while capability indicates the portion of an individual's talent that changes with training.

How important is genetic ability for training athletes up to the elite level? How much weight does training carry for developing Olympic champions? Is skill more important than ability or is ability more important than skill? Is individual difference from a genetic perspective a determining factor for peak performance? Obviously, a good understanding of these relationships helps teachers, coaches, or practitioners to effectively recruit and train athletes for the best outcomes (see Table 3.1).

TABLE 3.1. Concepts of technique, ability, skill, and capability

Technique	Ability	Skill	Capability
• form	• height of body	• result of action	• potential
• posture	• speed of running		• performance of training
• kinematics	• body shape		
• process	• motor perceptual		
• how to do	• hand-eye coordination		

For team sports, the requisite abilities for the various positions should be considered since each position on the team requires unique abilities. For example, on a basketball team, height is not as important for a guard as it is for a forward because the guard mainly needs to organize the play and distribute the ball to his/her teammates for scoring, while the height of a forward is critical for achieving success. Similarly, in soccer, the abilities required for a goalkeeper are vastly different from those of a striker; the goalkeeper needs swift hand movements, the ability to jump, and quick reactions, while a striker needs fast footwork, rapid speed, and the ability to penetrate the defensive line in order to score goals.

THEORIES OF ABILITY AND ITS IMPLICATIONS FOR PRACTITIONERS

The role of motor ability as it relates to motor performance has been extensively studied. Motor learning researchers and practitioners are always interested in finding the correlations between certain types of motor ability and specific motor performance (Bloomfield, Polman, O'Donoghue & McNaughton, 2007; Hrysomallis, 2011). To explain such relationships, several theories have been developed in the past, and we will discuss these theories in the next few sections.

Theory of Singular Global Ability

The theory of singular global ability states that an individual's motor ability can be applied to any sports skill (McCloy, 1934). According to this theory, if athletes have outstanding motor ability, they will be able to engage in many different sports. For example, if an individual is good at basketball, it is assumed that, with the right training, this person will also be good at other sports such as soccer, ice-hockey, swimming, volleyball, tennis, etc. A premise of the singular global ability theory is that all sports share similar ability requirements for peak performance (McCloy, 1934). In reality, some athletes at high schools do play several sports at a superior level of performance; they are perceived as universal athletes as they have the talents for many different sports. However, in contrast, some athletes are only good at one particular sport. For example, the basketball player Michael Jordan once proved to the world that he was the best basketball player in this universe. After his retirement from basketball, he tried to show the world that he would also be an outstanding baseball player by joining the Chicago White Sox minor league system, but he was not successful in playing baseball. Obviously, this example suggests two possibilities: (1) Michael Jordan only has the ability required to play basketball at the elite level, or (2) he does have the genetic ability to play baseball well, but missed the golden time for baseball training when he was young.

> **Singular Ability Theory**
>
> There is only one motor ability, so if an individual is good at one sport, he/she will be good at other sports as well.

Based on the singular global motor skill theory, Michael Jordan would have had the requisite ability to be an elite baseball athlete if he had been trained at an early stage. We will probably never know the answer since we cannot turn back time.

Theory of Many Specific Abilities

The second theory, proposed by Henry (1958), states that playing each particular sport requires specific abilities, which cannot be shared with other sports. For example, the ability required to be a swimming legend is different from that required to be an elite high jumper; a pianist's ability is quite different from the ability a gymnast requires to achieve peak performance, regardless of training. From the perspective of the specific ability theory, there is no universal ability which can be shared by different motor skills. In fact, some situations indicate that this theory is correct while in other situations it is controversial. Generally speaking, at the elite level of sports, the specific ability theory makes much more sense because the great majority of Olympic athletes only compete in one sport since they require very specialized abilities that cannot be shared by other sports.

> **Many Specific Abilities Theory**
>
> **Each sport requires specific abilities to reach full performance potential.**

Theory of Groupings of Abilities

The third theory is the grouping theory (Fleishman, 1964, 1965; Fleishman & Bartlett, 1969), which states that certain motor abilities can be shared by particular groups of motor skills with similar characteristics. For example, the ability a short distance runner requires (for 100 meter, 200 meter, and 400 meter races) is similar to that of a long jumper as both activities require extremely fast muscular speed in a very short time. That is why many of the same Olympic champions have won both these events. Likewise, table tennis and tennis players may share similar motor abilities, so a player of one of these sports could successfully adapt to the other with little difficulty since the rules, strategies, and technical structures of the two sports are very similar.

From the above, it is clear that different scientists look at the issue of ability from different perspectives and we should not make an absolute conclusion that one theory is better than the others since it all depends on the situation, the athletes, the coaches, and the particular sports events. These theories provide the different ways of interpreting the nature of ability and its application to motor learning settings.

People often wonder why there are so many differences in the performances of athletes trained by the same coach and under the same conditions. From the motor learning perspective, these differences are largely caused by the individual differences of the athletes, such as age, background, experience, motor ability, psychological well-being, physical make-up, emotional characteristics, etc. However, motor learning experts are particularly interested in knowing which elements of individual

> **Grouping Ability Theory**
>
> **Some sports may share similar motor abilities, so an athlete may play well in several different sports that share required abilities.**

differences are attributable to genetic factors that are stable and not easily changed. Once we find the solution to this, the next question is how coaches can provide the most effective training to maximize outcomes in the motor learning process. The first crucial step is for coaches or practitioners to understand the correlation between the abilities required and the particular motor skills for attaining performance potentials (Frost, 2009). The following discussion will elucidate this.

> **Underlying Abilities Are Required for Maximum Performance Potential**
>
> **For example, a high jumper needs:**
> - **Tall and lean body type**
> - **Fast twitch dominated**
> - **Explosive ability**
> - **Great coordination**

In every sport, athletes need to have the specific abilities that match the skills required for that sport in order, with the right training, to reach the highest level of performance. For example, a race-car driver requires extremely fast reactions to maneuver the car in order to avoid the opponents' vehicles; he/she also needs rapid eye-hand coordination to quickly and continuously turn the steering wheel to the right position. Once these innate abilities are identified, suitable athletes can be recruited for training since driving techniques are changeable traits which can be developed effectively. In gymnastics, the ideal athletes should have innate traits such as small body shape with a relatively low center of gravity, and extreme muscular strength with exceptional explosive ability; they must also be able to frequently change direction, position and speed, so they must constantly overcome inertia. Athletes with a tall, heavy body type may not be suited to gymnastics as they have great difficulty overcoming inertia. All the above examples illustrate that certain types of sports require athletes with particular abilities in order to reach the elite level. Without the requisite ability as a foundation or underlying support for the motor skills, athletes cannot perform the competitive skills and reach their athletic potentials.

VALIDITY OF TESTS FOR MEASURING MOTOR ABILITY

Since a learner's performance potential depends to a great extent on his/her underlying ability, practitioners make great effort when recruiting to identify athletes with the requisite abilities to attain peak performance. For example, when baseball coaches are looking for young people who could be trained to become elite baseball batters or pitchers, they need to know what type of testing is required to identify their underlying abilities. A boxing coach is interested in knowing what battery of tests to use in order to find potentially successful boxing athletes. Similarly, a soccer coach may develop his/her own evaluation system for recruiting talented young athletes for each position in the hopes that they might be Olympic stars in the future. Accurately identifying an athlete's underlying ability through appropriate testing is a scientific and challenging task and many times practitioners have their own approaches for doing this based on their previous experience (Baker et al., 2011; Williams & Reilly, 2000). This ability to correctly identify learners' potential is what ultimately puts these practitioners in a higher bracket. Scientists have proposed some approaches for identifying learners' abilities (Abbott, Button, Pepping, & Collins, 2005; Twist & Hutton, 2007).

Even though practitioners use different approaches to identify athletes' underlying abilities in an attempt to find potential elite athletes, one caveat to bear in mind is that some of the testing done in the laboratory may not reflect the real world (Durand & Salmela, 2001; Régnier, Salmela, & Russell, 1993). This is one of the reasons why some Olympic developmental coaches might miss excellent youngsters during the recruiting process. It is important that practitioners have a comprehensive perspective when recruiting.

ABILITY CAN BE CHANGED OVER TIME

Many athletes start their sports career at a very young age; for example, the Chinese government sponsors sport schools that recruit young children, often as young as three years old, to play sports. Recruiting athletes at such an early stage is very challenging because it is hard to know what underlying abilities to look for in such young children. One great challenge is that even though, from a theoretical perspective, ability is a stable factor which is difficult to change, human ability can be changed with age. For instance, a child might be shorter than average at the age of seven, but when he reaches 17, he might be much taller than most of his peers. Also, just because a child does not have much muscular strength at a young age, this does not necessarily mean that he/she will be physically weak as an adolescent. The reality is that many coaches or practitioners misjudge athletes' performance potential at the early stage of learning. Therefore, they should exercise caution whenever they are recruiting young athletes and the developmental perspective should be taken into consideration (Tourón & Tourón, 2011; Vaeyens, Lenoir, Williams, & Philippaerts, 2008).

> **Growing Process Changes Ability Potential**
> - **A shorter child does not imply a short person when fully grown**
> - **A weaker child does not imply a weak person when fully grown**

FACTORS CONTRIBUTING TO MOTOR PERFORMANCE BASED ON INDIVIDUAL DIFFERENCES

The ultimate goal of motor learning is to enhance motor performance through appropriate motor learning processes (see Table 3.2). There are many variables contributing to motor performance such as learners' characteristics, partially illustrated as follows:

1) Physical genetic makeup such as muscle type, body shape, and body structure, coordination, speed, motor perception, physical conditioning, etc.

2) Intellectual and cognitive ability for understanding teachers' instructions and decision-making skills.

3) Personality and psychological states such as their motivation, attitude, discipline, communication skills, control of anxiety, and attention style.

4) Age, gender, personal experiences, etc.

Each of the above aspects could directly influence the outcomes of motor learning and thus, teaching strategies should be based on the learners' physical, psychological, and personal characteristics. For example, the strategies for teaching motor skills to young children should focus on developing their cognitive understanding of how to perform the skills; the motor learning process should be entertaining and interesting for the learners so that their motivation to learn is enhanced. At the collegiate or elite level, learning how to perfect motor skills becomes a major task. Individually-based learning of motor skills is the most effective way to achieve training objectives.

TABLE 3.2. Three components contributing to motor performance

Learner's characteristics	Instructor's competence	Learning environment and condition
e.g., age, gender, experience, cognitive ability, genetic traits, and psychological characteristics	e.g., knowledge of sport science, athletic experience, knowledge of the sport, administration and communication skill, and human relations skills	e.g., non-distracting learning environment, facility and equipment, sports field and settings, and organization of training

Another factor contributing to motor performance is the competence of the teachers, coaches, or practitioners. These individuals have diverse backgrounds and different levels of competence; some have received solid training in sports science disciplines, while others might have very limited training in the field. Thus their level of knowledge of motor learning is quite varied. Incompetent instructors could lead learners to form bad habits as motor learning is not value-free. Once a bad habit is formed, it is very difficult to break it. Needless to say, the instructor's competence in teaching or coaching, especially for process-oriented motor skill learning, has a huge impact on students' motor learning processes.

Additionally, the learning environment is another factor influencing learning outcomes. A positive learning environment can help learners maintain the attention required for learning, cooperate positively with classmates or teammates, or increase their motivation to learn. A disrupted learning environment can distract learners' attention, affect their relationship with instructors, decrease their interest in learning, and hamper the learning progress. Choosing the right practice site or training facilities should be also emphasized for learning effectiveness because certain types of training require specific environments and facilities. Equally important, building a bridge between the theory and practice of the motor learning process is quite challenging but it is vital to the effectiveness of motor learning. The current reality is that for many years motor learning specialists have been conducting studies to try to understand the characteristics of an effective motor learning process for the various motor skills, and they have accumulated a great deal of knowledge in the area. However, unfortunately many of these research studies were in the form of lab-related experimental research. Teachers, coaches, or practitioners have found it challenging to make connections between the theory and practice. Thus, the outcome of the research is significantly compromised, especially for college undergraduate students who may have trouble applying the learned theories to practical settings and more detrimentally, many of these undergraduate students will enter the workforce as soon as they receive bachelor degrees.

HOW PRACTITIONERS ENGAGE IN MOTOR LEARNING BASED ON INDIVIDUAL DIFFERENCES

Motor Learning Process Based on Age Differences

Motor learning takes place in various settings such as elementary and high schools, or at collegiate levels, and the particular characteristics of students of different ages can have an impact on the learning process. Younger students usually have a short attention span and are unable to pay attention to instructors' verbal instructions for very long (Heller & Bach, 2007). Also, younger students often get bored easily and quickly during practice, so instructors should regularly structure variety into practice to retain their attention. Younger students are more interested in learning that is fun and includes contests or game-related activities, which will keep them involved for a longer period of time. Since younger students have less cognitive ability to comprehend instructors' verbal instructions, short, cue-related instructions are more effective. In addition, visual aids and demonstrations should be used in learning; in particular peer demonstrations are preferable since students see that their peers can perform the skill, which gives them the confidence to do the same movements (Weiss, McCullagh, Smith, & Berlant, 1998). Furthermore, younger students lack the physical ability to perform certain motor skills and this limitation could make them more prone to injury in the learning process, so prevention of injury during learning should be emphasized.

Obviously, older students are physically and cognitively more mature, so not only do they have better comprehensive ability, but they also have independent self-evaluation and self-improvement abilities; they can find the errors or problems in their learning and make their own revisions towards the designated goals. These students understand their learning objectives and have the self-discipline to engage in learning without requiring constant monitoring by the instructors. Age difference in the motor learning process should also be taken into account to maximize learning outcomes. Since motor learning can begin as early as two or three years of age, the learning process must be based on age as it relates to performance and to injury concerns.

Motor Learning Process Based on Students' Skill Levels

Students' motor skill levels vary from one individual to another according to their different backgrounds and experience. For example, some learners might have received great technical training in the past while many others might have received very little; skill levels could range from elementary school to Olympic levels. Thus, based on learners' skill levels, the motor learning process can be divided into three different phases: (1) cognitive phase, (2) motor phase (associate phase), and (3) autonomous phase, each of which has its own unique characteristics (Fitts & Posner, 1967). At the cognitive phase, the purpose of learning is to establish a proper image of how to correctly execute the particular motor skill; if the student mentally establishes a faulty image of the motor skill, an incorrect motor program will be formed. During the motor phase, the teaching objective should focus on eliminating incorrect or unwanted movements and developing more refined movement structures. In the last stage of learning, the autonomous phase, athletes have a well-established motor program and know what to do in practice and competition; their movement patterns are executed automatically, requiring limited attention. Depending on the level of the students being taught, instructors must view previous movement experience as a critical factor when designing training to fit specific groups of students.

Motor Learning Process Based on Physical Ability

The different motor skills require learners to exert various kinds of physical effort in order to complete the skills successfully and without injury. In some sports the risk of injury can be quite high, some examples being freestyle aero-jump skiing, figure skating, gymnastics, ice hockey, football, boxing, soccer, or other combat sports. If they do not have sufficient physical ability, athletes can easily get injured (Starkey & Johnson, 2006). Moreover, when athletes are exhausted, over trained, or lack the physical strength or conditioning, they could be even more prone to injury (Lieberman-Cline, 1996). Instruction should be based on the students' current physical ability and conditioning. In fact, overtraining and burnout are common phenomena for professional and Olympic athletes as win/loss records dominate coaches' and athletes' lives. One way to get ahead in competitions is to increase the amount of training that could harm athletes with overtraining at different levels (Budgett, 1998; Greenleaf, Gould, & Dieffenbach, 2001). If careful consideration is not given to the individual differences in athletes' physical ability, a negative impact on their well-being and poor performance is unavoidable.

Motor Learning Process Based on Psychological Make-up

Students' learning behavior is also reflected in their psychological make-up such as the psychological traits of anxiety, motivation, personal characteristics, personality, attitude, self-confidence, communication skills, etc., all of which can affect the learning process (Jarvis, 2006; Hankemeier, 2009). Inter-

estingly, all learners have their own unique psychological characteristics. For that reason, not only should instructors or practitioners have expertise in the technical skills, but they should also have knowledge of the psychology of learning in relation to the motor learning process. For example, some students may have low self-confidence and high levels of anxiety, which have a negative impact on the learning progress. A gymnast may hesitate to take a trial for fear of the potential risk; a soccer goalkeeper might be afraid of injury when diving to save the ball; an ultimate fighting athlete may be anxious about competing against a winning opponent; or a freestyle aero-jump skier may be fearful of falling and being injured. In fact, many athletes have failed or suffered injury due to fear. Many other psychological reasons can also affect learning outcomes, as described in Chapter 10, so it is essential for practitioners to be familiar with each learner's unique psychological characteristics in order to provide appropriate and effective training.

Motor Learning Process Based on Learning Styles

Learners are different in many ways, one of which is their learning style. For example, some students can learn better by doing, while others like to have a full understanding of the skill before trying it. Some students learn mostly through visual cues, life demonstrations, video-clips, etc., so any visually-oriented approaches could help them learn effectively. Learning progress is also different from person to person; some are fast learners while others might take longer (Richlin, 2006; Schmidt, & Lee, 2011). Some are independent thinkers while others are listeners and followers who do not tend to think or analyze independently. To effectively engage in the motor learning process, fully understanding students' unique learning styles would make learning a more effective and more enjoyable process.

Motor Learning Process Based on Social and Cultural Backgrounds

Students in the U.S. are very diverse in terms of their culture, ethnicity, language, tradition, customs, religion, value systems, beliefs, etc. and these individual differences could influence their learning processes. For example, students from East Asian countries such as China, Japan, Singapore, or Korea are relatively introverted; they work hard quietly, but they are unwilling to express their feelings or provide feedback to instructors. These students are used to obeying and will diligently engage in practice without challenging their instructors' authority. These learners have great discipline and follow the rules of learning, but they are usually less confident and less creative compared to Western students (Jaquish & Ripple, 1985; Lau, Hui, & Ng, 2004). On the other hand, students from Western countries are used to democratic learning approaches and tend to be highly confident regardless of their skill levels; they like to openly ask questions and make suggestions to instructors. They are more creative and are not afraid of challenging authority (Sawyer, 2006). The cultural differences of students can have a great effect on their learning, either positively or negatively, so it is important for instructors to recognize these differences in the social and cultural backgrounds of the students in order to provide effective teaching strategies.

Motor Learning Process Based on Students' Specific Needs

There are many differences among learners and some may have certain learning deficiencies that require specific attention, such as learning disabilities caused by injury, psychological barriers, abnormal personalities, mental or physical challenges, or phobias. For instance, a student who has had part of a lung removed may not be able to engage in very intense, demanding motor skill learning regimens. The instructor should be well informed of students' specific needs before the learning process begins. A partnership learning program could help special needs student with the required assistance. Also, a closed-circuit monitoring system is a useful approach for constantly observing those students who need special assistance. Some students may be able to perform motor skills successfully in non-competitive situations, but they have great trouble performing in competitive environments for fear of being injured, while others may have significant psychological trauma when they return to practice after an injury, which could be an enormous psychological barrier that prevents them from trying out new technical routines. In addition, some athletes are afraid of winning while others are afraid of losing. In reality, many learners require special attention in the motor learning process and instructors should pay attention to their characteristics and individual differences in order to provide them with appropriate teaching. In sum, learning should be an individually-based process for reaching maximum learning outcomes.

Practitioners engaged in the motor learning process should have a fundamental knowledge of basic sports science in the area of motor learning so that they can design training regimens, recognize the strengths and weaknesses of the training, modify training methods, and evaluate the learners' progress. They should also have a basic knowledge of research methods and integrate the current research findings into motor learning. Thus, practitioners or teachers could read scientific journals, conduct some basic applied studies, assess training progress objectively, and research appropriate training approaches. Understanding research methods also helps practitioners comprehend the science behind the training and make connections between theory and practice.

COURTESY OF BIGSTOCKPHOTO.COM

Key Terms to Remember

- *Individual differences* reflect on a person's differences in the areas of personality, attitudes, emotion, psychology, physiology, cultural perception, learning, or perceptual processes, etc., that account for variation in motor performance or motor behavior.

- *Singular global ability* references McCloy's (1934) theory of singular global ability states that an individual's motor ability can be applied to any sports skill.

- *Many specific ability theory* states that playing each particular sport requires specific abilities, which cannot be shared with other sports (Henry, 1958).

- *Groupings of ability theory* states that certain motor abilities can be shared by particular groups of motor skills with similar characteristics (Fleishman, 1964, 1965).

- *Motor skill* refers to a skill for which the primary determinant of success is the quality of the movement that the performer produces.

- *Technique* is a kinematic format, process, or body posture while motor skill is the end result, namely achieving the desired motor performance.

- *Motor ability* is a learner's genetic trait, upon which training or practice has little or no effect.

- *Capability* refers to an individual's potential to perform a motor skill through practice and training.

Student Assignments for Connecting Theory to Practice

- Based on your view, which individual differences are important to be considered during the motor learning process? Explain why.

- Distinguish the differences between the concepts of ability, capability, technique, and skill.

- Do you think that a person who has a great ability must have great techniques?

- As a coach or practitioner, can he/she effectively enhance an athlete's ability? Explain why?

- Which factors contribute to an athlete's capability?

- Do you feel any differences between the abilities of male and female athletes?

- To recruit 12-year-old Olympic developmental athletes, would you like to recruit more technically sound athletes or the athletes who have excellent abilities but lack of techniques. Please explain your rationale.

- Discuss the following theories: (1) general motor ability, (2) Henry's specificity hypothesis, and (3) groupings of abilities. Which theory do you believe most? Why?

- Have you ever thought about what some of your own dominant abilities might be? List three movement activities for which you feel particularly skilled. What abilities do you think you possess that allow you to perform these skills so well?

- If you are a basketball coach for the Olympic development team and you are recruiting 12 year-old basketball players (these players have already received three years of basketball training for your team), what are your criteria of selecting talented players?

- Conduct a task/skill analysis: (1) What abilities are needed for an elite basketball player? (2) What abilities are needed for an elite golfer? (3) What abilities are needed for the following athletes?
  - A novice basketball player?
  - An elite basketball player?
  - A novice tennis player?
  - An elite tennis player?
  - A novice racecar driver?
  - An experienced racecar driver?

- How can a coach or practitioner base training techniques on individual differences in order to positively contribute to the motor learning process?

- Explain the relationships between ability and skill.

- To achieve peak performance, does an athlete's ability play a more important role or his/her technique? Please explain the reasons behind your response.

- Engage in a task and ability analysis project

REFERENCES

Abbott, A., Button, C., Pepping, G., & Collins, D. (2005). Unnatural selection: Talent identification and development in sport. *Nonlinear Dynamics, Psychology, and Life Sciences, 9,* 61–88.

Baker, J., Schorer, J., & Cobley, S. (2011). *Talent identification and development in sport: International perspectives.* New York, NY: Routledge.

Bloomfield, J., Polman, R., O'Donoghue, P., & McNaughton, L. (2007). Effective speed and agility conditioning methodology for random intermittent dynamic type sports. *Journal of Strength & Conditioning Research, 21,* 1093–1100.

Bouchard, C., & Hoffman E. P. (2011). *Genetic and molecular aspects of sports performance.* Hoboken, NJ: John Wiley & Sons.

Budgett, R. (1998). Fatigue and underperformance in athletes: The overtraining syndrome. *British Journal of Sports Medicine, 32,* 107-110.

Durand-Bush, N., & Salmela, J. H. (2001). The development of talent in sport. In R. N. Singer, H. A. Hausenblas, & C. M. Janelle (Eds.), *Handbook of sport psychology* (2nd ed.; pp. 269–289). New York, NY: Wiley.

Fitts, P. M., & Posner, M. I. (1967). *Human performance.* Belmont, CA: Brooks/Cole.

Fleishman, E. A. (1964). *The structure and measurement of physical fitness.* Englewood Cliffs, NJ: Prentice Hall.

Fleishman, E. A. (1965). The description and prediction of perceptual motor skill learning. In R. Glaser (Ed.), *Training research and education* (pp. 137–175). New York, NY: Wiley.

Fleishman, E. A., & Bartlett, C. J. (1969). Human abilities. *Annual Review of Psychology, 20,* 349–380.

Frost, J. L. (2009). Characteristics contributing to the success of a sports coach. *Sport Journal, 12,* 1.

Greenleaf, H., Gould, D., & Dieffenbach, K. (2001). Factors influencing Olympic performance: Interviews with Atlanta and Negano US Olympians. *Journal of Applied Sport Psychology, 13,* 154–184.

Hall, S. (1999). *Basic biomechanics.* Boston, MA: WCB/McGraw-Hill.

Hankemeier, D. (2009). The athletic trainer's guide to psychosocial intervention and referral. Athletic training & sports health care: *The Journal for the Practicing Clinician, 1,* 239–240.

Heller, J., & Bach, G. (2007). *Coaching junior football teams for dummies.* London, UK: John Wiley & Sons, Ltd.

Henry, F. (1958). Specificity vs. generality in learning motor skills. In 61st Annual Proceedings of the College Physical Education Association. Washington, DC: College Physical Education Association.

Hrysomallis, C. (2011). Balance ability and athletic performance. *Sports Medicine, 41,* 221–232.

Jaquish, G. A., & Ripple, R. (1984-1985). A life-span developmental cross-cultural study of divergent thinking abilities. *International Journal of Aging and Human Development, 20,* 1–11.

Jarvis, M. (2006). *Sport psychology: A student's handbook.* New York, NY: Routledge.

Lau, S., Hui, A. N., & Ng, G. C. (Eds.) (2004). *Creativity: When East meets West.* River Edge, NJ: World Scientific Pub.

Lieberman-Cline, N., Roberts, R., & Warneke, K. (1996). *Basketball for women: Becoming a complete player.* Champaign, IL: Human Kinetics.

McCloy, C. H. (1934). Measurement of general motor capacity and general motor ability. *Research Quarterly of the American Physical Education Association, 5,* 46–61.

Payne, V. G., & Isaacs, L. D. (2008). *Human motor development: A lifespan approach.* Boston, MA: McGraw Hill.

Régnier G., Salmela J., & Russell, S. J. (1993). Talent detection and development in sport. In R. N. Singer, M. Murphy, & L. K. Tennant (Eds), *Handbook on research on sport psychology* (pp. 290–313). New York, NY: Macmillan.

Richlin, L. (2006). *Blueprint for learning: Constructing college courses to facilitate, assess, and document learning.* Sterling, VA: Stylus Pub.

Sawyer, R. (2006). *Explaining creativity.* Oxford, UK: Oxford University Press.

Schmidt, R. A., & Wrisberg, C. A. (2008). *Motor learning and performance: A situation-based learning approach.* Champaign, IL: Human Kinetics.

Schmidt, R. A., & Lee, T. D. (2011). *Motor control and learning: A behavioral emphasis.* Champaign, IL: Human Kinetics.

Singer, R. N. (1975). *Motor learning and human performance: An application to physical education skills* (2nd ed.). New York, NY: Macmillan.

Starkey, C., & Johnson, G. (2006). *Athletic training and sports medicine.* London, UK: Jones & Bartlett.

Tourón, J., & Tourón, M. (2011). The Center for Talented Youth Identification Model: A review of the literature. *Talent Development & Excellence, 3*, 187–202.

Twist, P., & Hutton, J. (2007). Identifying, understanding and training youth athletes. *IDEA Fitness Journal, 4*, 64–71.

Vaeyens, R., Lenoir, M., Williams, A., & Philippaerts, R. M. (2008). Talent identification and development programmes in sport: Current models and future directions. *Sports Medicine, 38*, 703–714.

Wang, J. (2009). Reaction time training for elite athletes: A winning formula for champions. *International Journal of Sport Science, 3*, 67–78.

Weiss, M. R., McCullagh, P., Smith, A. L., & Berlant, A. R.(1998). Observational learning and the fearful child: Influence of peer models on swimming skill performance and psychological responses. *Research Quarterly for Exercise and Sport, 69*, 380–394.

Williams, A. M., & Reilly, T. (2000). Talent identification and development. *Journal of Sport Sciences, 18*, 656–667.

Wrisberg, C. A. (2007). *Sport skill instruction for coaches.* Champaign, IL: Human Kinetics.

Roles of Sensory Sources to Motor Skill Learning Processes

OBJECTIVES

- Understand the relationship between performers and the environments
- Understand the target context, target skills, practice, and competitive conditions
- Understand the sensory system and types of sensory sources
- Understand the roles of proprioception and exterioceptions which are particularly related to motor learning and performance
- Describe and understand the motor learning process
- Understand information processing related to external stimuli and internal body feedback
- Understand the role of visual sensation to motor performance and skill acquisition
- Understand the role of auditory sensation to motor performance and skill acquisition
- Understand the applications of the sensory system in motor learning and performance during practice condition and competitive conditions

INTRODUCTION

This chapter discusses two very important aspects in terms of motor skill learning: the performer and the environment in relation to selecting and using sensory sources. While athletes at different levels (e.g., novice or experienced) might perform in the same types of environment (e.g., practice or competition, sunshine or rain, open or closed skill situations), their reactions to the particular environment will be quite different. Performers at various levels have different preferences when selecting and using sensory sources, and have different degrees of attentiveness when focusing on targets. For example, when a kickboxing athlete is attempting to block an opponent's attack, the neuro-muscular processes and mechanisms of punch blocking are far more complex than many people would imagine. Such a motor skill takes years of practice to be executed efficiently and accurately. The neuro-muscular process for performing the blocking shown in Illustration 1 involves various sensory system and different sensory sources in the following steps: (1) identify external visual and auditory information, (2) based on past experiences make a quick decision when and how to block an opponent's attack, and (3) send the proper electrical impulses to the relevant muscles to take the action (Schmidt & Wrisberg, 2008). For the kickboxing athlete to master the motor skills such as this successfully, he should engage in appropriate

COURTESY OF U.S. MARINE CORPS

training to develop necessary motor skills.

As another example, when dribbling a ball and trying to fake an opponent in soccer, novices will pay more attention to the dribbling player's body movement (that is why the novice can easily be faked), whereas experienced athletes focus on both the ball and dribbling player's body movement. They base their decision as to how to act on the direction in which the ball is moving, not on the dribbling player's body movement. Selecting appropriate sources of sensory information is very important in motor skill learning as students' and athletes' acquisition of motor skills relies on identifying and processing relevant information related to skill performance from numerous internal and external sensory sources (Clark et al., 2008; Schmidt & Wrisberg, 2008; Stallings, 1982). For example, performing a sport skill such as hitting a baseball, or receiving a football, volleyball, or tennis ball, requires athletes to use different sensory sources to detect and process task-relevant information (e.g., the speed and pattern of the motion of the ball, forward or backward spin, etc.), and make a decision on how to respond to the movement motion (Haggard, 1992; Sherrington, 1947; Wrisberg, 2007).

One of the most important pedagogical strategies in physical education and sports coaching, when teaching a new motor skill, is to use as much sensory information from as many sources and modalities as possible (e.g., providing verbal cues or descriptions, physical demonstrations, pictures, video, or other visual aids) to help students learn the skill effectively. Students and athletes are also advised to use all available sensory sources when they are engaging in motor skill learning and performance (Fairbrother, 2010). Using these available sensory sources, students can observe and experience a complete movement sequence to establish a motor skill pattern. They can detect their movement errors through their own performance (i.e., the feel of the movement), observation and video replay (i.e., visual) and external augmented feedback (i.e., verbal), and determine how to perform the skill correctly on the next trial (Fairbrother, 2010). The following section describes the relationship between the human body and the environment.

RELATIONSHIP BETWEEN PERFORMERS AND ENVIRONMENT

As indicated, motor skill learning is an integrated process between the human body and the environment (Ayres, 1972; Fisher et al., 1991; Levitt, 1995). To understand how students learn motor skills, teachers and coaches must address several important elements of motor skill performance (e.g., performer, target motor skill, and environment), and appreciate the relationships among these factors (e.g., how a performer executes a motor skill in a particular environment, or how the learning environment can be organized to optimize the performance of motor skills).

Teaching pedagogies and research in the area of motor learning focus on the interactions between student performance and the learning environment, and provide students with information on how to control the body (body awareness) in order to complete a movement in a particular environment (e.g., dance performance with a group and with music; Schmidt & Lee, 2011). Movement control training is necessary to improve body awareness and coordination among the individual parts in terms of speed, space, and position while performing skill movements, and to establish the relationship between body parts and the environment (e.g., dance with music and teammates) in which the performance will be presented. For example, the classification of a skill as closed or open is based on whether the environment is predictable or unpredictable (e.g., hitting a golf ball vs. batting a baseball), an important factor for athletes when deciding on a movement execution. In a stable and predictable environment, athletes need only to understand and master the correct movement patterns and execution in a self-paced fashion. Skill progression is achieved by repeating and reproducing the same movements in the stable environment over and over again until the desired goal is reached. However, in an unstable and unpredictable environment, athletes must not only master the motor skill components, but they must also learn to predict or anticipate the constantly changing environment, based on their past experiences, in order to be able to make adjustments to their movements. In many cases, the athlete is required to make automatic responses and produce movements according to some important features in the environment within a very short period of time (Shogan, 1999). In other words, the quality of the performance of open skills is not only dependent upon the movement production itself, but also on the selection, programming, and execution of the movements.

COURTESY OF DREAMSTIME

The reason that we address the relationship between performers and environments is because many students or athletes can demonstrate good skill performances during practice (e.g., 70% jump-shot rate) but are unable to achieve the same level of performance in competition, especially when facing strong opponents. This phenomenon can be attributed to the fact that the intensity and setting during practice do not match with the conditions in the competition setting (Weinberg & Gould, 2007; Gilchrist et al., 2009). Therefore, when teaching motor skills or coaching sport skills, the teacher or coach needs to consider the relationship between the performer and the environment and should use various practice methods to enable the athletes to demonstrate their characteristics and capabilities in different environments, whether during practice or competition. Performers also need to practice skills in environments or situations that are as close to the real competition environment as possible (e.g., against opponents of the same level; Browne et al., 2009; Hugh & Dean, 2002; Weinberg & Gould, 2007).

TARGET CONTEXT AND TARGET SKILLS

The *target context* is the environment or setting where a motor skill will be performed. The *target skill* is the selected motor skill that an individual needs to be able to perform for a particular sport in the identified *target context* (Brady, 1998; Schmidt & Wrisberg, 2008). As described above, while practicing or performing a motor skill, especially an open skill, the performer must consider the target context in which the motor skill will be executed. For example, accurate passing is an important motor skill (target skill) required to be able to perform as an elite soccer player in competition. The target context for a soccer player must be highly competitive practice and competition, with teams of a similar level. Soccer players practicing the targeted soccer passing skill need to use a highly competitive practice environment or situation that is as close to the real competition environment as possible (target context) (Williams & Hodges, 2005). However, in a high school recreational baseball class (less competitive target context), students might use a machine to pitch the baseball (or tee-stand) to increase their chances of hitting the ball. Athletes who want to be elite tennis players should create a more competitive situation as their target context in which to practice the target motor skill. They also should select a more competitive opponent, who uses high-speed serves and various angles of strokes, in order to increase the training intensity (e.g., a female tennis player might seek a male tennis player as practice partner). However, if the target skill is being practiced by a novice or recreational player, the target context will be less challenging: The practice partner will serve with a good pace so that the ball lands as close to the learner as possible to allow for an easy return, therefore keeping the ball in play. Both players should keep the same pace and path for each stroke so that the learner can easily return the ball.

Training enables athletes to demonstrate their characteristics and capabilities in different environments, whether during practice or competition. Since motor skill learning consists of practicing target skills in a target context in order to train the body to be aware of the external environment, the teacher or coach often needs to vary the practice conditions and create an environment that is similar to the one where the students will perform or compete (competitive conditions). For example, in a practice situation that is similar to the competition environment, students should not always hit the baseball from the tee (closed skill environment); they must practice hitting a thrown ball (open skill environment) at different speeds and angles, and with forward or backward spin (real competition environment). Therefore, important concepts for teachers and coaches to consider are individuals' characteristics (e.g., novice, high/low level of performance) and the target skill which they will demonstrate in the particular environment. These factors must be considered before providing instruction to students. For example, a technique which is appropriate in one environment may not be suitable in another situation.

TYPES OF CONDITIONS

Practice conditions and *competition conditions* are two different contexts and require different intensity levels of skill performance. As previously described, many athletes can demonstrate a perfect motor skill in practice conditions; they may not, however, perform the skill at the same level during competition conditions, especially when facing elite opponents, because the practice and competition settings are not the same (Weinberg & Gould, 2007). For example, a soccer player may not be able to pass the ball accurately to a teammate or dribble the ball past an opponent because of pressure from the opponent.

Or a tennis player may not be able to return an opponent's serve because the ball is travelling faster than in a practice setting. Many soccer players are unable to keep up the pace throughout an entire soccer game because their level of physical fitness and endurance is not high enough. The reason for this is that their training is not intense enough to prepare them for an actual competition. Therefore, trainers must create practice conditions that are as close to the real competitive environment as possible, for example with opponents at the same level.

SENSORY SOURCES

Proprioception refers to sensory information that comes primarily from sources inside a person's body detected by proprioceptors, which are located in the muscles (e.g., muscle spindles), tendons (golgi tendon organs), joints (joint receptors), and vestibular apparatus, etc. (Lephart & Fu, 2000; Sherrington, 1947). *Muscle spindles,* located within all skeletal muscles, are considered the most important proprioceptive sense organs for detecting the position and movement of body parts and limbs, including a sense of the limb's acceleration (Kraemer et al., 2012; Lephart & Fu, 2000; Proske, 2005). Muscle spindles are especially important in fine motor function control because these sensors have both sensory and motor connections with the central nervous system and the peripheral nervous system.

Golgi tendon organs are located at the junction of the tendon and skeletal muscles. These tendon organs are viewed as very important muscle receptors in relation to muscle movement. Each skeletal muscle consists of many tendon organ receptors to detect force or the particular position when changing the length of muscle tendons and body parts. *Joint receptors,* located in the joint capsule and ligaments of all synovial joints in the skeletal system, contribute to the information about change in the joint capsule and ligaments. These joint receptors work with other proprioceptors to provide the performer with both static and dynamic information about the joint position, body limb position, and kinesthetic awareness.

The *vestibular apparatus,* located in the inner ear, provides information about posture and balance during movement. The vestibular apparatus detects the position of the head during movement, provided by the saccule and utricle located in the inner ear. Information provided by the vestibular apparatus is critical in controlling, particularly, direction of movement, balance, and rotation with the change of the head's position. From motor learning and control perspectives, the head's position is very important. In the example of the "Fosbury Flop" high jump, athletes must keep their head straight at the moment of taking off in order to make the whole body rigid so that it is effectively using reaction force. When they are in the position to clear the bar, they should tilt their head backwards to help them to arch their back in order to avoid hitting the bar. When teaching high jump

motor skills, head control must be strongly emphasized as it plays a very critical role in controlling
body posture and thus in learning to execute the
motor skills effectively.

Proprioceptors can respond to stimuli that
impact on the corresponding body parts, transform
them into special signals and send them to the brain
for further analysis (Proske, 2005; Honeybourne et
al., 2000). These proprioceptors provide us with
information about the body parts and limbs, body
position in space prior to and during movement,
the relationship between body limbs, and the force
and acceleration produced from the muscles. For
example, gymnasts rely on the sensory information
provided by these proprioceptors to adjust their

body position while performing a sequential gymnastics movement routine. This is particularly true when the body is in the air, for example, when an athlete is performing a
complete triple somersault (1080°) in figure skating or a diving routine. Figure skaters
rely on these proprioceptors to control and coordinate body parts and limbs, and adjust
their body position to the best landing position throughout the entire routine (Spence &
Mason, 1992).

Exterioception refers to sensory information (visual, auditory, coetaneous) that comes
primarily from sources outside of a person's body (Webster, 2005). Exterioceptors provide
us with information about the movement pathway and speed, the relationship between
body parts and the environment, and auditory information related to dance with music.
Exterioception is an especially important source of sensory information when performers
execute a movement without visual assistance (Houk, 1991). *Vision* is probably the most
important sensor among all the senses related to motor learning due to the fact that it
greatly affects our motor skill acquisition and performance; there are significant differences when athletes perform a motor skill with and without vision. For most sports, vision
provides athletes with information about the movement in relation to the surrounding
environment, such as the anticipation of the path of a passed ball, and the speed of a served
tennis ball. For many closed sports like gymnastics and figure skating, vision integrates
proprioceptive sensors to help athletes sense the spatial and balance aspects in relation
to the other teammates and the environment. Therefore, it is important for teachers and
coaches to be aware of how vision affects instruction, and how it affects students' learning
and performance (Houk, 1991). The *auditory* sense is another major source of exterioception which provides information as feedback through sounds and music (Schmidt &

Lee, 2011; Schmidt & Wrisberg, 2008). Examples include coaches' and teachers' verbal augmented feedback, and dance with music and other dancers. It is especially important for people with vision impairment. Besides these two major sensory sources, athletes also rely on feeling and touch to sense information and changes within the environment where they are performing (Glencross & Piek, 1995). Teachers and coaches should guide or train students how to effectively use vision (observation), hearing (music or coach's verbal feedback), and touch (Tai chi push hand) to get the necessary information for a better performance. The feedback gained from any combination of these sources will provide students and athletes with information about their performance of the motor skill that they just executed (how well it went, what errors there were, etc.), so that they can make improvements for the next trial. From an information processing perspective, all human responses and movements rely on external stimuli and internal body feedback. Thus, students learning motor skills or athletes performing movements rely on the information they receive from internal and external sensory sources which they can then process. These sensory sources (proprioceptors and exterioceptors) can respond to stimuli that impact on the corresponding body parts and transform them into signals which are then sent to the brain for further analysis (Lephart & Fu, 2000). The following sections will discuss how human sensory sources contribute to motor skill learning and performance.

ROLE OF SENSORY SOURCES IN MOTOR LEARNING

The human nervous system consists of two primary sub-systems: the central nervous system and the peripheral nervous system. The central nervous system consists of the brain and the spinal cord, and the peripheral nervous system primarily consists of nerves that connect the body and the central nervous system. In the peripheral nervous system, there are many sensory receptors that are responsible for detecting the stimuli and changes in the environment, and passing that information to the central nervous system for processing and making decisions on actions. (Illustration 9). The human sensory system plays a very important role in motor skill learning and performance. It detects and provides necessary information about the changes in the external environment that can be used for making decisions about actions during the execution of a motor skill. For example, as a tennis player watches the ball just hit by the opponent, he must predict the possible direction of the ball, and make a quick decision as the best position to be in to return the ball (visual sensor). Similar scenarios like basketball passing, baseball batting, and soccer goaltending all need the player to use different sensory sources plus past experiences to make the best possible response. From the above-mentioned examples, there are two types of sensory sources that provide athletes with sophisticated information that can be used in planning and execution of performance.

Proprioception in Motor Performance

Proprioception plays two very important roles in terms of motor skill learning and performance. One is to sense the changes in the external environment and the other is to provide information for the correct body movement and position to the motor control system during motor skill execution (Cordo et al., 1994; Ghez et al., 1990; Rothwell et al., 1982; Vidoni, 2008). The proprioceptors respond to stimuli that impact on the corresponding body parts and transform the information into signals which are sent to the brain for further analysis. The motor control system can internally make an adjustment based on current and changing positions of muscles or joints that relate to the movement, and execute a correct and accurate performance. Therefore, in the process of motor skill learning and performance, proprioception plays an essential role in updating the feedforward commands derived from proprioceptors (e.g., vision) and provides information for body posture and position to the motor control system to make an appropriate adjustment during motor skill execution (Park, Toole, & Lee, 1999; Riemann & Lephart, 2002). The following discussions will provide several examples of how proprioception contributes to motor performance.

Motor skill learning, especially when new skills are being learned, is a complicated process that involves many different sensory contributions. A great many modifications and adjustments through practice are needed before a motor skill can be performed correctly and automatically (Cordo & Harnad, 1994; Kleinman, 1983). In this process, feedback that comes from internal and external sensory sources plays an important role. Some researchers have found that learning to control novel dynamics can only be acquired through the proprioceptive system (Taylor, 2007; Vidoni, 2008). Information from muscles, joints, skin, inner ears, etc. can be collected and sent to the central nervous system by the proprioceptive system to help identify the speed, posture or location of body segments (Brodal, 2010; Sherrington, 1947). After further analysis and comparison, adjustment information can then be generated and sent to the body's motor control system for execution. This kind of feedback and adjustment will not stop until the movement is performed correctly or meets the learner's requirement. Since the process is slow and may require one's full attention, it is good for new skill learning and stationary movement performance.

> **In motor skill learning and performance, proprioception plays an essential role in updating the feedforward commands and provides information to make an appropriate adjustment during motor skill execution.**

For example, the rings routine in gymnastics requires great strength in both arms (should be steady and firm with no shaking), good body posture (should be straight with no arching), as well as a good control of the rings (rings should be absolutely still) at the end of the each skill. The athletes mainly depend on their proprioceptive system to help them control their body posture and the rings, because the other feedback sources may be limited (as they cannot move their body freely) and maximum attention is required during each skill.

Contributing to Pre-feedback

The results of many studies have revealed that the proprioceptive system plays an important role in the process of feedforward control, through which the inner models of movement can be modified. In this process, some information from the visual system is needed as compensation. That is to say, the proprioceptive system, together with the visual system, can provide the nervous system with the environmental information. According to the changes of circumstances, some modification of the inner models of movement, formed during daily practice, will be made before the performance. Take the vault as an example, where an athlete should take part in a great many athletic events each year. At every event the environment and the apparatus are different. Even those athletes who are highly competitive should make adjustments to get used to the devices and environment. During this process, athletes should take advantage of their sensory proprioceptors to detect information such as the speed of each body segment, muscle tension, body postures, locations, etc. Based on this information, modifications will be made through the feedforward system during the next performance.

Focal and Ambient Vision in Motor Performance

Vision is an important sense that can help with the identification of object features and spatial locations. It greatly affects sport performance, at the quality level as well as the effectiveness of acquisition. The visual system provides feedback information to help the brain make decisions such as what skill should be used or what adjustment should be made to execute a motor movement. There is only a limited amount of time for athletes to make decisions during the performance of motor skills. They must possess the ability to translate visual images into accurate body movements to master the proper technique.

Focal vision and *ambient vision* play different roles during motor skill acquisition and competition. Taking soccer as an example, players not only have to focus their attention on the ball (dribbling or kicking the ball) through focal vision, but they also have to know where their opponents and teammates are by using ambient vision when dribbling or passing a ball. For all contact team sports like football, basketball, and Chinese martial arts, athletes must train their "vision sense" and be aware of the opponents around them, especially those behind them. Athletes should be trained to feel opponents' distance and speed through ambient vision. They should be aware of the whole field through their "vision sense" as they move. For soccer dribbling or passing, both focal and ambient vision become important because the players must protect the ball while keeping their peripheral vision on the other players around them.

Another example of the important role that vision plays in movement studies is balance control. Studies show that movement of sensory receptors in the vision system, such as the vestibulo-ocular receptors, coordinates with head motion to assist in balance stabilization.

When people stand with their eyes closed, postural sway will increase. This phenomenon occurs because the vision system can generate continuous updated information about the movement and position of the body segments in relation to each other and the environment. When students stand on one leg or walk with their eyes closed, all feedback information is completely lost, they will lose all sensory feedback, the coordination between head and body position (proprioceptor) will disappear, and body movements will become awkward and unbalanced. Walking on a balance beam without vision will cause a serious balance problem. We must, therefore, pay close attention when we teach balance exercises to students with visual impairment. This kind of ability which detects the relevant visual stimuli and perceives spatial relationships is essential in balance control.

Auditory Sense in Motor Skill Learning

Auditory sense is another important human sensation in motor learning. The auditory system can provide the nervous system with sound information derived from sound stimuli during motor performance. It is an important feedback source to assist movement learning or adjustment. Athletes can take advantage of sounds that are generated by the corresponding body segments or offered by the coach or other sources during movement performance. Such sounds can be taken as a special marker or notation to help the athlete identify the skill elements—such as speed or position of body segments, running pace, skill pattern, etc.—and execute a good performance. Taking the long jump as an example, a good jumping distance is strongly related to a good run-up, which greatly depends on an appropriate running pace. A good method for the training of the running pace is to take advantage of rhythmic sounds, such as a hand-clap from the coach or a rhythmic sound from the athlete's own mouth. More examples include blind martial arts masters and people with vision or hearing impairments who dance with music and teammates. These abilities must be developed through practice. Most elite athletes have special training in these abilities. On the other hand, noisy contest environments may be disadvantageous to an athlete's performance. Studies show that people who were exposed to a sound area had increased body sway (Brandt, 2003; Lakie, 2010). In addition, athletes' batting performance was reported to have a strong association with auditory sensitivity (Brandt, 2003; Lakie, 2010; Rose, 1997). Therefore, it is better for athletes to practice in different environments to get used to noisy situations so that the negative effect of sound stimuli can be diminished.

Key Terms to Remember

- *Pedagogical strategies* refers to a teaching style and method of instruction used in teaching motor skill.

- *Unpredictable environment* refers to an open environment that is not stable and changes in a way that an athlete or a player cannot fully comprehend and anticipate.

- *Practice variability* changes in the practice environment to provide a variety of practice conditions, for example, practice condition and competition condition.

- *Central nervous system* (CNS) consists of the brain and the spinal cord. It is within the CNS that sensory information is integrated, decisions are made, and signals are generated and are sent to the effectors (muscles and glands) to carry out responses (Coker, 2009).

- *Peripheral nervous system* consists primarily of nerves that extend from the brain and spinal cord, linking the body and the CNS (Coker, 2009).

- *Proprioception* refers to sensory information that comes primarily from sources inside a person's body detected by proprioceptors, which are located in the muscles (e.g., muscle spindles), tendons (Golgi tendon organs), joints (joint receptors), and vestibular apparatus, etc.

- *Exterioceptions* refers to sensory information (visual, auditory, coetaneous) that comes primarily from sources outside of a person's body (Webster, 2005).

- *Golgi tendon organs* refer to the receptors which are located near the junction between the muscle and the tendon, and signal the level of force in the various parts of the muscle (Schmidt & Wrisberg, 2008).

- *Auditory sense* is another major source of exterioception which provides information as feedback through sounds and music.

- *Focal vision* refers to the visual system people use primarily to identify objects; it uses the center of the visual field, leads to conscious visual perception, and is degraded in dim lighting (Schmidt & Wrisberg, 2008).

- *Ambient vision* refers to the visual system that allows people to detect the orientation of their body in the environment; it is non-conscious, takes in all of the visual field, and is used for action and movement control (Schmidt & Wrisberg, 2008).

Student Assignments for Connecting Theory to Practice

- List external stimuli related to basketball, soccer, volleyball, tennis, and other open motor skill related sports.

- Which sensory organs would athletes use to detect these external stimuli?

- Explain how athletes can manipulate external stimuli to enhance their ability to quickly and accurately identify external stimuli?

- What is pre-feedback and explain its role in the motor learning process?

- What is feedforward control and explain its role in the motor learning process?

- Explain when and how to properly use ambient vision in the sports of soccer and basketball.

- Explain when and how to properly use focal vision in the sports of soccer and basketball.

- Under what circumstances will an athlete be required to use auditory sensations to respond to external stimuli? You can give examples in the settings of sports, military, recreation, or other areas.

REFERENCES

Ayres, A. J. (1972). *Sensory integration and learning disorders.* Los Angeles, CA: Western Psychological Services.

Bard, C., Fleury, M., Teasdale, N., Paillard, J., & Nougier, V. (1995). Contribution of proprioception for calibrating and updating the motor space. *Canadian Journal of Physiology and Pharmacology, 73,* 246–254.

Brady, F. (1998). A theoretical and empirical review of the contextual interference effect and the learning of motor skills. *Quest, 50,* 266–293.

Brandt, T. (2003). *Vertigo: Its multisensory syndromes.* New York, NY: Springer-Verlag.

Brodal, P. (2010). *The central nervous system: Structure and function* (4th ed.). New York, NY: Oxford University Press.

Browne, S., Clarke, D., Henson, P., Hristofski, F., Jeffreys, V., Kovacs, P., . . . Simpson, D. (Eds.). (2009). *PDHPE application and inquiry second edition preliminary course.* Melbourne, Victoria, Australia: Oxford University Press.

Clark, M. A., Lucett, S., & Corn, R. J. (Eds.) (2008). *NASM essentials of personal fitness training.* Philadelphia, PA: Lippincott Williams & Wilkins.

Coker, C. A. (2009). *Motor learning and control for practitioners* (2nd ed.). Scottsdale, AZ: Holcomb Hathaway Publishers.

Cordo, P. J., Carlton, L., Bevan, L., & Carlton, M. (1994). Proprioceptive coordination of movement sequences: Role of velocity and position information. *Journal of Neurophysiology, 71,* 1848–1861.

Cordo, P., & Harnad, S. T. (Eds.) (1994). *Movement control.* Cambridge, UK: Cambridge University Press.

Fairbrother, J. T. (2010). *Fundamentals of motor behavior.* Champaign, IL: Human Kinetics.

Fisher, A., Murray, E., & Bundy, A. (1991). *Sensory integration theory and practice.* Philadelphia, PA: F. A. Davis Company.

Gilchrist, G., Hill, S., & Troesch, J. (2009). *Going for the green: Prepare your body, mind, and swing for winning golf.* New York, NY: Sterling Publishing Company, Inc.

Ghez, C., Gordon, J., Ghilardi, M. F., Christakos, C. N., & Cooper, S. E. (1990). Roles of proprioceptive input in the programming of arm trajectories. *Cold Spring Harbor Symposium on Quantitative Biology, 55,* 837–847.

Gjelsvik, B. E. (2008). *The Bobath concept in adult neurology.* Stuttgart, Germany: Thieme.

Glencross, D. J., & Piek, J. P. (Eds.). (1995). *Motor control and sensory motor integration: Issues and directions.* New York, NY: Elsevier.

Haggard, P. (1992). Multi-sensory control of coordinated movement. In J. J. Summers (Ed.), *Approaches to the study of motor control and learning* (pp. 195–232). New York, NY: Elsevier.

Honeybourne, J., Moors, H., & Hill, M. (2000). *Advanced physical education & sport: For A-level.* Cheltenham, UK: Stanley Thornes.

Houk, J. C. (1991). Outline for a theory of motor learning. In J. Requin & G. Stelmach (Eds.), *Tutorials in motor neuroscience* (pp. 253–268). New York, NY: Kluwer Academic/Plenum Publishers.

Hugh, R., & Dean R. (2002). Tough defense. In B. D. Hale & D. J. Collins (Eds.), *Rugby tough* (pp. 179–204). Champaign, IL: Human Kinetics.

Kleinman, M. (1983). *The acquisition of motor skill.* East Windsor, NJ: Princeton Book Co.

Kraemer, W. J., Fleck, S. J., & Deschenes, M. R. (2012). *Exercise physiology: Integrating theory and application.* Philadelphia, PA: Lippincott Williams & Wilkins.

Lakie, M. (2010). The influence of muscle tremor on shooting performance. *Experimental Physiology, 95,* 441–450.

Lephart, S. M., & Fu, F. H. (Eds.) (2000). *Proprioception and neuromuscular control in joint stability.* Champaign, IL: Human Kinetics.

Levitt, S. (1995). *Treatment of cerebral palsy and motor delay.* Oxford, UK: Blackwell Science.

Magnusson, M., Enbom, H., Johansson, R., & Pyykko, I. (1990). Significance of pressor input from the human feet in anterior-posterior postural control. The effect of hypothermia on vibration-induced body-sway. *Acta Otolaryngol, 110,* 182–188.

Park, S., Toole, T., & Lee, S. (1999). Functional roles of the proprioceptive system in the control of goal-directed movement. *Percept Motor Skills, 88,* 637–647.

Paulus, W. M, Straube, A., & Brandt, T. (1984). Visual stabilization of posture. Physiological stimulus characteristics and clinical aspects. *Brain, 107,* 1143–1163.

Proske, U. (2005). What is the role of muscle receptors in proprioception? *Muscle & Nerve, 31,* 780–787.

Riemann, B., & Lephart, S. (2002). The sensorimotor system, Part II: The role of proprioception in motor control and functional joint stability. *Journal of Athletic Training, 37,* 80–84.

Rose, D. J. (1997). *A multilevel approach to the study of motor control and learning.* Boston, MA: Allyn and Bacon.

Rothwell, J. C., Traub, M. M., Day, B. L., Obeso, J. A., Thomas, P. K., & Marsden, C. D. (1982). Manual motor performance in a deafferented man. *Brain, 105,* 515–542.

Schmidt, R. A., & Lee, T. D. (2011). *Motor control and learning: A behavioral emphasis.* Champaign, IL: Human Kinetics.

Schmidt, R. A., & Wrisberg, C. A. (2008). *Motor learning and performance: A situation-based learning approach* (4th ed.). Champaign, IL: Human Kinetics.

Sherrington, C. S. (1947). *The integrative action of the nervous system.* Cambridge, UK: Cambridge University Press.

Shogan, D. A. (1999). *The making of high-performance athletes: Discipline, diversity, and ethics* (pp. 75–76). Toronto, Canada: University of Toronto Press.

Spence, A. P., & Mason, E. B. (1992). *Human anatomy and physiology.* St. Paul, MO: West Pub. Co.

Stallings, L. M. (1982). *Motor learning: From theory to practice.* St. Louis, MO: The C.V. Mosby.

Taylor, J. A. (2007). *Human motor control and learning of novel dynamic forces and the influence of attentional control.* St. Louis, MO: Washington University in St. Louis.

Vidoni, E. D. (2008). *Proprioception is "central" to motor learning: Different consequences of peripheral and central proprioceptive disruption to sequence learning.* Lawrence, KS: University of Kansas.

Webster, D. (2005). *GCSE physical education: Revision guide.* FIF, UK: Letts Educational.

Weinberg, R. S., & Gould, D. (2007). *Foundations of sport and exercise psychology* (4th ed.). Champaign, IL: Human Kinetics.

Williams, A., & Hodges, N. (2005). Practice, instruction and skill acquisition in soccer: Challenging tradition. *Journal of Sports Sciences, 23,* 637–650.

Wrisberg, C. A. (2007). *Sport skill instruction for coaches.* Champaign, IL: Human Kinetics.

Movement Control Systems of Performing Motor Skills

OBJECTIVES

- Understand brain activity while engaging in motor skill movements
- Understand the closed-loop control system of performing open motor skills
- Understand the open-loop control system of performing closed motor skills
- Understand the key factors for effectively utilizing the closed-loop control system
- Understand Fitts' law – Speed/accuracy trade-off
- Understand how to strengthen the closed-loop control system for better performance
- Understand how to strengthen the open-loop control system
- Understand other considerations of implementing both closed-loop and open-loop control systems in motor learning process
- Understand how to integrate the two different control systems in the motor learning process
- Understand the specific nature of each sport activity and properly design training to maximize learning outcomes

INTRODUCTION

In sports, physical education, leisure, recreation, the military, and many other professions, participants are required to engage in various motor skills ranging from simple (walking or kicking) to complex (gymnastic routines, ice-hockey, or figure skating). In fact, all motor skills have their own distinctive characteristics that can be distinguished by either fine or gross motor skill control, by RT-based or non-RT based motor control, by the speed or endurance required, etc (Wang, 2009). Regardless of the type of motor skill, its execution is determined by the brain controls of the performer. Without proper brain control, a performer's muscles become paralyzed and useless. Ultimately, a human's skeletal muscles only serve to carry out the brain's commands as to what to do, and how and when to do it, by developing or relaxing muscular tension for executing the designated or intended movements (Sherwood, 2012).

The human nervous system is a very complex system that is in charge of receiving external stimuli such as hearing sound, seeing objects moving, feeling body pressure, or sensing internal kinematic feedback, etc. (Kalat, 2009; Lundy-Ekman, 2007). Based on all the above sensations, the brain relies on the immediate sensations as well as previous experiences to make a decision for action, and then the brain converts abstract program of skill action into electrical impulses sent to muscles to engage in coordinated movements. This process involves billions of nerve cells to coordinate with each other for completing a coordinated movement (Banerjee & Chakrabarti, 2008). Hence, motor learning is a brain controlling process for achieving specific goals at a particular time. For simple skills, such as throwing a dart at a static target or throwing a rock into the river, the learner might only need a few trials in order to attain perfect execution due to the simple brain controlling process. Conversely, a learner may require years to master complex motor skills such as ice hockey, gymnastics, or soccer. In short, the length of time and effort of motor learning process involved depends on the required precision and complexity of the control process for the specific skill.

Instructors should understand the unique controlling characteristics of the specific motor skills being learned in order to properly design the training methods for maximizing learning outcomes. For example, when teaching RT-based motor skills, such as boxing, basketball, soccer, tennis, or hockey, a major concern is how to shorten learners' RT when responding to external stimuli. In contrast, when teaching motor skills, such as weightlifting, diving, or gymnastics, consistency, coordination, and timing of action are pivotal aspects of the controlling process. In sum, all human skill movements are the result of neuro-muscular control processes since both brain and muscles work together to produce desired human movements (Rose & Christina, 2006). Coordinated skill movements are not easily accomplished unless extensive and proper training is provided for the brain to send the appropriate signals to the muscle groups. Ultimately, precise, flawless, and coordinated movements must be consciously controlled by the central nervous system whose functions should be trained through well-organized practice. In order to illustrate how a coordinated motor skill is executed, it is necessary to briefly describe the human central nervous system and the different components of the brain that are involved in human movements.

BRAIN ACTIVITY UNDER VOLUNTARY CONTROL

Watching an elite baseball player hitting a pitched ball is not as simple as people would normally think because the complex integration of various parts of the nervous system must coordinate to accomplish this act. The baseball batting movement relies on a complex interaction of higher brain centers with spinal reflexes performed together with precise timing. In order to effectively teach athletes and motor skill learners, it is necessary to understand how the human brain controls skeletal motor movements. The first stage in performing a voluntary movement occurs in subcortical and cortical motivational areas which send signals to the association cortex which forms a "rough draft" of the planned movement. The abstract movement plan is then sent to both the cerebellum and basal ganglia. These movement structures of the "rough draft" are then converted into precise temporal (timing) and spatial excitation programs. Respectively, the cerebellum plays an important role for making fast movements, while the basal ganglia are more responsible for charging slow or deliberate movements. Through the processes from the cerebellum and

COURTESY OF U.S. AIR FORCE

basal ganglia, the intended motor program is sent through the thalamus to the motor cortex that further forwards the information down to spinal neurons for "spinal tuning" and finally to skeletal muscles (Powers & Howley, 1997). As the movement progresses for performing RT-based motor skills, it is monitored by sensory endings in the muscle spindles, Golgi tendon organs, and joint censors. These sensory endings update the cerebellum and basal ganglia, so that the cerebral cortex can analyze the current movement situation and, based on external environmental demands, make decisions to modify the motor programs if necessary, and further send corrective nerve signals back to the relevant muscle groups for the next movement (Stefan, Kunesch, Cohen, Benecke, & Classen, 2000).

TWO TYPES OF MOTOR CONTROL PROCESSES

The performing of movements is a complex neuro-muscular controlled process that includes two types of processes, the *closed-loop control process* and the *open-loop control process*. These are illustrated as follows: (1) the closed-loop control motor system controls human movements that respond to unpredictable external stimuli, such as motor skills in the sports of basketball, soccer, volleyball, tennis, team handball, boxing, and others. Without external stimuli, the performer cannot make decisions to develop an action plan for a movement (DiStefano, Stubberud, & Williams, 1995; Schmidt & Lee, 2011). (2) The open-loop control system refers to that system, which controls human movements without requiring a response to ever-changing external stimuli for the motor skills, such as diving, swimming, weight-lifting, gymnastics, figure skating, high jumping, long jumping, etc.

Closed-loop Control System

The closed-loop control system refers to the human motor control system, which is activated in reaction to external unpredictable stimuli in order to achieve a specific movement goal (Schmidt & Wrisberg 2008). To illustrate the specific mechanisms of the closed-loop human control system, we can use a home-thermostat system as an analogy. A thermostat constantly controls the temperature in a house at the level set by the resident. For example, when the temperature is set at 70 degrees, the thermostat will be shut down if the temperature rises above 70 degrees and will be turned on if it drops below. The thermostat will be automatically shut down or turned on according to the immediate temperature in the house. In order for this system to work, there are several key elements that must be part of the process: a) executive (thermostat), b) feedback (temperature), and c) effector (fan). If any of these components are missing, the closed-loop control system will not work. The decision for turning the thermostat (executive) on or off depends solely on the room temperature (feedback). The fan (effector) carries out the executive's order to blow cool or warm air into the room. Based on this system, the change in the feedback causes a decision to be made by the executive and then an action is taken by the fan to blow the air into the room. If there is no change of temperature, no action will be taken. This model illustrates how human movements are controlled by a closed loop control system.

Characteristics of a Closed-loop Control System

1. External environment is unpredictable.
2. Any decision and action must rely on the changing external environments.
3. Quick reaction and speedy action is crucial to success of action.
4. Action cannot be determined in advance.

As can be seen in Figure 5.1, the key components of the closed-loop control system include feedback (external stimuli and intrinsic feedback), the brain (executive) for decision-making, and the muscle (effector) for carrying out the movements. Generally, unpredictable external stimuli are related to game situations such as teammates' movements, opponents' actions, travel of a ball, open space, flow of competition, etc. An athlete's eyes, ears, and skin sense these external stimuli and transfer the information to the sensory cortex, which immediately recognizes them and facilitates the motor cortex in selecting a response and programming an action. Once the motor cortex has programmed an action, an abstract concept will be transformed into electrical impulses that are sent to the relevant muscle groups for a coordinated movement. During the process of performing an action, the muscle spindle, Golgi tendon organ, joint sensors, and vestibular appendix sensory nerves continuously send the nerve signals of the immediate movement information to the cerebral cortex for the commands of the next movement. Based on immediate extrinsic and intrinsic feedback, the brain will continuously make decisions to command the muscles to carry out the consequent movements based on the immediate external and intrinsic feedback (Grossberg, 1980).

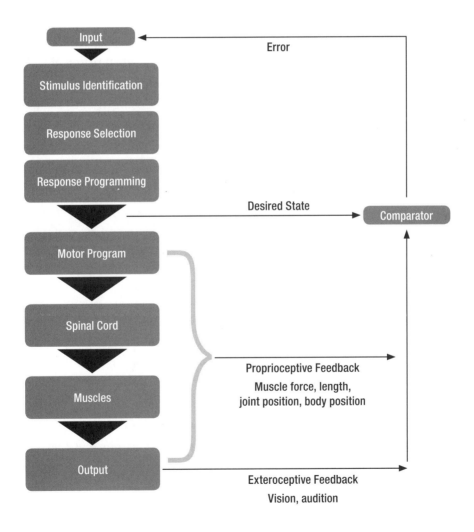

FIGURE 5.1. Closed-loop control system. (Schmidt & Wrisberg, 2008)

The key factors for effectively utilizing the closed-loop control system

SPEED OF DECISION MAKING

When performing impellent reaction based motor skills, one of the two key elements for successfully carrying out the closed-loop control system is the speed of a performer's decision-making in response to unpredictable external stimuli (game situations) because the situation changes rapidly from moment to moment. Any delay in responding to external stimuli could result in failure, such as a boxer being knocked down by an opponent within a split second, a soccer player failing to block a ball passed by an opposing striker, or a basketball player missing a shot in the last second of the game due to a slight hesitation. Hence, the development of prompt decision-making skills in reaction to unpredictable external stimuli, controlled by a closed-loop control system, is a critical component of training regimens for RT-based motor skills.

TIMING OF MOVEMENT CONTROL

Although speed of movement is obviously an important factor when performing RT-based motor skills, timing of movement control is another essential element for successfully executing these skills. For example, in soccer, tackling an opposing dribbler's ball too early could easily result in failure to steal the ball from that opponent, and likewise in boxing, blocking an opponent's fake punch prematurely could result in being knocked down by the opponent. Also, a rapid baseball bat swing does not ensure success in hitting the ball effectively unless the timing is perfect during the moment of contact. Practitioners must not overlook the importance of controlling the timing of executing RT-based motor skills by solely focusing on speed of decision-making. Furthermore, timing of executing a motor skill is also an imperative component of performing certain motor skill.

ACCURACY OF MOVEMENT CONTROL

In addition to the two above factors contributing to the success of movement performance of RT-based motor skills, accurate and precise movement control is the third crucial component contributing to the effectiveness of the closed-loop control system when executing RT-based motor skills. In particular, in the high-level competition environment, it is easy for athletes to perform fast actions, but it can be a tremendous challenge to perform them while achieving precise movement control. For example, when observing collegiate soccer competitions, we often see that many athletes have very fast actions, but they lack accuracy. As a result, the players on both teams constantly chase the ball back and forth due to inaccuracy of passing or collaborating among the teammates. Thus, for RT-based motor skills, accurate control of movements and fast speed of decision-making should be deemed as equally important elements of the training focus for the closed-loop control system. To illustrate the relationship between speed and accuracy, we need to introduce the speed/accuracy trade-off theory in motor learning settings.

Key factors for effective utilization of the closed-loop control system

- **Speed of decision making**
- **Timing of movement control**
- **Accuracy of movement control**

Fitts' Law of Speed-accuracy Tradeoff

Speed of responding to external stimuli and accuracy of movement control are two essential components of the closed-loop control system. According to *Fitts' law of speed-accuracy tradeoff theory,* when speed of an action increases, accuracy of performing a motor skill decreases, and vice versa. Basically, when performing RT-based motor skills, a performer can manipulate the speed in order to increase or decrease accuracy based on environmental demands. This principle is critically important in practical situations. For example, for beginners, speed of movement should not be the main factor; learning the correct patterns of motor skills is the key element that should be emphasized. Thus, practitioners should compromise speed for accuracy at the cognitive stage of learning (Coker, 2004). Conversely, in high-level competition, the goal of training for these athletes is to increase speed of movement control while still maintaining accuracy. It is a great challenge to accomplish both goals simultaneously. When observing a performer competing in RT-based sports, it becomes clear that when speed is increased, errors consistently increase as well; when speed decreases, accuracy of movement control increases. The following section illustrates the rationale behind the speed-accuracy tradeoff theory.

REASONS FOR THE SPEED-ACCURACY TRADEOFF PHENOMENON

The reasons for the speed-accuracy tradeoff are as follows: (1) to execute RT-based motor skills commanded by the closed-loop control system, a performer has to identify external stimuli, make a decision about what to do, and program and send proper signals to muscles to carry out the designated movements. Furthermore, proprioceptive and external feedback will be continuously sent to the brain for making the next decision of action. Obviously, the more time a performer has to process the information, the greater the accuracy he or she can accomplish (Schmidt & Lee, 2011). If there is only a short time for analyzing and processing internal and external feedback during the progress of performing motor skills, this could increase errors in the execution. There is clearly a positive linear relationship between available decision-making time and accuracy of movement execution. In addition, from a psychological perspective, when a high demand for rapid speed of movement executions is required, the anxiety level of an athlete is elevated, which, in turn, negatively affects the accuracy of movement control.

TWO EXCEPTIONS TO THE USE OF THE SPEED-ACCURACY TRADEOFF

The first exception to the use of Fitts' law in motor skill learning is when engaging in temporal and spatially oriented motor skills. The temporal feature refers to timing and the spatial element is related to the three-dimensional environment. Hitting a baseball, heading a soccer ball, or spiking a volleyball are examples of executing temporal and spatially-oriented motor skills because all these actions require precise timing and are undertaken in a three-dimensional environment. Fitts' law of speed-accuracy tradeoff cannot be applied to this type of motor skill. The second exception to Fitts' law is when an athlete engages in a forceful motor skill action such as hitting a baseball or golf ball, or throwing a javelin or discus.

Strengthening the Closed-loop Control System for Better Performance

The closed-loop control system serves as the controlling system of a performer responding to unpredictable external situations by accepting the stimulus, selecting the proper response, and programming for an action to be executed with speed and precise timing. To accomplish these goals, proper training should be arranged to develop the closed-loop control system for any learners who engage in these types of motor skills.

In practical settings, countless unpredictable external stimuli with numerous variables such as timing, speed, shapes, patterns, specific representations, etc., are presented to performers in different settings. Not only does a performer need to deal with a wide variety of unpredictable external stimuli, but quick reaction and precise control of movement actions are also essential for implementing RT-based motor skills controlled by the closed-loop control system. Therefore, if athletes or performers cannot develop the closed-loop control system to a highly sophisticated level, they will not be able to meet the environmental demands. The following strategies can be used to strengthen the closed-loop control system.

MAKING FULL USE OF FOCAL AND AMBIENT VISIONS

One of the important mechanisms of the closed-loop control system is the use of either focal or ambient vision, or both, to properly detect external stimuli –in a timely manner - in order to make accurate decisions for engaging in coordinated movements (Knudson & Morrison, 2002). Focal vision refers to the performer using his/her vision to identify a specific object or person from the environment (Schmidt & Lee 2005; Rose, 1997).

COURTESY OF GEEK PHILOSOPHER PHOTOS

For example, a baseball outfielder must very carefully watch the direction and speed of travel of a flying ball in order to catch it. A basketball receiver must watch an upcoming ball to catch it for the next movement and a martial arts master needs to be aware of an opponent's punch or kick at any given moment to defend himself/herself. The vision used in these various settings is focal vision that mainly identifies an object or focuses on a specific point.

Depending on the situation or environmental demands, a performer either uses focal vision or *ambient vision,* which refers to observation of the peripheral fields of the environment (Berencsi, Ishihara, & Imanaka, 2005). For example, in soccer or basketball competitions, a passer must observe a wide range of the field to identify the teammate who is in the best position for receiving a pass. In practical settings, the performer sometimes needs focal vision and sometimes ambient vision to detect the relevant external stimuli for proper decision-making. Practitioners must teach learners to determine in which situations to use focal or ambient vision in order to accomplish the required goal. Without such training, a soccer player may only focus on the ball all the time while he/she is dribbling and not be able to see where his/her teammates are and which player is in the best position to receive a pass. Such a bad habit can last a lifetime once the poor pattern has been developed. Using appropriate vision for executing the particular motor skill is one of the essential processes of using the closed-loop control system.

MANIPULATION OF EXTERNAL STIMULI IN PRACTICE

The response of the closed-loop control system relies on external stimuli such as a ball, teammates, opponents, or game flow pattern that can be manipulated with different colors, shapes, patterns, forms, speed, timing, or backgrounds. The more varied the external stimuli a performer encounters, the less time he/she needs to identify these stimuli and the more effectively he/she can respond to them. Manipulation of the external stimuli presented to the performer should be a vital component of training for engaging in RT-based motor skills in order to develop the capability of the closed-loop control system. For instance, in baseball practice, balls of different sizes, with different surface friction or color can be used to change the speed of traveling and meet the demands of training. Obviously, a smaller and denser ball can travel faster due to the decreased friction between the ball and the air. By using a ball with a color that is easier to see, such as one with black darts on a white background, a performer can shorten his/her RT at the stimulus identification stage. Likewise, in soccer, external stimuli can be manipulated through the use of balls with different air pressure, size, or surface texture or by playing on different soccer fields (wood floor or grass). With such changes, the rebound, speed, and controllability of the ball will differ significantly. In addition, external stimuli can be manipulated in specific ways depending on practitioners' intentions and training requirements to accomplish the goals. For example, when training to receive a soccer ball, the variables of external stimuli could include: distance between ball and player, different angles of rebound of the ball, varied heights, speed, direction, force, format (curve or not) of incoming balls, receiving with or without defenders, and in hot, cold, or rainy weather. By using this concept, practitioners can creatively manipulate external stimuli using many different types of formats according to the motor skills and sports being practiced. The main goal is to make unpredictable external stimuli become predictable stimuli. Once this has been achieved, performers will be able to execute any RT-based motor skill effectively and swiftly.

FULLY UTILIZING INTRINSIC FEEDBACK BASED ON TYPES OF SKILLS

To make an appropriate decision controlled by the closed-loop control system, not only does a performer need to detect external stimuli, he/she also needs to fully utilize proprioceptive feedback, such as the current body states of muscular tension, speed of action, joint positions, body and head orientation, etc. The brain continuously compares external stimuli with proprioceptive feedback to make the correct decision for the next action. Sensitive self-awareness of the immediate body movements can be strengthened with deliberate and effortful attention after an action is completed. Such practice is important as it can improve accuracy of movement executions for RT-based motor skills.

EMPHASIZING QUICK DECISION MAKING

Since the closed-loop control system is responsible for carrying out RT-based motor skills, quick decision-making and reduction of RT should be the core of technical training for strengthening the system. An accurate and appropriate decision depends on a *speedy decision-making process*. Any slight delay will render the decision meaningless with the resulting loss of the opportunity to respond effectively to the external demand. In reality, whoever gets ahead of the environmental demand in a particular situation becomes the winner. In Chapter 7, many strategies will be introduced for reducing RT when engaging in RT-based motor skills.

To strengthen the closed-loop control system when training for engaging in RT-based motor skills, different focuses of motor control must be emphasized based on the particular motor skills involved. For example, motor controls could be stressed for balance, spatial orientation, precise timing, fine movements, speed, collaborating with partner(s), strength and coordination, etc. Once the practitioner has identified the particular RT-based motor skills required in a particular situation, the correct closed-loop control system can be effectively strengthened to accomplish the goals of training. Ultimately, the main purpose of skill training is to develop specific patterns of the neuro-muscular control process that give precise, timely, and proper nerve signals to the relevant muscles for executing the designated motor movement (Keogh & Sugden, 1985).

> ## Strategies for strengthening the closed-loop control system
>
> - **Make full use of focal and ambient visions**
> - **Manipulate external stimuli in practice**
> - **Fully utilize intrinsic feedback based on types of skills**
> - **Emphasize quick decision making**

Open-loop Control System

The open-loop control system (Figure 5.2) is responsible for controlling non-RT based motor movements which do not require external stimuli to make a decision for taking an action. Thus, the required mechanics of the open-loop control system include only the executive and effectors since the performer can plan in advance how he/she will carry out a motor skill. Once a decision is made, the command will be sent to the muscles to carry out the actions without requiring any incoming external feedback to complete the movement. Such motor skills include high jumping, long jumping, gymnastics, diving, figure skating, weightlifting, swimming, disc throwing, etc.

One of the unique characteristics of this type of motor skill is that competition conditions are exactly the same as practice conditions so the environment of competition is predictable and stable and performers do not need to respond to unpredictable external

stimuli. To successfully perform non-RT based motor skills commanded by the open-loop control system, the consistency of movement executions should be emphasized. For example, a long jumper needs to have a consistent approach phase with precise steps during practice and competition alike; any inconsistent approach steps could result in undesirable consequences of

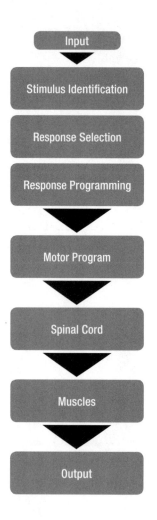

FIGURE 5.2. Open-loop control system. (Schmidt & Wrisberg, 2008)

performing. Advanced decision making and consistent movement execution are critical elements of performing this type of motor skill.

Even though there is no requirement to make decisions based on external stimuli when engaging in non-RT based motor skills controlled by the open-loop control system, it is still important for the performer to be aware of the proprioceptive feedback in order to compare it with the outcome of the performance just completed. The performer's proprioceptive feedback is always considered after an action has been taken, not during the action (Riemann & Lephart, 2002). For example, since basketball free shooting is a non-RT based motor skill controlled by the open-loop control system, a shooter has to make a decision in advance as to how to shoot the ball without taking into consideration any possible intervention by defenders. After the shot is taken, the shooter must compare the result of the shot with the intrinsic feedback (proprioceptive feedback) so that the brain can develop a proper perspective as to whether the shot was successful in order to decide whether an adjustment is necessary for the second shot.

> ## Characteristics of an Open-loop Control System
>
> 1. **External environment is predictable.**
> 2. **Performer can make decisions in advance without worrying about the changes of external stimuli.**
> 3. **Emphasize maximum consistency of action.**

Clearly, the open-loop control system should be used for carrying out non-RT based motor skill executions that are determined well in advance, since practice and competition conditions are exactly the same. When preparing for high jumping contests, the critical training focus should involve learning how to use biomechanical principles to maximize vertical distance, so the elements of approach steps and speed, techniques of take-off, being airborne and landing should be emphasized. Utilization of external feedback and quick decision-making are irrelevant for an open-loop control system. There are many motor skills controlled by open-loop control systems some of which require the performer to achieve the maximum horizontal or vertical distance, while others require maximum speed, such as 100-meter, 200-meter, or 400-meter races. As non-RT based motor skills are required for a variety of purposes, the specific motor skills controlled by the open-loop control system should be well developed. The following diagram illustrates the process of the open-loop control system for controlling non-RT based motor skills.

Other Considerations

The above information illustrates how the closed- and open-loop control systems of the brain organize, coordinate, and direct the human body to implement RT and non-RT based motor skills. It is evident that, as every controlling process has its own unique characteristics, the training method for each control system should have a different focus. However, in practical settings, sometimes certain motor skills fall into one category of the motor skill type, which may not exactly correlate with the theoretical model of the designated control system. For example, pairs figure skating is considered to involve non-RT based motor skills because all the movements are part of pre-determined routines which are exactly the same in practice and competition. All the actions of performance can be planned ahead by following strict sequences of movements. However, sometimes a skater has to jump into the air to execute certain movements and her partner has to catch her. In this case, the jumper must execute her movements perfectly in order for her partner to be able to catch her smoothly. Thus, while in theory pairs figure skating is considered to involve non-RT based motor skills, in reality, the control system for certain portions of the performance is the closed-loop control system because a performer's actions must rely on external stimuli. Similarly, the sport skill of downhill skiing is performed under stable and unchanging situations, so theoretically it is regarded as a non -RT based motor skill. But from a practical point of view, a skier cannot remember all the characteristics of the specific hill conditions and situations so he/she must constantly make body adjustments to keep good balance in order to prevent falling. Any delay or hesitation in making body adjustments could easily result in falls. To prevent falls, a performer's RT in responding to external stimuli (hill conditions) should be one of the major training emphases. Thus, from a theoretical perspective, while downhill skiing is considered to be a non-RT based motor skill, in reality, to engage in this type of motor skill, the closed-loop control system must be used to successfully carry out the movement sequences. For the above reason, practitioners should have a creative mind to analyze the nature of the particular motor skill that they are teaching or coaching in order to properly develop a training regimen to accomplish the goals of training.

Since non-RT based motor skills controlled by the open-loop control system are executed under consistent and unchanging conditions with an advanced planning format, the goal of training is to develop the performer's accurate and sharp image of the proper movement patterns in the brain so that an expected movement skill can be executed with maximum certainty over and over again. Watching and analyzing video-clips or life demonstrations of accurately executed motor skills can effectively stimulate and enhance the blueprints in the performer's brain (Mulder, Zijlstra, Zijlstra, & Hochstenbach, 2004). These blueprints of the precise movement images are the ultimate mechanism determining the success of movement executions controlled by the open-loop control system. In addition, mental imagery training can help performers consolidate accurate motor skill images. According to Darling (2008), and Taylor and Wilson (2005), mental imagery combined with technical practice will produce better learning outcomes compared to many other training methods of motor learning. Internal and/or external mental imagery could be applied to technical training for reinforcing and strengthening correct technical images of executing motor skills (Orlick & Partington, 1988; Taylor & Wilson, 2005).

Repeatedly practicing motor skill routines under optimal physical conditions is another important variable to consider because performing correct and precise motor skill coordination is a major training objective. Coordinated neuromuscular movements can only be achieved through numerous repetitions. Accordingly, maximum consistency or maximum certainty come with repeated practice and training so that patterns of neuromuscular coordination can be eventually established and stabilized.

Key Terms to Remember

- The *nervous system* is a very complex system that is in charge of receiving external stimuli such as hearing sound, seeing an object moving, feeling body pressure, or sensing internal kinematic feedback, etc., and responding to those external stimuli accordingly.
- *Executive* refers to a decision-making center such as the human brain.
- *Effector* refers to the human muscles that are the only body tissues to carrying out actions.
- *Comparator* refers to as an analyzing center to compare the intended action and the actual consequence of the action to see the deviation or accuracy in order for the brain to make the next proper decision for ongoing activity.
- The *closed-loop control system* controls human movements that respond to unpredictable external stimuli.

- The *open-loop control system* refers to that system which controls human movements without requiring a response to ever-changing external stimuli for the motor skills, such as diving, swimming, weightlifting, gymnastics, figure skating, high jumping, long jumping, etc.

- *Fitts' law – Speed/accuracy trade-off* occurs when the speed of an action increases and the accuracy of performing a motor skill decreases, or vice versa.

- *Intrinsic feedback* refers to the kinematic feedback, such as the internal feedback from Golgi tendon organ, muscle spindles, vestibular apparatus, cutaneous sensation, etc.

- *Extrinsic feedback* refers to any feedback from outside of the body such as an opponent's attack, a flying basketball or soccer ball, sound, teammates' actions, etc.

Student Assignments for Connecting Theory to Practice

- To execute open motor skill movements, what motor control system is taking control of human motor movements?

- To execute closed motor skill movements, what motor control system is taking control of human motor movements?

- How can a practitioner manipulate external stimuli to maximize students' learning outcomes?

- What is the purpose of a practitioner to manipulate external stimuli for training?

- What types of stimuli are considered to be external stimuli?

- What is the role of intrinsic feedback? Please explain the relationship between extrinsic and intrinsic feedback.

- To train basketball, soccer, or volleyball athletes, should a practitioner enhance athletes' closed loop control system or open loop control system? Explain why.

- To train high jumping, long jumping, gymnastics, diving, or 100-meter dash, should a practitioner enhance athletes' closed loop control system or open loop control system? Explain why.

- Is reaction time an important factor related to close loop control system or related to open loop control system?

- What is the important implication for understanding two control systems relating to practitioners' motor learning engagements?

- Explain why speed is such an important factor of motor learning process for closed loop control system? Give examples to illustrate your response.

REFERENCES

Banerjee, R., & Chakrabarti, B. K. (2008). *Models of brain and mind: Physical, computational, and psychological approaches.* Oxford, UK: Elsevier.

Berencsi, A., Ishihara, M., & Imanaka, K. (2005). The functional role of central and peripheral vision in the control of posture. *Human Movement Science, 24,* 689–709.

Coker, C. A. (2004). *Motor learning and control for practitioners.* New York, NY: McGraw-Hill.

Darling, T. (2008). *Technical application of sport imagery.* Dissertation, Monroe, Louisiana: University of Louisiana Publisher.

DiStefano, J. J., Stubberud, A. R., & Williams, I. J. (1995). *Feedback and control systems.* New York, NY: McGraw-Hill.

Grossberg, S. (1980). How does a brain build a cognitive code? *Psychology Review, 87,* 1–51.

Kalat, J. W. (2009). *Biological psychology.* Belmont, CA: Wadsworth Cengage Learning.

Keogh, J., & Sugden, D. A. (1985). *Movement skill development.* New York, NY: Macmillan.

Knudson, D. V., & Morrison, C. S. (2002). *Qualitative analysis of human movement.* Champaign, IL: Human Kinetics.

Lundy-Ekman, L. (2007). *Neuroscience: Fundamentals for rehabilitation.* St. Louis, MO: Saunders Elsevier.

Mulder, T., Zijlstra, S., Zijlstra, W., & Hochstenbach, J. (2004). The role of motor imagery in learning a totally novel movement. *Experimental Brain Research, 154,* 211–217.

Orlick, T., & Partington, J. (1988). Mental links to excellence. *The Sport Psychologist, 2,* 105–130.

Powers, S. K., & Howley, E. T, (1997). *Exercise physiology: Theory and application to fitness and performance.* Madison, WI: Brown & Benchmark Publishers.

Riemann, B. L., & Lephart, S. M. (2002). The sensorimotor system, part II: The role of proprioception in motor control and functional joint stability. *Journal of Athletic Training, 37,* 80–84.

Rose, D. J. (1997). *A multilevel approach to the study of motor control and learning.* Needham Height, MA: Allyn & Bacon.

Rose, D. J., & Christina, R. W. (2006). *A multilevel approach to the study of motor control and learning.* San Francisco, CA: Pearson Benjamin Cummings.

Schmidt, R. A., & Lee, T., D. (2011). *Motor control and learning: A behavioral emphasis.* Champaign, IL: Human Kinetics.

Schmidt, R. A., & Wrisberg, C. A. (2008). *Motor learning and performance: A situation-based learning approach* (4th ed.). Champaign, IL: Human Kinetics.

Sherwood, L. (2012). *Human physiology: From cells to systems.* Hong Kong, China: Cengage Learning.

Stefan, K., Kunesch, E., Cohen, L. G., Benecke, R., & Classen, J. (2000). Induction of plasticity in the human motor cortex by paired associative stimulation. *Brain, 123,* 572–584.

Taylor, J., & Wilson, G. (2005). *Applying sport psychology–Four perspectives.* Champaign, IL: Human Kinetics.

Wang, J. (2009). Reaction-time training for elite athletes: A winning formula for champions. *International Journal of Coaching Science, 3,* 67–78.

Motor Programs and Stages of Motor Skill Learning

OBJECTIVES

- Understand motor programs and stages of motor learning, motor program, and schema theory
- Understand generalized motor program, specific motor program, and grouped motor program
- Understand the implication of motor program in Fitts and Posner's three stages of motor learning
- Understand training approaches for distinctive stages of motor skill learning
- Understand types of goals and goal settings in motor learning
- Understand rewarding systems integrated into goal setting programs
- Understand the integration of theory into practice

INTRODUCTION

Coker (2004) indicated that "a mechanism at the core of the central command-based construct is the motor program, and a motor program is an abstract representation of a movement plan that contains all of the motor commands required to carry out the intended action when there is a stimuli or a particular environment." According to this definition, learning a motor skill is just like building a motor program, and then storing it into memory for future use when needed. The schema theory for discrete motor skill learning (Schmidt, 1975; Schmidt & Lee, 2005) proposes the production of rapid discrete movements involves units of action (motor programs) that are retrieved from memory and then adapted to a particular situation. The schema theory suggests that an appropriate program is simply retrieved from memory and executed when a specific movement is required. For example, once biking, skiing, or golf skills are stored in long term memory, they remain and will not be forgotten. Under the definition of motor program and schema described in the above studies, a schema is a set of rules relating various outcomes of an individual's actions to the parameter values chosen for the motor program, and the motor program of all skills and movements must be built and stored in our memory, waiting for retrieval. However, our brain has limited space, and cannot store all motor programs for all skills. In practical and competition settings, some athletes can complete motor skills and movements which they have never done before. Some students can perform a new movement or skill very well even in the first trial without practice and having a previously stored motor program for that skill. This phenomenon challenges the schema theory in terms of storing the motor program in memory and retrieving it when needed. In order to clearly describe the motor program theory, and understand the nature of motor skill learning, there are three categories into which motor programs are classified. These three categories of motor programs might help explain different situations of motor learning.

GENERALIZED MOTOR PROGRAM (GMP)

Schmidt (1975) proposed that every movement does not require a separate motor program for its execution and the motor program is more general in nature. This GMP represents a class of actions or pattern of movement that can be modified to fit into different motor programs. Just like a simple basketball lay-up movement pattern (motor program), it can be customized by different players and performed very differently (modified). Schmidt indicates that the generalized motor program concept gives a solution for both the storage and the novelty problem in terms of learning/performing a learned or untaught skill. It says that "by modifying the parameters such as force and timing of the movement you could have a single motor program that could be customized for different patterns. Therefore, a general class of movements may be governed by a single GMP, which can be scaled to meet the current task demands."

> **Fitts and Posner (1967) suggest that the learning process is sequential and that we move through specific phases as we learn.**

Consequently, some elements of the generalized motor programs are thought to be relatively fixed from trial to trial, and a standard feature of the movement, which can be modified to produce unique movement events. For example, movements like baseball, golf, and cricket swings involve a basic pattern of a backswing and a forward swing motion that are governed by the swing GMP. Movements like kicking a football in soccer or American football involves a basic leg swing backward and forward kick pattern. Therefore, having learned one motor skill program, the pattern of that learned skill will

COURTESY OF MEDIA FOCUS

assist in learning another skill with a similar pattern. The overall duration and amplitude of that movement, as well as the specific muscles to use (parameters), may depend on the distance that the baseball, golf ball, or soccer ball will travel.

SPECIFIC MOTOR PROGRAM (SMP)

The execution of any motor program has a specific order and sequence that are mandatory to follow. For example, a right hand stroke in tennis and a right hand stroke in badminton require different motor skill programs. Although there are similarities in certain motions in tennis and badminton movement (major motor program pattern), the specific motor program for a tennis stroke is different from badminton in parameters. Both motor programs have a specific order and sequence when executed. Therefore, a specific motor skill for different sports (tennis and badminton) may be governed by a single SMP for that specific skill, which can be retrieved to meet the immediate task demands. For example, two different styles of high jump. Although these two motor skills are a high jump, their motor programs are different, and the executions required using different techniques and skill, and require different jump abilities, just like two different sports skills require a different training.

GROUPED MOTOR PROGRAM (GRMP)

For sequentially related sports and activities that require several specific motor programs with logical connections to coordinate each other (e.g., triple somersaults in gymnastics, or the long jump and high jump in track and field), the specific motor programs of these sport events are relatively fixed. For example, the sequence of steps in performing a long jump includes the approach, take off, the body and limbs movement in the air for balance, and finally, the landing. The approach, going from slow to fast and gradual accelerating to an appropriate speed for taking off, includes several motor programs, and these programs are grouped and coordinate with each other.

> **A specific motor skill for different sports (tennis and badminton) may be governed by a single SMP for that skill, which can be retrieved to meet the immediate task demands.**

The mechanical element and relationship among each motor program are relatively fixed, (e.g., time, force, and rhythm). Breaking the logical connections and fixed relationship between these motor programs will reduce the quality of the performance and skill execution, resulting in the motor skill not being performed properly. For example, in throwing a discus in track and field for right-handed individuals, the right leg and right arm must move after the left leg and arm during the spin, and leg movement must be faster than the arm movement. If any limb movement does not follow this fixed structure, the technique of the motor skill will be incorrect, and outcome of the throw will not be ideal. The kicking skill in soccer also consists of several logically connected motor programs. For

> **Teachers and coaches must teach novices the motor program pattern and the fixed mechanical sequences first, and then teach execution based on the individual conditions.**

example, the approach to the ball, placement of the non-kicking foot next to the ball, the backward and forward swing of the leg, as well as the final contact with the ball are all required for correct execution of the skill. The fixed kicking motor program requires players to execute the kicking movement one after the other following the correct sequence and timing. Any movement that does not follow the sequence and timing (e.g., executing a forward leg swing too early) will affect the completion and quality of the next motor skill program, and eventually will affect the execution of the entire movement. Note that while all athletes, no matter if they are novice or experienced players, will follow the same sequence and timing, the speed of execution (slower for novices and faster for experienced players) is different depending on the level of the athletes. Therefore, teachers and coaches must teach novices the motor program pattern and the fixed mechanical sequence first and then, teach execution based on the individual conditions.

DEEP STRUCTURE OF MOTOR SKILL LEARNING

The deep structure of motor skill learning is another factor that plays an important role in all aspects of motor skill learning and performance and it contributes varying influences on the quality of skill performance under different conditions. For example, the execution of throwing a discus described above must follow the deep structure (the timing and sequence) of each movement to guarantee a quality completion with the best result of a throw. This deep structure is based on the principle of biomechanics and human anatomy to regulate such movement structure under a specific timing and sequence, which movement should be executed faster while another movement should be slower. This example indicates that teachers and coaches must understand the nature of the deep structure of each motor movement when teaching/coaching a motor skill. The two most important elements of the deep structure of motor skill learning are: relative timing and sequence. The relative timing for any motor skill or motor program is relatively stable and unchangeable, and the parameters for each motor skill can be modified based on the individual conditions under which the skill is executed. For example, during the long jump approach and take off, or a tennis forward stroke, the relative timing is the same and unchanged whether performed by a novice or experienced athlete. Novices' approach for the long jump might be slow in speed, but the rhythmic structure is the same as elite athletes (starting slow with gradual acceleration, and take off at the end). The elements that can be changed are the parameters of the motor program, for example in the long jump approach, elite athletes might have a longer distance to cover, run with greater speed or longer strides, and in turn, jump farther in distance. Also, there are more parameters that can be changed after taking off (e.g., take off velocity and angle) to determine what techniques an athlete should select to achieve the best results.

PARAMETERS OF MOTOR SKILL LEARNING

As previously indicated, the GMP represents a class of actions or pattern of movements that can be modified to fit into different motor programs. For example, a generalized kicking motor program can be customized by different players and performed very differently (different force and muscle used in long pass, short pass, and in/out pass). In a GMP, there is a deep structure of motor skill that is fixed, such as the sequence and structure of each individual motor program. However, the parameters of each motor program are adaptable and easily modified from one performance to another to produce variations of a motor response. Thus, the GMP could be customized for different patterns by modifying the parameters such as force and timing of the movement to become a single motor program.

A common example could be the walking and running motor program. The patterns of walking and running are the same, and people can walk slow or fast by modifying the timing. With this adaptable feature, all GMP can be modified for a particular motor program. (e.g., learning skating on carpet for a beginner at the early learning stage, and increasing the difficulty for the advanced level in the late learning stage for competition). It is true that we teach a generalized program in our physical education classes, and we modify the parameters of the learned general motor program based on the competition intensity and environment (e.g., ice surface in skiing) and opponents' skill level (national team or college team). Examples of parameters that can be modified include movement time, duration, muscle force, and speed.

FITTS AND POSNER'S THREE STAGES OF MOTOR LEARNING

For both novice and experienced athletes learning a new motor skill, they will go through a similar learning process where their skill will gradually develop, while they will concentrate less and less on what they are doing. From the GMP to SMP perspectives, a generalized motor program pattern related to that new motor skill can be retrieved, if any exist, and the SMP can be established by modifying parameters of the GMP based on the characteristics of new motor skills. Although a novice and an experienced athlete will go through a similar process when learning a new motor skill, an experienced athlete can learn faster than a novice because he/she might have more similar motor programs stored in memory that he can connect with the new skill. Fitts and Posner (1967) proposed a three-stage skill acquisition model to describe the learning process as related to a new motor skill (see Figure 6.1). Let's discuss how the Fitts and Posner three-stage skill acquisition model fits the theory of motor program and schema theory.

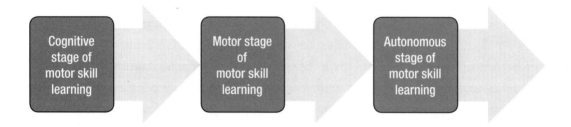

FIGURE 6.1. The three-stage skill acquisition model. (Fitts & Posner, 1967)

Cognitive Stage of Motor Skill Learning

Fitts and Posner's three-stage skill acquisition model (1967) indicates that in the cognitive stage, learners acquire new skills by observing a teacher's demonstration of the new skill. In the early learning stages of acquiring a new skill, students experience a lot of new information and make a lot of errors at the same time. They need a lot of feedback to correct errors, but they can only take two or three pieces of feedback at a time. If a teacher provides too much detailed feedback, students tend to be confused by too much stimulation to concentrate on learning the general motor program of the skill being taught. Teachers should simplify the demand of the new motor skill (e.g., not mention some unimportant details that are easy to correct or can be added later on) to help students focus on understanding the nature of the general motor program (thus, students will make fewer errors, and teachers will not need to provide too much feedback to confuse them). Visual abilities at this stage play an important role in skill acquisition, and teachers and coaches should use visual techniques, (e.g., physical demonstration or video) to introduce the new skill, and tell students exactly what to look at during their observation (good teaching strategies could be: physically moving students through the skill motion (e.g., tennis stroke), physical demonstration plus simple and clear feedback to guide the performance of a quality

stroke). The purpose of the cognitive stage is to observe the GMP pattern, and not focus on a specific motor program. Therefore, teachers and coaches who provide too much detailed information and feedback may not help them understand the GMP during this stage. For example, in teaching a sequential routine movement, teachers should teach the major movement (e.g., teaching Tai Chi or a dance sequential movement routine without focusing too much on the details of hand or foot placement). They should focus on the movement routine first and then correct the hand/foot position after students have learned the movement routine. Transferring learning from other similar motor skills will be helpful at this stage, and teachers should indicate and demonstrate the similarities and differences between these two skills to establish the GMP of the new skill (e.g., the difference between the flexibility of the wrist/elbow in badminton and the locked wrist/elbow in tennis). With a good teaching strategy such as knowledge transfer, students can understand and perform the GMP of the new skill, and move through the first stage in a short period of time.

Motor Stage of Motor Skill Learning

In the associative stage, the basic skill pattern developed in the cognitive stage must be improved, and the new motor skill must be further enhanced through practice and refinement. The purpose of this stage is to modify the parameters of the GMP, and establish a new specific motor program that matches the taught motor skill and the condition of execution. This is normally done under a closed-loop control situation so that the SMP can be established and added to the GMP pattern through parameter modification (e.g., practice baseball batting skill from a tee, shooting basketballs while grounded in one spot to establish a personal shooting pattern and accuracy before moving to jump shots). During the associative stage of motor skill acquisition, students will gradually rely less on the visual sensors, and become more dependent on proprioception by which we control our body and limb position by "feel" during performance. Students need a great deal of practice to refine and stabilize the motor skill pattern and reduce the frequency of errors, as well as improve the speed, accuracy, and consistency of movements. In addition, students should establish their own SMP by acquiring and improving the abilities to produce various new movements to respond to various situations for the competition (e.g., under an open-loop control situation to practice baseball batting from a variety of pitches, shooting basketballs from different spots). Teachers and coaches should gradually increase the difficulty and complexity of the practice situation, aiming to make them similar to the competition environment. For example, changing different opponents in table tennis, badminton and tennis during practice, or changing play positions in basketball and soccer to allow athletes to experience and familiarize themselves with different environments.

Autonomous Stage of Motor Skill Learning

In the autonomous stage, the motor skill has become automatic, and the learner has acquired and refined the motor skill. The motor skill can be performed without mental effort, and practice should be carried out under an open-loop control system, random and varied, with specificity training so that the individual SMP can be classified and established independently from the GMP pattern. By reaching this stage, students can perform the skill with little conscious effort, and they are free to concentrate on other things around them (e.g., opponents during competition). For example, an elite basketball player can control and dribble the ball at full speed, change directions to bypass the defensive players, and determine the best strategy (various execution skills) to reach the basket. Like many NBA basketball teams and European football teams, their year-around practices are not only for maintaining their physical fitness, but these world class-level elite athletes still continue their intensive practice and training in order to maintain and improve their skill level. They continue to seek challenges and comparative teams to enhance their skills, and coaches must create such environments to stimulate their players' high intensity performance. We also noticed that some athletes will continue to practice basic skills (e.g., a baseball player practicing batting skill from a tee or machine, basketball players shooting hundreds of balls from the foul line). We must understand, however, that elite athletes practicing basic skills are not doing so for skill acquisition, but for stimuli to enhance their skill for the new competitive situations they are facing or they have faced at the previous game, and find solutions to improve their performance when the situation occurs again.

RECOMMENDED TRAINING APPROACHES FOR DISTINCTIVE STAGES OF MOTOR SKILL LEARNING

Cognitive Stage

Successful learning of a new motor skill requires repetitive practice and intensive training. In the *cognitive stage* as discussed earlier, students experience a lot of new information and make a lot of errors. They need a lot of precise and specific feedback to correct errors and need blocked and constant practice for consistency and proper skill pattern development. Therefore, a great deal of practice plus clear and specific instructional feedback must be provided to help students establish a motor skill pattern as soon as possible. The training environment in this learning stage should be relatively stable. The constant practice with immediate feedback may be the only choice to effectively establish the new skill pattern during this stage.

Motor Stage

During the second stage, students at the motor stage will further acquire the new skill through various approaches and situations, such as, blocked and random practice, varied practice, simulation training, part/whole, fractation practice, and learning transfer, to refine the motor skill. Athletes at this stage have understood the movement sequences and skill components, but have not completely managed the parameters of the skill (e.g., relative timing and rhythm of the GMP). Practice at this stage is normally still under relatively stable and controlled situations so that the skill pattern can be established, and a high quality performance can be achieved more consistently. Through blocked and varied practices, students will gradually be able to decide to select a better way to execute the skill under different situations. Coaches at this stage should arrange many specific skill practices, followed by appropriate feedback, and progressively increase the complexity of the practice situations. For example, for an open skill like baseball batting, coaches can start to use a pitched ball instead of the tee. Random practices, varied practice, and random/varied practice can be used in basketball shooting. For a closed skill like archery, golf, or javelin, coaches should ask students to practice under different weather or speed conditions which are close to the possible competition condition (e.g., windy or raining conditions). In gymnastics and dance, Part vs. Whole skill practices can be used. Evidence suggests that blocked practice produces better performance while establishing the GMP, and the random practice is more effective for execution of learned motor skill in various situations and competitions.

Autonomous stage

Under the autonomous stage, the athlete has learned the motor skill, and it has become automatic, and can be performed with little mental effort. The training should use the random, varied, and intensive practice, and should be carried out under an open-loop control system to continue to improve and maintain the quality level of the motor skill. Athletes at this stage require challenge and the intensity necessary to enhance their skill development. Teachers and coaches must create a challenging practice environment to allow athletes to maintain their physical fitness and skill level toward their peak performance. Training should focus on accuracy, consistency, and control of the skill, and should become precise (basketball shooting rate). Athletes should be able to detect their own mistakes after every trial, and know how to correct them in the following trial. For example, elite golf players can detect their mistakes immediately after the swing, so that they continue to correct their movement without the coach's feedback. Basketball players will immediately know

whether the ball is a good or bad shot immediately after the ball is released. In this stage, coaches should continue to create challenges and comparative environments to stimulate their players' high intensity performance.

GOAL SETTING FOR EACH STAGE OF MOTOR LEARNING
Goal Setting for Long- and Short-term Goals

Goal setting is an important and powerful technique to motivate students and athletes to achieve higher performance during acquisition of motor skills. Locke and Latham (2002) suggested that goals affect individual performance through four mechanisms: 1) goals direct action and effort toward goal-related activities and away from unrelated activities, 2) challenging goals lead to higher effort than easy goals, 3) goals result in persistence to exert more effort to achieve high goals, and 4) goals motivate the use of existing knowledge to attain a goal. Goal-setting theory is a psychological strategy to help students and athletes to break down a general goal (long-term goal) into specific achievable goals (short-term goals) in order to motivate and encourage students to learn and practice during motor skill acquisition. By breaking the long-term goal into a series of specific short-term goals, teachers and coaches can gradually guide students and athletes to achieve the shot-term goals one-by-one. Students and athletes must initiate a commitment to set up a goal for a task, and it will not motivate a person's effort without the commitment. For example, setting a goal of running four 400 meters in 50 seconds each for a training course will motivate athletes to reach the set goal for each 400 meter run during that training course. For a seasonal goal of a 400 meter run of 48 seconds, the first short-term goal might be 49 seconds for the first two months, and then 48.5 seconds for the next two months, and then, reach the final goal of 48 seconds by the end of season. Goals motivate athletes to exert effort to meet training demands and persist over time. When students and athletes have a clear goal set by themselves, the goal will affect their behavior, change their attitude, and enhance their performance, eventually influencing their training outcome.

Realistic Goals and Challenging Goals

If a goal is unrealistic, it will not be helpful. Therefore, to make a goal useful, it has to be specific and achievable. On the other hand, the goals that students and athletes set should not be too easy so that they do not have to work hard to achieve it. As well, the goal should not be too difficult and unrealistic so that it is impossible to reach (i.e., participating in three sports teams in one season or taking six courses in one semester and getting all "As" from all courses). Therefore, the goal must be realistic and appropriate so that a student and athlete feels motivated during its implementation. It is important for an individual to reach the goals in a short period of time in order to stay motivated. For example, for the long-term goal of losing ten pounds in six months, students should break this long-term goal into smaller goals, such as, working out twice a week to lose five pounds in the first two months, and working out three times a week to lose three pounds for another two months, and finally, lose a total of ten pounds in a half year. The most important thing in setting realistic

> Goal setting is a very important and powerful technique to motivate students and athletes to achieve higher performance during learning and acquisition of motor skills.

and challenging goals, and being able to continue to be motivated, is to carefully set realistic short-term goals so that students will feel motivated if they can see the improvement and be able to periodically achieve the short-term goal.

Performance Goal

Performance goal setting is based on an individual's current performance and setting a goal that focuses on improvement in the future. Proper performance goal setting will greatly affect one's performance, and avoid failure and disappointment. For example, each student and athlete will have an annual goal in terms of motor skill performance in either skill proficiency (correct skill) or performance result (can push shot put farther, or can jump higher than last year). As discussed earlier, the performance goal can be set as a long-term goal and short-term goal based on realistic and challenging targets with which the individual feels comfortable. For example, a proper performance long-term goal for a novice can be "swimming 50 yards across the swimming pool independently by the end of semester" and the short-term performance goal can be to float on the water independently in the first month, swim with head under water independently during the second month, swim with proper head position independently for 25 yards during the third month, and finally, swim 50 yards using proper techniques by the end of the semester. With these carefully set goals, students have clear short-term goals to achieve for different periods, which eventually lead to the final long-term goal. Again, goals that are too easy or too difficult will negatively affect students' achievement.

Process Goal and Outcome Goal

These two goals are closely related and connected during different stages of motor learning. The process goal is focused on the performer's skill execution, measuring the techniques, and other physical conditioning (e.g., physical fitness level). The outcome goal emphasizes the final result that the performer achieved, like the distance in shot put, and time for a 100-meter dash by the end of the learning period. Achieving the process goal due to good techniques and great physical fitness will lead to achieving a better outcome goal (overall continuum of performance). Academic or training measurements are always based on both the process goal and outcome goal to benchmark the criteria in certain key areas and assess these goals periodically, in order to provide feedback to students for improvement and lead them toward the final outcome goal.

Reward Systems Integrated Into Goal Setting Programs

Goal-setting is an effective strategy for leading students or athletes toward a pre-set long-term goal and short-terms goals. Therefore, goals must be challenging, but realistic and achievable in order to motivate students to challenge themselves and achieve the goals. Achievement must be recognized and awarded, so a reward system that relates to the students' achievement should be established to recognize those students who achieve the final goal. Students and athletes will feel the appreciation and recognition for their hard work. For example, teachers can give those students who achieve the short-term goal a free play period, or can reward athletes when they

> A reward system should be integrated into goal setting so that hard-working and outstanding students and elite athletes can be encouraged along with short-long terms goals.

have reached the goal in competition (announcement, material award). Teachers can issue a better grade or issue certain academic achievement distinctions. An outstanding athlete or student award can be conducted more formally at annual ceremonies to recognize those students and athletes (e.g., annual prize presentation, outstanding student scholarship award).

COURTESY OF BIGSTOCKPHOTO.COM

Key Terms to Remember

- *Motor program* is an abstract representation of a movement plan that contains all of the motor commands required to carry out the intended action when there is a stimuli or a particular environment.

- *Schema* refers to a set of rules relating the various outcomes of a person's actions (e.g., short distance of a throw) to the parameter values the person chooses to produce those outcomes (e.g., small amount of force) (Schmidt & Wrisberg, 2004).

- *Generalized motor program (GMP)* refers to the general memory representation of a class of actions that share common invariant characteristics. It provides the basis for controlling a specific action within the class of actions (Magill, 2011).

- *Specific motor program* is any motor program that has a specific order and sequences.

- *Grouped motor program* (GMP) for sequentially related sports and activities is a motor program that requires several specific motor programs with logical connections to coordinate each other.

- *Motor skill* is a goal-oriented act or task that requires voluntary body and/or limb movement that must be learned (Coker, 2004).

- *Relative time* is the proportion of the total amount of time required by each of the various components of a skill during the performance of that skill (Magill, 2001).

- *Cognitive stage* is initial stage of learning when a learner is first introduced to a motor task. The learner must determine the objective of the skill as well as the relational and environmental cues that control and regulate the task to be learned (Fitts & Posner, 1967; Shea, Shebilske, & Worchel, 1993).

- *Associative stage* is the second phase of learning, and is reached only after performers have completed sufficient amounts of practice. In this stage, the frequency and magnitude of errors are greatly reduced, processing time becomes more efficient, and overall performance becomes more consistent (Young, LaCourse, & Husak, 2000).

- *Autonomic stage* is the third stage, and is reached when the motor skill has become automatic, and can be performed with little mental effort.

- *Goal-setting theory* is a psychological strategy to help students and athletes break down a general goal (long-term goal) into specific achievable goals (short-term goals or objectives) in order to motivate and encourage students to learn and practice during motor skill acquisition.

- *Performance goal setting* is based upon an individual's current performance and setting a goal and objective that focus on improvement in the future. Proper performance goal setting will greatly affect one's performance, and avoid failure and disappointment.

Student Assignments for Connecting Theory to Practice

- Discuss the following theories: (1) general motor ability, (2) Henry's specificity hypothesis, and (3) groupings of abilities. Which theory do you believe most? Why?

- Have you ever thought about what some of your own dominant abilities might be? List three movement activities for which you feel particularly skilled. What abilities do you think you possess that allow you to perform these skills so well?

- If you are a basketball coach for the Olympic development team and you are recruiting 12-year-old basketball players (these players have already received three years of basketball training) for your team, what are your criteria for selecting talented players?

- Conduct a task/skill analysis: (1) what abilities are needed for an elite basketball player? (2) what abilities are needed for an elite golfer? And (3) what abilities are needed for an elite gymnastic athlete?

REFERENCES

Coker, C. A. (2004). *Motor learning and control for practitioners* (5th ed.). Boston, MA: McGraw-Hill.

Coker, C. A. (1996). Accommodating students' learning styles in physical education. *Journal of Physical Education, Recreation and Dance, 67*(9), 66–68.

Fitts, P. M., & Posner, M. I. (1967) *Human performance.* Oxford, UK: Brooks and Cole.

Locke, E. A., & Latham, G. P. (1990). *A theory of goal setting and task performance.* Englewood Cliffs, NJ: Prentice-Hall.

Locke, E. A., & Latham, G. P. (2002). Building a practically useful theory of goal setting and task motivation: A 35-year odyssey. *American Psychologist, 57,* 705–717.

Magill, R. A. (2011). *Motor learning and control: Concepts and applications* (9th ed.). New York, NY: McGraw-Hill.

Schmidt, R. A. (1975). A schema theory of discrete motor skill learning. *Psychological Review, 82,* 225–260.

Schmidt, R. A., & Lee, T. D. (2005). *Motor control and learning: A behavioral emphasis.* Champaign, IL: Human Kinetics.

Schmidt, R. A., & Wrisberg, C. A. (2004). *Motor learning and performance: A problem-based learning approach* (3rd ed.). Champaign, IL: Human Kinetics.

Shea, C. H., & Kohl, R. M. (1991). Composition of practice: Influence on the retention of motor skills. *Research Quarterly for Exercise and Sport, 62,* 187–195.

Shea, C. H., Shebilske, W. L., & Worchel, S. (1993). *Motor learning and control.* Boston, MA: Allyn & Bacon.

Young, D. E., LaCourse, M. G., & Husak, W. S. (2000). *A practical guide to motor learning* (2nd ed.). Peosta, IA: Eddie Bowers Publishing, Inc.

Young, D. E., & Schmidt, R. A. (1992). Augmented kinematic feedback for motor learning. *Journal of Motor Behavior, 24,* 261–273.

Contribution of Information Processing and Speedy Decision-Making to Effective Motor Skill Performance

OBJECTIVES

- Understand the concept of reaction time and three different models of reaction time
- Understand the neuro-process of reaction time
- Understand the structure of reaction time
- Understand how reaction time can be changed through training
- Understand the strategies for delaying an opponent's reaction time
- Understand the strategies of shorting self reaction time through proper training
- Understand the ways to apply information processing principles to sports settings

INTRODUCTION

In Chapter 3, we discussed the classification of motor skills into RT and non-RT based motor skills (open vs. closed motor skills). Obviously, when individuals engage in an RT-based motor skill, the speed at which they can respond to external stimuli is a deciding factor in their success. For example, it is crucial for a boxing athlete to respond instantly to an opponent's attack; a soccer player should immediately block an opponent's shot to prevent a goal being scored; a football player must quickly block a ball-carrier's attack. All these examples illustrate the importance of the speed of the reaction to the opponents' attacks (external stimuli). Any slight delay in the reaction will cause the defender to lose the combat. The speed of an individual's response to external stimuli represents his/her information processing ability (Crabtree & Antrim, 1988). One athlete could have a very fast information processing ability in responding to external stimuli, while another may be slow to react (slow information processing ability). When engaging in RT-based motor skills, the speed of information processing is a vital element for success. From a motor learning perspective, we use RT as a measurement of this process (Delignieres, Brisswalter, & legros, 1994).

THREE MODELS OF REACTION TIME

Reaction time is the interval between an individual's seeing the external stimulus or stimuli and starting to act, and it usually indicates the speed at which the information can be processed (Crabtree & Antrim 1988). This measure of RT is used to indicate the level of performance of athletes who are engaged in RT-based motor skills in competition or combat. The following illustration depicts the specific structures of the RT model. Based on the different types and the number of external stimuli that vary from situation to situation and sport to sport, RT is normally divided into three different categories: (1) simple RT, (2) choice RT, and (3) discrimination RT. The differences between these three different RT models are described below.

The Simple Reaction Time Model

Simple RT refers to situations where only one external stimulus correlates with one fixed response (Klemmer, 1956; Schmidt & Lee 2011). For example, in experimental studies we can use a red light to serve as an external stimulus. An individual sits facing a desktop with a response button and is required to use his/her index finger to push the button when he/ she sees the red light come on. The time interval between this individual's seeing the red light come on and starting to push the button is referred to as simple RT. It is called simple RT because this mechanism only has one stimulus and one response, in which the relationship is fixed.

TABLE 7.1 Reaction time model

Ready	Set . . . Go	Pre-motor time	Motor time	Jump
Forwarding	Prepare	Reaction time	Reaction time	Movement time

The practical question is how we can apply the illustrated model (Table 7.1) to actual sports or other settings. For instance, if a soccer offender only learns one skill to beat an opponent, once the defender realizes this, he/she requires only a very short RT to respond because only one skill is needed in defense. Therefore, in the practical setting of a sports training regimen, the coach should teach as many fake offensive movements as possible, and by doing so, the RT model switches to the choice RT model that requires a defender to spend a much longer time to make a decision as to how to defend against the offensive players.

Choice Reaction Time

The second model, choice RT, refers to the time needed for selecting and responding to one stimulus out of several choices of stimuli (Scott, Whitwam, & Wilkinson, 2007). In experiments, five different colored lights such as red, green, yellow, blue, and orange are set up and, one at a time, are turned on randomly; the student has no way of knowing ahead of time which particular colored light will come on. The rules we set are as follows: the individual must use his/her thumb to push the button when the red light is on, the index finger for the green light; the middle finger for the yellow light; the ring finger for the blue light; and the small finger for the orange light. Thus, a specific finger is used to push the button when a pre-set and correlated light is on. The time delay between the individual's seeing the light come on and starting the action is called choice RT.

Bearing this principle in mind, in competitive combat sports (RT-based sports), a performer should learn a variety of offensive plays, attacking or faking movements. Thus, a defensive position must learn a variety of defensive plays in order to block a variety of offensive attacks. To do this defenders require a much longer RT than when responding to an offender who can only execute one skill.

Discrimination Reaction Time

The third RT model is discrimination RT which requires that an individual only reacts to one specific stimulus, even though multiple potential stimuli are presented, and remains motionless when any other stimulus appears. In experiments, when we use the five different colored lights employed for the choice RT model, the athlete must react to the green light when it comes on, but not to any of the other four lights. This mechanism is called discrimination RT.

Based on the research on the three different RT models, it is clear that choice RT requires the longest time for an individual to process information in order to accurately push the button. The reason for this is that he/she must process information involving many possible choices which requires more attention, and thus a longer time is needed to make the best decision to match the specific situation. It is also apparent that discrimination RT requires a relatively longer time than simple RT since, in this case too, the athlete needs to make a choice from a number of options. The simple RT model requires the least RT because there is only one external stimulus matching one fixed response thus, the athlete has only has one option.

To successfully execute RT based motor skills, rapid processing of information and quick decision-making in response to external stimuli should be perceived as the focal element of motor skill training. RT is commonly used as a critical measure when evaluating athletes' skill level (Brown, Kenwell, Maraj, & Collins, 2008; Collet, 1999; Der & Deary, 2006; Mero & Komi, 1990). RT can be shortened through proper training, but practitioners should have a comprehensive understanding of the neuro-mechanical process of RT so that they can effectively plan appropriate and specific training to help learners or other related professionals decrease their RT and make accurate decisions when performing RT-based motor skills for peak performance.

NEURO- PROCESS OF REACTION TIME

From the above descriptions we can clearly see how the amount of time required to respond to one or more external stimuli is based on the types and the number of stimuli presented to an individual at a given time. Continuing on from the presentation of the three different RT models, let us now explain the mechanics of RT including its different phases and the characteristics of each phase. Training programs can be purposefully designed to help individuals shorten their RT at each specific phase in order to maximize their performance potentials.

The structure of RT can be divided into two phases: (1) pre-motor time, which is the time used for processing information and for decision-making, or cognitive time, and (2) motor time, the time used for overcoming inertia of the moving limbs (Botwinick & Brinley, 1962; Botwinick & Thompson, 1996). Both phases determine how much time is needed to respond to external stimuli. Specifically, a performer needs to focus on reducing the pre-motor time, which can be done through appropriate training. The second phase of RT, motor time, is determined by two factors: (1) the weight of the moving limbs or body parts, and (2) the speed of the electrical impulse traveling from the brain to the relative muscles. It is clear that it is very difficult to change the motor time of RT because the weight of an individual and the speed at which electrical impulses travel from the brain to muscles are relatively stable and cannot be changed easily, so the focus during training should be on learning how to reduce the pre-motor time, the time it takes to process information, the so-called cognitive time. In the next section, the mechanisms of information processing will be extensively discussed.

INFORMATION PROCESSING AT THE PRE-MOTOR TIME (COGNITIVE TIME)

The pre-motor time (information processing) phase of RT can be divided into three distinct stages: (1) stimulus identification, (2) response selection, and (3) programming (Wrisberg & Shea, 1978). At the stimulus identification stage, as is clear from the name, before taking an action, an individual must first identify the actions of the opponent(s) or other external stimuli. For example, because the opponent's action is unpredictable, a boxing athlete must identify his opponent's attacking tactic before he can defend himself/herself. The athlete must rely on the types of external stimuli the opponent presents in order to make a decision as to how to block the attack. This decision-making process relies on immediate external stimuli for countering the opponent's attack. This stage of information processing is referred to as the stimulus identification (Schmidt & Wrisberg, 2008). Table 7.2 illustrates an applied model of the various factors affecting each stage of the pre-motor time and motor time of reaction time structure in sports situations (Wang, 2009).

The second stage of the pre-motor time is the response selection stage (Schmidt & Wrisberg, 2008). For example, once a boxing athlete identifies the opponent's particular punching pattern, he/she must select a response of how to defend himself/herself based on the type and direction of the incoming punch. The last stage of the pre-motor time is the response programming stage, in which the athlete's decision, an abstract concept, is programmed into a transferrable command converted to electrical impulses that are sent to the relative muscle groups for the next action. The time needed for the programming stage depends on the complexity of the particular motor skill. The more complex the motor skill, the longer the time required for programming (Schmidt & Lee, 2011).

TABLE 7.2. Applied reaction time model (adopted from Wang, 2009)

Pre-motor Time (Cognitive Time) (With training, pre-motor time can be shortened)			Motor Time (Motor time is hard to change, even with training)
Information Processing Stage			Initiation of a Movement
Detection of Game Situation Stage	Decision-Making Stage	Programming Stage	Time for Overcoming Inertia to Initiate a Movement
Factors Affecting This Stage of RT	Factors Affecting This Stage of RT	Factors Affecting This Stage of RT	Determining Factors of Motor Time
(1) Clarity (sharpness) of the color of the stimulu. *(2) Intensity (brightness) of the color of the stimulus* *(3) Contrast of background and stimulus.* *(4) Loudness of sound if it is auditory stimulus*	*(1) Uncertainty or unpredictability of game situations* *(2) Potential alternatives of attacks and counter-attacks* *(3) Compatibility between attacks and responses.* *(4) Motivation* *(5) Fatigue*	*(1) Complexity of motor skill* *(2) Level of accuracy*	*(1) Weight of the moving limbs or body parts* *(2) Age of the athlete* *(3) Genetic makeup of the nerve system*

THE FACTORS AFFECTING PRE-MOTOR TIME OF RT

Based on the aforementioned analysis, each stage of pre-motor time is determined by distinctive factors and therefore, motor skill learning should follow the related principles to reduce RT for enhancing performance. On the other hand, motor time is more genetically determined so it cannot be reduced. Thus, the main focus should be on providing appropriate training in order to reduce that portion of RT that can be changed to achieve peak performance. Once practitioners understand the specific factors that affect each stage of the pre-motor time, they can create training conditions to manipulate various factors to accomplish their goals. The following discussions provide extensive information on which factors affect the pre-motor time.

Stimulus Identification Stage

From the information processing perspective, an individual must detect the external stimulus or stimuli before he/she can make a decision. The stimulus identification stage is the time it takes to detect the external stimulus or stimuli. There are two factors that determine how much time is needed for identifying a stimulus or stimuli, the first of which is the color contrast between stimulus and background (Schmidt & Lee, 2011). The research shows that when there is a sharp contrast between stimulus and background, less time is needed for an individual to identify the stimulus. For example, when a martial arts master wears a black outfit at night when the sky is dark, there is very little contrast between the black outfit (stimulus) and black sky (background), so an opponent finds it very difficult to see his actions. Conversely, if the martial arts master wears a white outfit at night, his actions can be seen much more easily due to distinct contrast between the white outfit (stimulus) and the black sky (background). Thus, wearing a black outfit would have a greater advantage than wearing a white outfit at night. Similarly, in a soccer game, if the players on a team wear a green uniform, socks and cleats, it is difficult for the opponents to identify their actions due to the low contrast between the green uniform (stimulus) and the green grass (background). In turn, this would lengthen the opponents' RT. Conversely, when a team wears a white uniform there is a sharp contrast between their uniform (stimulus) and the grass (background), allowing the opponents to identify their actions more quickly. With this concept in mind, in practical settings, professions could use this principle to manipulate color contrast between stimulus and background in order to accomplish the designated goals. For example, soldiers fighting in mountains or forests tend to wear camouflage colored uniforms that blend in very well with the colors of the environment so they cannot easily been seen by the enemy.

The second factor affecting the length of the stimulus identification stage is the brightness of the stimulus color (Schmidt & Wrisberg, 2008). For example, a baseball batter requires a longer RT to identify the ball's curve when it is dull white than when it is bright white. The research shows that the brightness of the stimulus is also an important factor affecting the stimulus identification stage of RT. For this reason, coaches, teachers, or practitioners can manipulate the sharpness and brightness of stimulus colors in order to shorten or lengthen the RT of stimulus identification. During training for many sports, we can manipulate the colors of the stimulus and background in order to change the RT of the stimulus identification stage. Lastly, an individual's familiarity of stimulus also affects RT in the stimulus identification stage. The more familiar an individual is with the stimulus, the less time is needed for this individual to identify that stimulus.

Three elements affecting stimulus identification stage

1. **Contrast between stimulus color and background**
2. **Brightness of color**
3. **Familiarity of the stimulus**

Response Selection Stage

The second stage of information processing in the pre-motor time is referred to as the response selection stage. Firstly, we need to recognize that the information processing involved in choice RT requires an individual to make a choice out of many different external stimuli. For example, if a basketball offender wants to beat a defender (bypass a defender) he/she can use a variety of methods to do this. To be able to effectively block the offender's attack, the defender must learn many different defensive plays. Unfortunately, the defender has no way of knowing which particular skill the offender might use at any given time so he/she must react to the offender's immediate action to make a quick decision as to how to block. Thus, offenders would like to lengthen their opponent's RT (decision-making time) while defenders would like to shorten their RT to disrupt the offender's attack as quickly as possible. The following factors reveal the critical elements related to the required RT during the response selection stage. The first element is the number of different ways in which a basketball offender is able to beat the defender. If an offensive player could execute many alternative ways of beating the defender, it requires the defender to use more cognitive time deciding which response to choose in defense. Likewise, if a martial arts master can hit an opponent in 40 different ways, the opponent must learn so many defending approaches to block any one of those potential attacks. Thus, the more different types of attack there are, the more RT is required at the response selection stage.

Another factor affecting the response selection stage is the compatibility between stimulus and response: the greater the compatibility between stimulus and response, the shorter the RT required. For example, it is difficult for a right hand dominant table tennis player to compete with a left hand dominant player, because the left-handed player creates spins that are opposite to the right-handed player's motions, thus a longer RT is required. Generally, in many sports competitions, encountering a left hand dominant athlete creates a great challenge for right hand dominant athletes due to the incompatibility between stimulus and response. Thus, the compatibility between stimulus and response is an important factor in determining how much RT is needed at the response selection stage.

The last factor affecting RT at the response selection stage is the familiarity of incoming stimuli. For example, if a martial arts master has never competed against an opponent who practices a new style of Japanese fighting, this master will require a longer RT to process the information and make decisions as to how to respond to the attack. Obviously, the predictability of an opponent's incoming attack also has a crucial impact on RT at the response selection stage. That is why many athletes wisely fight strategically by randomizing their

> **Four factors affecting response selection stage**
>
> 1. Available response alternative
> 2. Compatibility between stimulus and response
> 3. Familiarity of stimulus
> 4. Amount of practice

attack actions and thus increasing the uncertainty level of play in order to disrupt the opponents' defense.

Programming Stage

The last stage of the pre-motor time phase is the response programming stage, which is the time required to program an abstract decision into a command transferred with electrical impulses to the relative muscle groups for an action (Latash & Lestienne, 2006). The time an individual needs to program a command is largely based on the complexity of the skill. As a rule, the more complex the skill is, the more RT is needed for the programming stage (Schmidt & Lee, 2011). In order to speed up the process, an athlete should always use as simple a skill as possible to accomplish goals in order to reduce RT at this stage because an elaborate skill execution requires more attention and energy expenditure and thus takes longer to program. In addition, there is a greater possibility of making unnecessary mistakes when skills are complex. With a comprehensive understanding of the structures and mechanisms of the pre-motor time of RT, practitioners can purposefully and effectively design training regimens to reduce RT at each of the respective stages for RT-based sports motor learning.

In the above sections we have reviewed the factors that affect RT, including the three stages of pre-motor time, stimulus identification, response selection, and response programming. Perform-

> **Main Factor Affecting Programming Stage**
>
> **Complexity level of the response**

ers' goals should reduce their RT when responding to unpredictable external stimuli and conversely force opponents to lengthen their RT in competitive situations. In the next section, the strategies performers can use to shorten their RT and delay their opponents' RT will be introduced.

THE STRATEGIES FOR DELAYING AN OPPONENT'S RT

a. *Make actions unpredictable* so that opponents have no way of knowing what will happen next. Unpredictable actions can take many different forms, such as using a variety of different skills, randomizing the order of skill executions, utilizing different strategies or tactics, lining up with varied formations, setting up new play strategies, etc. The greater the number of unpredictable actions that occur, the longer RT opponents require.

b. *Increase the number of alternative skill movements* so that opponents must spend more time at the response selection stage, as described above. Whenever possible, coaches should teach athletes as many different ways as a possible to beat or attack their opponents, which in turn forces the opponents to choose from a variety of different defense options thus increasing their RT. It is essential that coaches teach a variety of skills to enhance athletes' ability to attack.

c. *Make actions more incompatible* between stimulus and response. Some examples of this are using new or unconventional strategies, having unfamiliar new players against opponents, using undesirable techniques against traditional play, having left hand or foot dominant players against right hand or foot dominant players, etc. The rule of thumb is that any different ways of competing that are unique or could cause opponents to require a longer time to process information are good strategies to utilize. Once coaches and practitioners understand the principles of the above four major factors that contribute to the RT of information processing during the pre-motor time, they can freely and purposefully design training accordingly to force opponents to lengthen their RT.

d. *Randomize offensive action from the temporal and spatial perspectives.* This means that an athlete should manipulate the arrangement of the order of using different skill patterns. For example, a tennis player could randomize the orders of his/her serving patterns so that the opponent has difficulty predicting what type of serve will be delivered. Returning an unpredictable serve or play requires longer RT.

e. *Attack the opponents' weaknesses,* which makes it difficult for them to block the attack or defend themselves thus lengthening their RT. For example, if a soccer defender's left foot skills are weak, the offender should make an effort to kick the ball towards his/her left side in order to gain an advantage of play since more RT is needed to block the opponent's attack.

Summary of Delaying Opponent's RT

a. Make actions unpredictable.
b. Increase alternatives of offensive skill movements.
c. Make actions more incompatible.
d. Randomize offensive actions.
e. Attack the opponent.

THE STRATEGIES FOR SHORTENING AN ATHLETE'S RT

a. *Be familiar with all the styles of play of the opponent.* Athletes should become familiar with their opponents' styles of play, their defensive and offensive moves, in order to quickly counter their attacks. For example, an ultimate fighting athlete should carefully study all the opponent's attacking movements including kicking, punching, and wrestling either by left or right limb. The more familiar one becomes with the opponent's moves, the less RT one requires for combat. An athlete's familiarity with the opponent's styles of play has a negative linear relationship with his/her required RT. Therefore, as much appropriate practice as possible is always recommended for reducing an athlete's RT.

b. *Make incompatible stimuli become familiar ones.* Incompatibility between external stimuli (opponent's attacks) and response is a critical factor influencing an individual's RT, as mentioned above. In order to decrease incompatibility, athletes should engage in simulation training by competing with teammates whose style of play is similar to the opponents'. For example, during practice a Chinese Olympic table-tennis player would commonly play against a teammate who imitates the opponent's style such as a left-handed player or a player with a unique style. Such simulation training helps the athlete decrease the incompatibility of competing with a player with a particular style. This principle can be applied to many sport settings.

c. *Anticipation for advanced planning.* In order to reduce an athlete's RT, anticipation of the incoming stimulus or stimuli is an effective strategy because the time required for the response-selection stage will be eliminated due to a decision being made before an opponent's action is taken. For example, it is extremely difficult for a soccer goalkeeper to react quickly to a penalty shot as the distance from kicking spot to goal line is only 12 yards. A short distance in addition to a powerful penalty shot makes for a goalkeeper with a deficient RT to react to the incoming ball. Most elite goalkeepers like to make a decision as to which way they are going to dive to catch the ball before the penalty shot is kicked instead of after. Such a strategy eliminates the time required for response-selection so the RT is significantly reduced. If the prediction is correct, there is a good chance the ball will be caught by the goalkeeper; obviously, if the prediction is incorrect, he/she will fail.

d. *Make actions simple, easy, and fast.* An athlete executing a motor skill movement can either use a complex and elaborate approach or a simple, direct, and easy approach. According to (Schmidt & Lee, 2011), programming a complex motor skill requires longer RT than programming a simple motor skill. It is recommended, whenever possible, that elite athletes use the simplest skill possible with the minimum energy required to complete the action for the shortest RT and the most effective outcome. A boxing athlete should use the simplest and quickest method to block an opponent's attack instead of using complex and intricate movements.

> ## Strategies to Shorten an Athlete's RT
>
> a. Be familiar with all the styles of play of the opponent.
> b. Make incompatible stimuli become familiar.
> c. Anticipate events to aid in advanced planning.
> d. Make actions simple, easy, and fast.

In RT-based sports, many teams experience a performance gap between practice and competition. Some athletes who demonstrate great skills during practice may not excel in competition. Part of the reason for this void is that their skills are more appropriate for demonstration environments, uncompetitive situations, or relatively slow scrimmages. To maximize the potential of athletes in competitive environments, effective coaches, or practitioners should understand the nature of the sports they are coaching so that they can structure appropriate training procedures. Thus, the central issue of training should focus on how to effectively shorten athletes' RT so that they can quickly respond to external and unpredictable game situations. With proper training, all three stages of RT can be shortened.

In addition, coaches and practitioners must have a comprehensive understanding of the characteristics of high-level competition and be able to formulate training regimens accordingly. To achieve this they should regularly update their knowledge base and apply scientific principles to their training programs.

APPLICATION OF INFORMATION PROCESSING PRINCIPLES TO SPORTS SETTINGS

In the previous section we discussed the three phases of the information processing model as well as the importance of processing information quickly to reduce RT for achieving peak performance. In this section we will discuss the relationship between attention and information processing and, in particular, how to make fake moves effectively in order to beat opponents or bypass defenders based on the mechanism of RT. The fake move is perceived as one of most challenging motor skills to learn and yet this skill is widely used in many different sports and other professions. When one has a clear understanding of the information processing pattern of the defender, proper fake moves can be learned effectively. Even though there are a wide variety of sports events, the principles of fake moves are the same.

Let us first analyze the characteristics of a defender's information processing patterns at the stimulus identification, response selection, and programming stages. At the stimulus identification stage, athletes identify external stimuli with a parallel pattern, meaning that they can accept many external stimuli at once without their attention being compromised.

For example, athletes can simultaneously observe the positions of their teammates and of their opponents, the travel of the ball, and the flow of the competition without any disruption of their attention pattern. In other words, an athlete can accept many different stimuli at a given moment without loss of attention; this information processing pattern at the stimulus identification stage is referred to as the parallel attention pattern. Once the stimuli are identified, athletes need to select a response or make a decision as to how they are going to react to the immediate external stimuli. Because an athlete can only make one decision at any given time, the information processing pattern at the response selection stage is a series relationship (Schmidt & Wrisberg, 2008). In other words, the athlete must make one decision before making the next decision. Lastly, once a response has been selected at the response selection stage, this abstract decision must be programmed and sent to the relevant muscles for the action. At this stage, the information processing pattern is also a series relationship since the athlete can only execute one action at any given time. Understanding the specific patterns of information processing at each of the three stages helps us develop appropriate strategies for making fake moves and beating an opponent in an effective way. In the next paragraph, we will describe specific approaches for making fake moves based on a defender's information processing patterns.

The purpose of a fake move is to deceive the opponent by swinging one's body to one side and then suddenly moving to the opposite side. In this type of movement the first fake swing motion is the first stimulus, and the second swing motion in the opposite direction is the second stimulus. This movement consisting of two consecutive and closely connected stimuli is referred to as the *double stimulus paradigm*. The time interval between these two stimuli is known as the *interstimulus interval*. The effectiveness of a particular fake motion depends to a great degree on the interstimulus interval (Schmidt &. Wrisberg, 2008).

To beat an opponent, a soccer offender could make a fake move first and then immediately swing in the opposite direction to bypass the opponent. Whether or not this fake move is successful largely depends on how much time (interstimulus interval) the offender takes to execute the first swing motion. If an offender spends too little time (less than 40 ms) engaging in the first fake move before swinging in the opposite direction in an attempt to bypass the opponent, this short interstimulus interval allows the defender to identify the offender's first fake move, but not enough time to make a decision and program it. Thus, once the offender has moved in the opposition direction, the defender can immediately stop processing the information in response to the first fake movement, and swing in the opposite direction to block the offender's move. Therefore, when an offender has a too-short fake move, the defender can respond prematurely by stopping the information being processed at the stimulus identification stage. So we can conclude that a small range or quick fake move is ineffective to beat an opponent.

An increased interstimulus interval beyond 60 ms gives the defender enough time to process the information (identify stimulus, select a response and program) in response to the fake move. According to Fairbrother (2010) and Schmidt and Wrisberg (2008), once the processing of the information has gone through the response selection stage, it cannot stop until the entire defensive action has been completed. Thus, the offender can use this time delay to swing in the opposite direction in order to beat the opponent. Based on the available research data, it is very clear that if an offensive player executes a fake swing motion with an interstimulus interval of 50–60 ms, this will achieve the goal of successfully faking out the opponent (Schmidt & Wrisberg, 2008).

If the offender takes more than 60 ms to execute the first fake swing motion, the interstimulus interval is relatively longer. In this scenario, the defender has enough time to respond to the first fake move, but when the offender swings in the opposite direction, the defender also has time to swing back to effectively block the offender's actual attack action. Thus, according to the above principle, if the offender spends too much time on the first fake move, the defender has sufficient time not only to respond to his/her first fake move, but to block his/her second action as well.

In sum, the offender must spend an optimal time to execute the first fake move (interstimulus interval), neither too little nor too much. Thus, athletes should be taught the following guidelines for executing fake moves: (1) the first fake move should be executed by using about 50-60 ms; (2) the fake move must be performed to appear as realistic and authentic as possible; (3) the transition from the first fake move to the second true action must be sudden, and (4) the offender must keep an optimal distance (neither too close to nor too far) from the defender to avoid the ball being disrupted or giving the defender enough space to engage in the second blocking.

Key Terms to Remember

- *Reaction time* is the interval between an individual's seeing the external stimulus or stimuli and starting to act, and it usually indicates the speed at which the information can be processed.

- *Simple RT* refers to situations where only one external stimulus correlates with one fixed response.

- *Choice RT* refers to the time needed for selecting and responding to one stimulus out of several choices of stimuli.

- *Discrimination RT* requires that an individual only reacts to one specific stimulus, even though multiple stimuli are presented, and remains motionless when any other stimulus appears.

- *Pre-motor time* is the time used for processing information and for decision-making, or cognitive time.

- *Motor time* is the time to use for overcoming inertia of the moving part of the body.

- *The double stimulus paradigm* is a movement consisting of two consecutive and closely connected stimuli.

- *Interstimulus interval* is the length of time separating the onsets of two stimuli in a double-stimulation paradigm (Schmidt & Wrisberg, 2008).

Student Assignments for Connecting Theory to Practice

- Describe the information-processing activities that might occur in the stimulus-identification, response-selection, and response-programming stages for a soccer goalie.

- Describe the information-processing activities that might occur in the stimulus-identification, response-selection, and response-programming stages for a tennis player (please identify the specific skill).

- Describe which factors affect reaction time and how you can shorten and lengthen the reaction time. Please apply these principles to different sport situations.

- Describe how you can reduce reaction time for yourself and force your opponents to increase their reaction time. (Use examples of boxing, soccer, and basketball training. Identify the situations and be specific.)

REFERENCES

Botwinnick, J., & Brinley, J. F. (1962). An analysis of set in relation to reaction time. *Journal of Experimental Psychology, 63,* 568–574.

Botwinnick, J., & Thompson, L. W. (1996). Premotor and motor components of reaction time. *Journal of Experimental Psychology, 1,* 9–15.

Brown, A. M., Kenwell, Z. R., Maraj, B. K., & Collins, D. F. (2008). "Go" signal intensity influences the sprint start. *Medicine and Science in Sports and Exercise, 40,* 1142–1148.

Collet, C. (1999). Strategic aspects of reaction time in world-class sprinters. *Perceptual and Motor Skills, 88,* 65–75.

Crabtree, D., & Antrim, L. (1988). Guidelines for measuring reaction time. *Perceptual and Motor Skills, 66,* 363–370.

Delignieres, D., Brisswalter, J., & legros, P. (1994). Influence of physical exercise on choice reaction time in sports experts: The mediating role of resource allocation. *Journal of Human Movement Studies, 27,* 173–188.

Der, G., & Deary, I. J. (2006). Age and sex differences in reaction time in adulthood: Results from the United Kingdom Health and Lifestyle Survey. *Psychology and Aging, 21,* 62–73.

Fairbrother, J. T. (2010). *Fundamentals of motor behavior.* Champaign, IL: Human Kinetics.

Erlanger, D., Feldman, D., Kutner K., Tanya, K., Kroger, K., Festa, J., & Broshek, D. (2003). Development and validation of a web-based neuropsychological test protocol for sports-related return-to-play decision-making. *Archives of Clinical Neuropsychology, 18,* 293–316.

Goldstein, E. B. (2009). *Sensation and perception*. Independence, KY: Wadsworth Cengage Learning.

Klemmer, L. (1956). Time uncertainty in simple reaction time. *Journal of Experimental Psychology, 51*, 179–184.

Latash, M. L., & Lestienne, F. (2006). *Motor control and learning*. New York, NY: Springer.

Magill, R. A. (2010). *Motor learning and control: Concepts and applications*. Boston, MA: McGraw-Hill.

Mero, A., & Komi, P. V. (1990). Reaction time and electromyographic activity during a sprint start. *European Journal of Applied Physiology, 61*, 73–80.

Schmidt, R. A., & Lee, T. D. (2011). *Motor control and learning: A behavioral emphasis*. Champaign, IL: Human Kinetics.

Schmidt, R. A., & Wrisberg, C. A. (2008). *Motor learning and performance: A situation-based learning approach*. Champaign, IL: Human Kinetics.

Scott, W. A. C., Whitwam, J. G., & Wilkinson, R. T. (2007). Choice reaction time: A method of measuring postoperative psychomotor performance decrements. *Anaesthesia Journal of the Association of Anaesthetists of Great Britain and Ireland, 38*, 1162–1168.

Wang, J. (2009). Reaction time training for elite athletes: A winning formula for champions. *International Journal of Sport Science, 3*, 67–78.

Wrisberg, C. A., & Shea, C. H. (1978). Shifts in attention demands and motor program utilization during motor learning. *Journal of Motor Behavior, 10*, 149–158.

Assessment and Evaluation of Motor Performance

OBJECTIVES

- Define assessment for learning and assessment of learning
- Define assessment and its relationship to motor skill acquisition
- Describe the purposes of assessment and evaluation
- Understand the progress in motor performance and skill acquisition
- Understand new strategies of learning
- Understand techniques of assessment and evaluation of motor skills
- Understand the importance of using statistics to analyze motor performance
- Understand the assessment instrument
- Understand the importance of assessment methods and the nature of experimental and descriptive research methods

OBJECTIVES OF ASSESSMENT AND EVALUATION OF MOTOR PERFORMANCE

When assessment is moving from the direction of "Assessment of Learning" toward "Assessment for Learning and Assessment as Learning" (Mok, 2010), assessment becomes an integral aspect of effective motor skill acquisition and performance. It also becomes a vital element of the skill learning process (e.g., Assessment as Learning). The objectives of assessment are for placement, achievement, classification, motivation, prediction, and for learning according to your professional needs. Thus, assessment must have a clear and specific goal and purpose. For motor skill acquisition and performance, assessment and evaluation can help teachers and coaches in flowing perspectives. Assessment is a very important process during motor skills acquisition, as it can help teachers or coaches identify problems that might affect students or athletes' motor skill development. From the measurement and evaluation perspective, assessment refers to a process that includes measurement, evaluation, diagnosis, and prescription (Baumgartner, 2007; Miller, 2006).

In the current school physical education context, most physical education teachers measure students' performance based on the motor skill they taught, and provide performance outcome information (e.g., 2.5 meters on a standing jump) to students. They fail to further identify students' skill or performance problems based on the results they measured, and provide feedback on how the problems can be corrected.

Today, the trend of motor performance assessment is moving from "assessment of learning" to "assessment for learning," in which assessment is not only used to reflect on students' progress and achievements in their studies, but also to become a systematic and ongoing process of performance diagnosing and prompt provision of feedback to assist students' learning. Therefore, the primary objective of assessment in movement studies is to assess students' learning process, and evaluate their progress in order to facilitate students' learning effectiveness.

UNDERSTAND LEARNING PROGRESS

Assessment, especially formative assessment, is critical to students in terms of their learning progress. The key for formative assessment is "feedback". Feedback must be timely and specific in order to be effective. For example, the teacher or coach should provide feedback immediately or shortly after performance to allow students to receive the performance outcome information, or allow students to conduct self-evaluation before receiving feedback: Late feedback, on the other hand, may reduce the informational function of feedback because the student might have forgotten how he/she just performed. During motor skill acquisition, students progressively develop their motor skills and knowledge through three learning stages. They acquire and master the motor skills through repetitive practices to develop sequential and temporal movement patterns and to refine movement parameters such as speed and force.

Through assessment and appropriate feedback, students will be able to understand the movement patterns and skill concepts being taught (Derri & Pachta, 2007). The assessment and evaluation process will help students understand the progress of the skill acquisition. For example, teaching students a high jump technique requires the teacher to involve them in the process of teaching and learning which includes listening to the teacher's introduction of the skill, observing the teacher's demonstration, following the teacher's instruction to physically imitate and practice the skill, making necessary adjustments based on the teacher's feedback or answers to students' questions, and gradually being able to successfully perform the skill independently. Through practice under the teacher's supervision, students will develop a strategy that enables them to integrate the new knowledge into practice. A formative assessment with feedback along with the learning process might help students evaluate the quality of their performance, detect their own errors, and understand their own learning and progress.

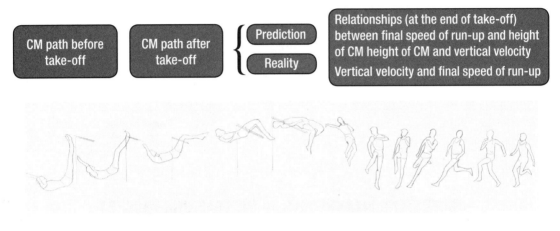

FIGURE 8.1. The record of the center of mass of a high jumper reveals the high-jumping movement pattern.

The following describes the typical learning process in a physical education class: The teacher describes and provides the instruction about a skill, gives a formal demonstration to help students understand what she/he just described, and then, asks students to imitate and practice. If some students do not know how to execute the skill or made an error during practice, the teacher will describe and demonstrate the correct movement again and again until they perform the skill correctly (Goldberger & Gerney, 1986). Through this learning process, students gradually master the skill.

However, from a physical education pedagogy and assessment for learning perspective, this process has different applications at different learning stages, and the effectiveness of assessment and feedback can be different from the stages of learning (Table 8.1); therefore, it cannot simply be applied to all the teaching practices. Teachers must understand the characteristics of each stage, and assess students' performance and provide feedback accordingly. For example, the assessment at the first stage, the cognitive stage, focuses on helping students to establish a motor skill pattern through a great deal of practice plus very clear and specific instructional feedback for errors. At the second stage, the motor stage, assessment should focus on refining the motor skill by providing specific, as well as varied practices, including simulation practice, and part/whole practice with precise feedback and demonstration for the skill improvement and consistency. In the final stage of learning, the autonomous stage, skill is becoming automatic, and the athlete needs to be able to adapt movement patterns to any specific performance situation. Assessment should be used to challenge students or athletes to perform the skill at the desired level of intensity to enhance their abilities to apply these skills at various practical situations (Sullivan, Kantak, & Burtner, 2008).

TABLE 8.1. Three stages and characteristics

Stage	Name	Characteristic
First	Cognitive stage	Establish a motor skill pattern
Second	Motor stage	Refining the new motor skill
Third	Autonomous stage	Skill is becoming automatic

UNDERSTAND WEAKNESSES OF THE LEARNING PROCESS

Assessment is crucial for students' learning process because it provides them with feedback on their motor skill performance and learning progress. Assessment not only helps students understand the correct learning process, but also helps them gain knowledge of understanding their own strength and weakness of their skill performance; appropriate feedback allows students to understand how to perform and how to improve. A formative assessment with feedback along with the learning process might help students judge the quality of their performance, detect their own errors, make proper corrections immediately following each performance trial, and gain an in-depth understanding of their own learning and progress.

Students' learning process is not like a sponge ball absorbing water. They must physically and mentally engage in the motor skill learning process by observing others, practicing the skill, and developing the motor program. Fitts and Posner's (1967) learning stages describe the students' learning experiences in the process. Students must practice and refine the motor skill, must respond to the teachers' comments and feedback, and make necessary adjustments during the learning process. As students have different levels of motivation and attitudes toward motor skill learning and practice, teachers must also use a number of evaluation methods to assess their students' progress so that their strengths and weaknesses can be identified. Adopting different types of assessment provides an opportunity for all students to progress at their own rate and in different ways. For example, at a high jump practice, the teacher makes comments on each trial based on observation, and helps each student understand his/her problem, and how to improve his/her performance.

Although different students might have similar problems, the ways to correct the problem can be very different depending on their skill level and ability (e.g., girls/boys, experienced performer/beginner), as well as their understanding of the motor skill learning process (novice and experienced at different learning stage). Some students might require more cognitive understanding to establish the general movement patterns, some might need more practices to refine the global movement, while others might need to practice parts of the skill to correct errors before practicing the whole skill (Boyle & Ackerman, 2004).

DEVELOP NEW STRATEGIES AND MAKE COMPARISONS OF LEARNING PROGRESS AMONG LEARNERS

Today, teachers are on the edge of a significant opportunity to facilitate students' learning through various teaching methods and technologies and effective formative assessment. Assessment for learning (AFL) is currently a new teaching strategy widely used by teachers and coaches. Teachers in the education system have integrated the AFL into their teaching to provide students with appropriate feedback along their learning process. Using formative assessment establishes an active learning environment to encourage integration between students and teacher, and teachers provide feedback to students to ensure that they are on the right track.

Many new strategies have been adopted by teachers, such as goal setting and positive reinforcement. For example, setting a goal in more intangible areas (e.g., short-term objectives) such as dribbling a soccer ball to pass two opponents allows students to see their performance outcome immediately. Another example is a *peer tutor,* where the teacher or coach invites peers to demonstrate various performances (good or bad), uses the peer's skill pattern as an example to show where the mistake and correct movements are, or compares the difference of performances among students, and encourages students to observe the peer's performance and help each other. The teacher can also receive feedback from students through those interactions, and will adjust his/her teaching strategies to meet the students' needs. Through these strategies, both teacher and students can observe others' teaching/learning process, and the teacher can monitor students' learning progress along with the whole education process. Provision of feedback for error detection and correction according to individual situations is also part of the learning process. Teachers must use varying teaching strategies to accommodate students' needs.

PROVIDE INFORMATION ABOUT LEARNERS' STATUS IN MOTOR SKILL LEARNING

When assessing and evaluating students' performance, the teacher will find that there are various stages of performance status for students, as well as many skill patterns and abilities for any single movement. These differences come from different learning stages and experiences. For examples, when teaching badminton skills in the first lesson, it is

The measurement of motor performance is critical for both teacher and student to understand motor learning and development.

expected that students will have varying levels of experience and skill levels in badminton, which can be an advantage in terms of learning from a cognitive perspective. Therefore, the teacher must be able to differentiate students' skill development and learning strategies so they can provide appropriate feedback information to help them acquire skill under different learning stages.

Students can learn and improve their skill under their own pace of learning progress (Boyle & Ackerman, 2004). As mentioned in Chapter 6, for example, feedback provided to students about their performance at different learning stages will be different based on their experiences and abilities. Some students may need more verbal instruction while others may require more demonstrations (different learning style or abilities). Some students need to focus on the details of performance (stage of refining the movement), and others might want general instruction (stage of building up motor program pattern). Feedback must be provided timely and appropriately, although more feedback is not always good (Sullivan, Kantak, & Burtner, 2008).

TECHNIQUES FOR ASSESSMENT AND EVALUATION OF MOTOR SKILLS

Performance Measurement

The measurement of motor skill performance is required to identify an individual's performance level. It is critical for both teacher and students to understanding the status of motor learning and acquisition. Students will not know how their performance is unless it has been measured and feedback provided. The fundamental purpose of performance measurement is to improve performance, evaluate how well students perform a motor skill, and provide information regarding their performance to motivate students to strive for perfection. Performance assessment provides valuable information to the teacher and students with regards to whether the learning outcomes are in line with what was intended or should have been achieved.

Error Measurement

From a measurement and evaluation perspective, the teacher and coach provide the exact score for basketball shots (5 out of 10), exact measurement of height and distance for high jump or long jump, distance for shot put and javelin, and seconds for running or reaction time. The teacher/coach uses a numerical score and compares it with others to evaluate students' performance. For other types of sports like gymnastics and soccer, for example, accuracy is used to describe the quality of a passing or shooting in soccer (e.g., results in ball possession or missed goal), and error measure is used to evaluate the accuracy of performance in gymnastics, (e.g., the points are deducted from a perfect score to judge a gymnastic routine performance). There are three methods commonly used to measure performance when executing a motor skill. These methods provide different types of feedback and a comprehensive evaluation of students' performance. These three methods are: absolute error (AE), constant error (CE), and variable error (VE). *Absolute error* refers to the absolute difference between the actual performance on each trial and goal (Magill, 2011)

which indicates a record of the average amount of error. For example in archery, the distance of six arrows hit the center of the target, and the AE record how much error there is. *Constant error* refers to the signed (+/-) deviation from the goal (Magill, 2011), which indicates the average of the distance that arrows hit close to or away from the center. CE provides information on the direction of error which the arrows were shot at the target, and it is more useful for teacher to know students' actual performance. *Variable error* refers to the information of consistency or the variability which an individual or a group's performance on a motor task (Magill, 2011).

RETENTION MEASUREMENT

A retention test measures how much information a student has retained after having learned a motor skill. The retention test determines an individual's ability to retain the same level of motor skill performance after a period of no practice. Retention is an important indicator of the effectiveness of the teaching method and of students' learning. For example, students who can perform motor skills up to 80% by the beginning of next class session would indicate they have retained a great amount of information related to skill performance. Biking and swimming can be a perfect example to describe the retention of a child who has learned these skills at an early age, and who can bike or swim after ten years of no practice due to extensive initial learning experience. In terms of motor skill learning, the teacher/coach is concerned, not only with retaining the motor skill but also transferring it to daily life or competition. Students should be able to transfer a skill learned in a class (or drill) setting to a real game setting. Students who can demonstrate a good technique in practice (e.g., high percentage shooting rate in basketball) but who cannot perform well in a real game present a problem, as those who cannot transfer the learned skill to a new yet similar motor skill. Therefore, the teacher and coach must provide different practical settings to enhance both retention and transfer. There are many tests and measurement instruments to examine retention and transfer. For example, a retention test occurs after students have learned a skill under a teacher's supervision, and the teacher gives a retention test to these students again days or weeks after teaching is completed. The retention test is to determine how much these students have retained. The more a student has retained the more effective the condition was in learning the skill (Thomas, 1980).

"Assessment for Learning" utilizes formative assessment to measure students' learning process and their learning progress. Another type of assessment called "outcome measurement," uses summative assessment to measure their final performance outcome. These two measurements in physical education have a different focus: one examines how a novice student's learning occurs and develops; in this case, assessment is closely linked with the student' learning process which describes how he/she performs a new motor skill, and which provides feedback on those incorrect movements for further practice. The teacher/coach focuses on the details of the skill by using observation or some other instruments such as a camera with a biomechanical analysis system, to analyze performance and provide appropriate feedback.

During the three learning stages, the assessment focus varies depending on the students' learning progress; a number of assessment measures can be used to evaluate both teaching effectiveness and strategies and student learning progress (e.g., videotaping and biomechanical analysis). Accuracy of performance is compared to standard form and detailed indicators such as time, distance, or learning/performance curves are used to describe the learning progress. For experienced learners or athletes, summative measurement is used to evaluate performance outcome at the end of a training session; the results are then used to describe what students have achieved. Score, rating scales, and percent gains based on established standards serve as indicators to demonstrate students' learning results. The results of the "outcome measurement" indicate teaching and learning effectiveness (Barclay & Newell, 1980).

BETWEEN MEASUREMENT AND WITHIN MEASUREMENT

In applied motor development and motor behavior analysis, assessment of motor development and behavior change before (pre-measure), during (between or repeated measures), and after (post measures) the learning process are used to describe students' skill acquisition progress. Graphics of performance curves are useful indicators to analyze the changes in students' behavior (Figure 8.2.). For example, pre-post measures are used to compare significant differences on a new training method between/among groups through statistical t-test or ANOVA analysis. The ABA Single Subject Design is used to evaluate student behavior change under the new treatment during a pre-intervention baseline phase (A), an intervention phase (B), and a post intervention withdraw phase (A). The study "Effectiveness of TGFU Teaching Strategy on Motivation of Participating in Physical Activities" is a good example to describe these measures (Gonnella, 1989).

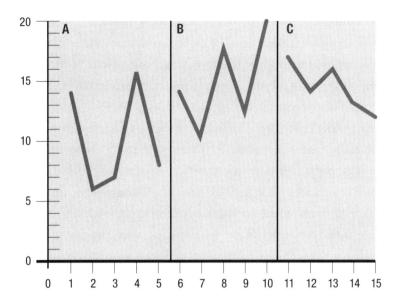

FIGURE 8.2. Criteria of elite motor skill performance.

MAXIMUM CONSISTENCY

It is a common belief that "practice makes perfect." Although it is not absolutely correct, it is commonly accepted that the more a person practices, the better his/her performance will be. The importance of practice in motor skill acquisition has been widely recognized (Ericsson, et al, 1993; Williams & Hodges, 2005). In sports training and competition, the primary purpose of practice is to improve an athlete's ability to maximize the consistency of his/her performance. To date, practice of a routine (e.g., gymnastics routine) starts at an early age, and in certain sports, athletes begin serious training very early (e.g., gymnastics) and maintain a daily intensive training for many years until reaching elite athlete standard. Accuracy and consistency in performance become a criterion for the Olympic competition, and athletes are now using thousands of hours of practice to secure the highest consistent performance in order to maintain a high level performance at the world level competition, especially for sports such as gymnastics, diving, golf, and table tennis (Shea & Kohl, 1990).

REQUIRE MINIMUM TIME OF COMPLETING AN ACTION WITH LEAST ENERGY EXPENDITURE

Energy expenditure refers to the amount of energy an athlete uses to perform a motor skill, or complete a routine like floor exercise in gymnastics. An elite athlete's physical performance and training level is influenced by physiological, psychological, and biomechanical factors. Movement efficiency refers to an athlete's ability to perform a motor skill using the least expenditure of energy, because the more skillful athlete at elite level will activate only those muscle fibers required to produce the appropriate movements, extra muscle contractions require more energy expenditure, (usually at novice level), but do not contribute to effective power output (Coyle, Spriet, Gregg, & Clarkson, 1994). It is a general agreement that elite athletes use less energy to complete a same motor program routine compared with regular athletes. For example, in a 100-meter swimming competition, average athletes with incorrect or inefficient body movement will generate much more unnecessary internal or external resistances because they have to, not only focus on movement skill, but also how their body movement coordinates with their breathing. These extra resistances will increase the expenditure of energy and cause early fatigue.

In contrast, the elite swimmer's movements will be automatically executed without spending extra energy on strokes and breathing. As a result, an elite swimmer's movement will be more efficient in the swimming pool, and will spend less energy than other swimmers. In sports such as gymnastics (e.g., apparatus event), figure skating, and ice hockey, the average athletes will use much more energy when they perform the skill, and at the same time work against their own body to maintain coordination with the apparatus and avoid falls. Team sports like basketball can be another example to support the statement.

REQUIRE MINIMUM TIME TO COMPLETE AN ACTION WITH LEAST ENERGY EXPENDITURE OF ELITE ATHLETE

Elite athletes will have a great advantage during team sports competition, as their experience and high skill level allow them to execute skills automatically. Their performance is clean, smooth, and more relaxed. In contrast, the average athlete faces higher intensity and more competitive opponents, and must spend more energy playing against high-level players. Therefore, these athletes will use more energy than elite athletes when playing the same game. As stated earlier, "practice makes perfect." Efficient performance causes the least expenditure of energy.

COURTESY OF U.S. ARMY

PRE-REQUISITES OF EFFECTIVE ASSESSMENT AND EVALUATION

Understand Nature of Particular Motor Skills

Assessment and evaluation is one of several integral aspects in physical education, sports training, and sport science, and offers many benefits for teachers, coaches, and students by understanding the nature of motor skill. Assessment and evaluation is important for teachers, as it helps them decide what they want students to learn and how to guide them in their learning. It can also help the teacher to design appropriate goals and objectives for their teaching. Assessment and evaluation are important for coaches as well, as it assists them in training athletes according to motor learning principles, and providing feedback to help them improve their performance. Assessment and evaluation are important for students because they offer feedback to students about their learning and performance, and help them understand their strengths and weaknesses. Feedback during practice facilitates students' motor skill learning. For example, a functional test can diagnose a problem and measure the student's learning progress, which in turn will allow him/her to see a weakness that must be strengthened. Verbal instructions, demonstration (or video), and feedback greatly helps the students understand incorrect aspects of the performance which must be changed.

Understand Basic Statistic Methods

Statistics is the mathematical tool to convert all raw data collected from assessment into a meaningful evident to describe students' performance and achievement (Baumgartner & Jackson, 2007; Miller, 2006). In movement studies, statistics involve collecting, organizing, analyzing, and interpreting data from professional perspectives. Currently, many teachers give reports based only on the raw data, they fail to use statistics to organize the data into a meaningful manner for a particular purpose, or use organized data to identify students' motor skill and performance problems. Therefore, without appropriate statistical analysis, data obtained from assessment are useless and wasted (Bloomfield & Wilson, 1999). The two main types of statistics used in sports science and school are descriptive statistics such as frequency distribution, central tendency, variability and probability theory, standard score (t-score and Z-score), and *inferential statistics* such as t-test and analysis of variance (ANOVA), correlation and regression, and more. These statistical methods can be used for school grading and report, survey and election statistical analysis, social studies on attitude, health status profile, sports participation interests, and medical related analysis. For example, "Patterns of participation in recreation activities among primary school students" is a good example for using the above statistics methods to analyze data. Only the data that have been statistically and appropriately analyzed can be trusted, and can then be used to interpret assessment results and draw conclusions (Atkinson & Nevill, 2001).

Understand the Purpose, Strengths and Weaknesses of Assessment Methods

Assessment includes measuring motor performance, evaluating analysis of test results, identifying performance problems, and providing a report and suggestions. The purposes of assessment normally include, but are not limited to, providing feedback to motivate students, diagnosing students' strengths and weaknesses, evaluating students' achievement and program development, and predicting students' progress (formative assessment for learning). Assessment can give teachers feedback on student learning, evaluate teaching and training programs, indicate strength and weakness on the program implementation, monitor the teacher's performance, and improve teaching effectiveness (assessment for quality assurance).

> **Understanding the Purpose of Assessment**
>
> **Assessment includes measuring motor performance, evaluating the test results, identifying performance problems, and providing feedback and suggestions.**

There are many formal and informal assessment instruments commonly used to assess learners' motor performance; some are simple and easy to operate, and others are more complex and require more time. These assessment instruments can be categorized into the following area: 1) health-related fitness tests including cardiorespiratory endurance, flexibility, muscular strength and endurance, and anthropometry and body composition; 2) skill-related fitness tests such as agility, balance, power, and coordination; 3) functional fitness test for community-residing older adults, 4) assessment for special population; and 5) assessment instruments for various sports skills (Table 8.2). The table below includes the list of assessment instruments in physical education. Teachers and coaches must fully understand the function of each instrument, and select the appropriate instrument to meet the purposes of the assessment. (Baumgartner, Jackson, Mahar, & Rowe, 2007; Miller, 2006).

COURTESY OF SHIHUI CHEN

> This Whole-body Air-Displacement Plethysmography chamber (BodPod) is a system measuring body composition. It uses a very precise scale to measure body mass and volume by sitting inside the BodPod. The body density can be calculated through the following formula: Density = Mass/Volume

TABLE 8.2. Assessment instruments in physical education

Agility	a. AAHPERD Shuttle Run b. Barrow ZigZag Run c. SEMO Agility Test

Balance	d. Static Balance Tests (Stork Stand, Bass Stick Test)
	e. Dynamic Balance Tests
	    • Johnson Modification of the Bass Test of Dynamic Balance
	    • Balance Beam Walk

Cardiorespiratory Fitness Tests	a. 12-Minute and 9-Minute run b. 1 mile and 1.5 mile runs c. 12-Minute Cycling Test d. YMCA 3-Minute Step Test
Flexibility	a. Sit and Reach b. Trunk and Neck Extension c. Shoulder-and-Wrist Elevation
Muscular Strength, Endurance, and Power	a. Sit-up Test (strength) b. Sit-up Test (endurance) c. Abdominal Curls d. Pull-ups Test for Strength e. Pull-ups Test for Endurance f. Modified Pull-ups for Endurance
Anthropometry and Body Composition	Measure Body Posture Measure Body Composition
Physical Fitness	a. The FitnessGram b. AAHPERD Health-Related Physical Fitness Test for College Students c. South Carolina Physical Fitness Test d. YMCA Physical Fitness Test e. ACSM Fitness Test f. The Canadian Physical Activity, Fitness & Lifestyle Appraisal: • AAHPERD Youth Fitness Test
Older Adult	a. Functional Fitness Assessment for Adults over 60 Years b. Functional Fitness Test for Community-Residing Older Adults

Special Population	a. Perceptual-Motor Performance Tests
	    • Purdue Perceptual Motor Survey
	    • Ayres Southern California Perceptual-Motor Tests
	b. Motor Performance Tests
	    • The Broininks-Oseretsky Test of Motor Proficiency
	    • Test of Gross Motor Development
	c. Physical Fitness Tests
	    • FitnessGram Modification for Special Populations
	    • AAHPERD Motor Fitness Tests for the Moderately MR

TABLE 8.2. Assessment instruments in physical education (continued)

Sports Skills	a. Badminton • French Short-Serve Test • Scott and French Long-Serve Test b. Golf • Clevett's Putting Test c. Racquetball • Racquetball Skills Test d. Tennis • AAHPERD Tennis Skills Test e. Team Sports (Basketball) • AAHPERD Basketball Skills Test • Soccer (McDonald Soccer Test) f. Softball • AAHPERD Softball Skill Test g. Volleyball (Brumbach Volleyball Service Test)

Key Terminology to Remember

- *Assessment for learning* is the process of seeking and interpreting evidence for use by learners and their teachers to decide where the learners are in their learning, where they need to go, and how best to get there. (Assessment Reform Group, 2002)

- *Assessment as learning* is based in research about how learning happens, and is characterized by students reflecting on their own learning and making adjustments so that they achieve deeper understanding. (Western and Northern Canadian Protocol, 2006)

- *Assessment of learning* refers to strategies designed to confirm what students know, demonstrate whether or not they have met curriculum outcomes or the goals of their individualized programs, or to certify proficiency and make decisions about students' future programs or placements. (Western and Northern Canadian Protocol, 2006)

- *Formative assessment* is a process used by teachers and students during instruction that provides explicit feedback to adjust ongoing teaching and learning to improve students' achievement of intended instructional outcomes. (McManus, 2006)

- *Performance measurement* is the ongoing monitoring and reporting of program accomplishments, particularly progress towards pre-established goals.

- *Retention measurement:* A retention test measures how much a student has retained after having learned a motor skill.

- *Maximum consistency* is a common belief that "practice makes perfect." Although it is not absolutely correct, it is commonly accepted that the more a person practices, the better his/her performance will be.

- *Energy expenditure* refers to the amount of energy an athlete uses to perform a motor skill, or complete a routine like floor exercise in gymnastics.

- *Assessment and evaluation* is one of several integral aspects in physical education, sports training and sport science, and offers many benefits for teachers, coaches, and students by understanding the nature of motor skill.

- *Statistics* is the mathematical tool to convert all raw data collected from assessment into a meaningful evident to describe students' performance and achievement.

- *T-test* is a statistical test, which reveals if there is(are) significant relationship(s) between two or more variables.

- *One-way/Two-way ANOVA* is statistical comparison(s) between two or more groups with one/more independent variables.

- *Linear correlation* indicates a strong correlation either in a positive or negative way with a linear pattern.

Student Assignments for Connecting Theory to Practice

1. Describe the characteristics of the proper instructions for cognitive stage, motor stage, and autonomous stage.

2. Describe the advantages and disadvantages of demonstrations by instructor and peer.

3. Give three examples of segmentation practice (use proper sports skills).

4. Give three examples of simplification practice.

5. Why do practitioners use slow-motion practice? Under what circumstances can coaches use slow-motion practice?

6. Describe different ways of structuring simulation training.

7. Before implementing a skill-training program, what preliminary areas of the learners should be carefully considered?

8. Describe the recommended internal focus (broad or narrow) before ice skating competition.

9. Describe the recommended internal focus (broad or narrow) before basketball competition.

10. Describe the recommended external focus (broad or narrow) before basketball competition.

11. Under what circumstance should a coach use distributed practice?

12. Under what circumstance should a coach use massed practice?

REFERENCES

Assessment for Learning. Retrieved from http://archive.excellencegateway.org.uk/page. aspx?o=131258

Atkinson, G., & Nevill, A. M. (2001). Selected issue in the design and analysis of sport performance research. *Journal of Sports Science, 19*, 811–827.

Barclay, C. R., & Newell, K. M. (1980). Children's processing of information in motor skill acquisition. *Journal of Experimental Child Psychology, 30*, 98–108.

Baumgartner, T. A., Jackson, A. S., Mahar, M., & Rowe, D. (2007). *Measurement for evaluation in physical education and exercise science* (8th ed.). Boston, MA: McGraw-Hill.

Bloomfield, J., & Wilson, G. (1999). Flexibility in sport. In B. Elliott (Ed.), *Training in sport: Applying sport science* (pp. 239–283). Chichester, UK: John Wiley & Sons.

Boyle, M. O., & Ackerman P. L. (2004). Individual differences in skill acquisition. In A. M. Williams & N. J. Hodge (Eds.), *Skill acquisition in sport* (pp. 84–102). New York, NY: Routledge.

Coyle, E. F., Spriet, L., Gregg, S., & Clarkson, P. (1994). Introduction to physiology and nutrition for competitive sport. In D. R. Lamb, H. G. Knuttgen, & R. Murray (Eds.), *Perspectives in exercise science and sports medicine, Vol. 7: Physiology and nutrition for competitive sport* (pp. xv–xxxix). Carmel, IN: Cooper Publishing Group.

Derri, V., & Pachta, M. (2007). Motor skills and concepts acquisition and retention: A comparison between two styles of teaching. *Revista Internacional de Ciencias del Deporte, 9*, 37–47.

Ericsson K. A., Krampe R. T., & Tesch-Römer, C. (1993). The role of deliberate practice in the acquisition of expert performance. *Psychological Review, 100*, 363–406.

Fitts, P. M., & Posner, M. I. (1967). *Human performance*. Oxford, UK: Brooks and Cole.

GAO-11-646SP. (2011). *Performance measurement and evaluation: Definitions and relationships*. Retrieved from http://www.gao.gov/assets/80/77277.pdf

Goldberger, M., & Gerney, P. (1986). The effects of direct teaching styles on motor skill acquisition of fifth grade children. *Research Quarterly for Exercise and Sport, 57*, 215–219.

Gonnella, C. (1989). Single-subject experimental paradigm as a clinical decision tool. *Physical Therapy, 69*, 601–609.

Hall, K. G., & Magill, R. A. (1995). Variability of practice and contextual interference in motor skill learning. *Journal of Motor Behavior, 27*, 299–309.

Magill, R. (2011). *Motor learning and control: Concepts and applications*. New York, NY: McGraw-Hill.

McManus, S. (2006). *Attributes of effective formative assessment*. Retrieved from http://www.ncpublicschools.org/docs/accountability/educators/fastattributes04081.pdf

Miller, D. (2006). *Measurement by the physical educator* (5th ed.). New York, NY: McGraw-Hill.

Mok, M. C. (2010). *Self-directed learning oriented assessment: Assessment that informs learning & empowers the learner*. Hong Kong, China: Pace Publishing Ltd.

Schmidt, R. A., & Wrisberg, C. A. (2000). *Motor learning and performance: A problem-based learning approach*. Champaign, IL: Human Kinetics.

Shea, C. H., & Kohl, R. M. (1990). Specificity and variability of practice. *Research Quarterly, 61*, 169–177.

Sullivan, K., Kantak, S., & Burtner, P. (2008). Motor learning in children: Feedback effects on skill acquisition. *Physical Therapy, 88*, 720–732.

Thomas, J. R. (1980). Acquisition of motor skills: Information processing differences between children and adults. *Research Quarterly for Exercise & Sport, 51*, 158–173.

Western and Northern Canadian Protocol. (2006). Rethinking classroom assessment with purpose in mind. Retrieved from http://www.edu.gov.mb.ca/k12/assess/wncp/rethinking_assess_mb.pdf

Williams, A. M., & Hodges, N. J. (2005). Practice, instruction, and skill acquisition in soccer: Challenging tradition. *Journal of Sports Sciences, 23*, 637–650.

Wulf, G. (1991). The effect of type of practice on motor learning in children. *Applied Cognitive Psychology, 5*, 123–134.

Instruction and Feedback in Motor Skill Learning

OBJECTIVES

- Understand roles of instruction and feedback to motor learning and processes
- Understand neuro-stimulation and memory perspective of establishing proper cognitive images
- Understand proper instruction and feedback based on learners' age, experience, cognitive ability, and skill levels
- Understand types of feedback and its applications to motor skill learning
- List all different types of feedbacks and describe their characteristics
- Understand the strategies providing feedback at cognitive stage
- Understand the strategies providing feedback at motor stage
- Understand the strategies providing feedback at autonomous stage
- Understand providing feedback based on outcome-oriented motor skills
- Understand providing feedback based on open and closed motor skills

INTRODUCTION

For the last century, the roles of instruction and feedback have been addressed as essential aspects of the motor skill learning process. There are many ways to provide learners with information feedback about their performance during their motor skill practice (Edwards, 2010). The two most common ways to assist learners to learn or perform a motor skill correctly and effectively are verbal instructions and physical demonstration. However, effective methods of providing instructions for learning a motor skill depend on many variables such as the type of skill and the purpose of instruction. This chapter will help readers better understand 1) the natural connection between human brain information-processing mechanisms and motor skill learning and retention; 2) how to establish a correct image based on proper instruction and feedback through transferring information from the short-term memory to the long-term memory; 3) the latest research by comparing it with traditional teaching and coaching methods; and 4) how augmented feedback can facilitate the learning process and lead to effective learning and performance of motor skills.

ROLES OF INSTRUCTION AND FEEDBACK IN MOTOR SKILL LEARNING PROCESSES

The neuro-stimulation and memory perspective for establishing proper cognitive image memory theory has been integrated into the cognitive neuroscience and cognitive psychology areas, and the two fields became an interdisciplinary theory a number of decades ago (Baars & Gage, 2012; Banich, & Compton, 2010). Memory theory plays an integral role in terms of motor skill learning. According to Van Dijk (2006), motor skill learning processes interact with cognitive and sensory processes, and this best summarizes the neurological nature of a human's learning. Brain imaging involves analyzing activity within the brain while various cognitive tasks are performed. This allows us to link behavior and brain function to help understand how information is processed. Cognitive neuroscience approaches to memory attempt to understand the brain processes and systems that are involved in different forms of memory and learning. For example, what part of the brain is responsible for memorizing movements and what part is responsible for memorizing words? (Feinstein, 2009; Sherwood, 2011). Cognitive psychology approaches to memory investigate the internal mental processes of thought, such as visual processing, memory, and problem solving, to show how people mentally represent information (for example, how does seeing affect a person's beliefs (Shea, Shebilske, & Worchel, 1993)?

Human memory is very important in motor skill learning as well as in understanding how motor skill-related information is stored and retrieved, and promotes learning because of past experiences (Figure 9.1). Memory usually consists of both long-term and short-term memory. Long-term memory refers to the memory that can last a few days or as long as decades and a life span, and allows humans to store information over a long period for retrieval when needed (for example, riding a bike or driving a car). Short-term memory is a temporary message of neural connections that can only store information for a short period, maybe only a few seconds (Foster, 2008). Through rehearsals, information in the short-term memory can be transferred to the long-term memory. For example, when

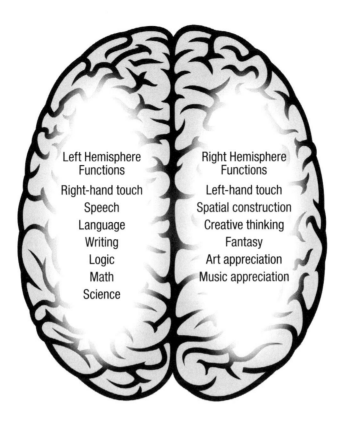

Left Hemisphere
Functions

Right-hand touch
Speech
Language
Writing
Logic
Math
Science

Right Hemisphere
Functions

Left-hand touch
Spatial construction
Creative thinking
Fantasy
Art appreciation
Music appreciation

FIGURE 9.1. The left and right brain hemispheres specialize in different functions. Split-brain research suggests that functions are divided as indicated.

you glance at a picture, the image of the picture is stored in your short-term memory for a few seconds, and then might become unclear unless you rehearse it. When we refresh the image of the picture in our memory, or glance at it again within a different period of time, the short-term image will become a long-term memory that lasts a few days, if you are interested in the picture (or if it is important to you). From the perspective of movement studies, teachers and students are interested in understanding how the information on motor skills is stored and retrieved, and how the information from past experiences can be retrieved for learning new skills (for example, learning to play tennis based on previous experiences of playing squash).

From the perspective of motor skill learning processes, establishing proper cognitive images (short- to long-term memory) is the premise for building a correct neuromuscular movement or motor skill performance. And learning and establishing a correct motor skill depends on proper motor programs that include correct instruction and feedback, and repeated practice (Haskell et al., 1977; Thomas et al., 1988). Thus, building up a proper cognitive image is the most essential aspect in terms of motor skill learning and retention.

For example, when a student observes a teacher's demonstration, a short-term image is established. Then, if the student is interested in learning the skill and the demonstration is followed by practice with appropriate instruction and feedback, then he/she will finally learn the skill through repetition, and the short-term memory will be transferred to the long-term memory. Atkinson and Shiffrin's (1968) Multiple-Store Model in Figure 9.2 shows three "stores" of human memory: sensory memory, short-term memory (limited capacity, short duration), and long-term memory (potentially unlimited capacity and duration). Attention and rehearsal explain how data is transferred (Plotnik & Kouyoumdjian, 2010; Sternberg, 2000). The Multiple-Store Model makes good sense from the perspective of motor skill learning processes, and provides a framework for kinesiology teachers and sports coaches to understand the importance of memory (Magnussen & Helstrup, 2007).

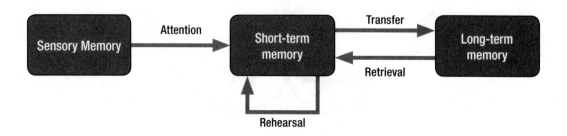

FIGURE 9.2. Multi-store model.

ESTABLISHMENT OF PROPER MOTOR PROGRAMS (HABITS) WITH CORRECT INSTRUCTION AND FEEDBACK

After establishing appropriate cognitive images of a motor skill, the learner must establish the correct neuromuscular movement or motor skill performance transferred from the cognitive images. One of the most important elements for establishing a correct motor skill performance is practice, which needs to be guided by the right instruction, and the most significant way in which a teacher or coach can provide the instructional guidance to students is through augmented feedback. For optimal effectiveness of motor skill learning and performance, feedback needs to be carefully scheduled and delivered, depending on the type of skill and whether the learner is experienced or a novice. For example, feedback for swimmers should be provided after the drill, but feedback for gymnastics can be done either during or after practice.

Recent research studies have raised questions regarding how much feedback is appropriate. The results of these studies indicate that more feedback is not always better

(Brookhart, 2008; Thomas, Lee, & Thomas, 2008). The most interesting issues discussed in the research literature are how much feedback we should provide for our learners, how often we should provide it, and when it should be delivered to our learners. For example, Walsh, Ling, Wang, and Carnahan (2009) suggest that too much feedback can impair learning. Their study showed that when instructors are interacting with and instructing students with large amounts of feedback, there are many temporary effects of feedback that will influence performance. However, when the feedback is removed during the retention phase when students perform independently, their performance deteriorates. The question is: What is the optimal frequency for the delivery of feedback to the learner during practice? The answer to the question depends on the learners' age, experience, cognitive ability, skill levels, etc.

In addition, the type and amount of feedback that should be delivered also depends on the characteristics of the various learners. In a regular physical education class, teachers and coaches provide feedback to students after every trial. However, this method may not be effective. Anderson and Magill's (2005) study indicates that adults who practice motor skills under conditions 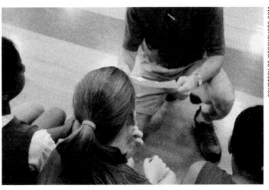 of reduced feedback perform with greater accuracy and consistency compared to those who are provided with feedback during every trial (Anderson, Magill, Sekiya, & Ryan, 2005). Clearly, the appropriateness of instruction and feedback varies according to the individual learner's age, experience, cognitive ability, and skill levels, and the feedback is optimally effective only when it is suited to the individual learner's particular situation and the specific learning scenario. For example, during the initial stage of learning a skill, corrective feedback is commonly used by teachers, whereas at the intermediate level, suggestive feedback is more effective in enhancing skill performance (Kirk, MacDonald, & O'Sullivan, 2006; Weinberg & Gould, 2010). It is well established that students' experience and cognitive ability play an important role in learning. Sullivan's study (Sullivan et al., 2008) investigated the effect of feedback given during practice on acquisition and retention of a motor skill in children. Their research revealed the very interesting fact that children have different information processing capabilities compared with adults (Sullivan et al., 2008). Children of different ages have different cognitive learning processes because selective attention varies with age. For example, younger children have more difficulty in maintaining attentional focus than older children. These differences in cognitive ability may influence the effectiveness of children's learning and performing motor skills. This is because younger children are more engaged on a daily basis in fundamental physical motor activities such as running, jumping, kicking, skipping, and throwing, and other eye-hand coordination motor skills, in their natural environment. When children are young, their learning follows a natural progression through a development sequence, and their skill level during the different learning stages will also influence their ability to pay attention to feedback. Therefore, feedback that is effective for adults might not be effective for children. The "more feedback is not always better" finding demonstrated by many studies is absolutely true in terms of children's learning, especially during the first learning stage. Sullivan's study (Sullivan et al., 2008) also indicates that children may require more practice trials with appropriate feedback to promote a more accurate and stable internal representation of a motor skill. Studies related to the environment and context in which the feedback is presented show that the feedback given on a student's performance in one situation might not be appropriate in a different setting. A particular skill might work very well when performed in one environment but be quite inappropriate in another. For example, in javelin throwing there are a number of environmental factors (e.g., wind, running speed, the athlete's individual style) which determine whether or not a throw is good. Teachers and coaches therefore need to consider environmental and context factors when providing feedback. The characteristics of a movement that are necessary for its successful execution in different contexts or scenarios must be specified so that students understand how to perform the skill correctly in a given environment.

TYPES OF FEEDBACK AND THEIR APPLICATIONS TO MOTOR SKILL LEARNING

While it has been shown that feedback is one of the most important elements in motor skill learning; it is also the most critical form of guidance a learner can receive from teachers and coaches (Chen, Kaufman, & Chung, 2001). Students will learn less effectively and at a lower rate, and will have more difficulty reaching high-level proficiency if they do not receive well-prepared instruction and performance feedback. Therefore, understanding different types of feedback is very important in terms of effective learning.

Feedback can be intrinsic or extrinsic and both types are useful learning aids. *Intrinsic feedback,* also called sensory feedback, comes directly through the senses (including visual, auditory, proprioceptive, and tactile) of the person who is performing the skill. For example, experienced soccer or basketball players can sense whether they kicked the ball well or shot toward the basket.

Extrinsic feedback, also called augmented feedback, comes from the outside environment and external sources. Augmented feedback refers to information that does not come directly from the performer's senses, but is imparted by the teacher or coach, for example by verbal instructions and comments about his/her performance. Augmented feedback includes Knowledge of Results (KR) and Knowledge of Performance (KP) as well as augmented sensory feedback. KR focuses on feedback related to the outcome of a learner's activity, and is the information provided about the results of a performance after completion of the motor skill (e.g., a good or bad performance). For example, when we teach a student to pitch a baseball overhand, providing feedback in the form of KR indicates to the student the accuracy and speed of the pitching trial (e.g., "Too high," or "Great! Right in the middle"). In other examples, a teacher or coach can tell an archery/shooting athlete that his score is "up-right of 9 points" or inform a track athlete of the number of seconds each lap of a 10K race took. For athletes who are visually impaired or blind, extrinsic feedback on all their movements is extremely important. Each movement completed must be followed immediately by verbal or manual feedback and compared with previous movement experiences and the athlete's intrinsic feedback so that he/she can establish a correct image. KP focuses on the movement pattern executed to achieve the goal, and is the information or comments provided to evaluate the quality of the movement performance. KP as augmented feedback is widely used by teachers and coaches. Some examples of this would be instructing a high-jumper to place his/her jumping leg slightly forward before taking off to provide better vertical force, telling a student to place his/her foot slightly forward when kicking a rolling ball, or replaying a videotape to show an athlete his/her body movement position during a performance. In other examples a teacher or coach might tell a javelin thrower that the throwing arm should extend farther back, or a basketball point shooter that he should keep his arm at a higher position when releasing the ball. Feedback in the form of KP on overhand baseball pitching could focus on giving the performer information about his/her hand movement and swing, upper body and lower body coordination, and body position when releasing the ball. When students are learning or performing a new motor skill, both KR and KP need to be firmly scheduled into the training to facilitate their skill acquisition.

COURTESY OF U.S. MARINE CORPS

Over the years, many research studies have focused on the effectiveness and utilization of augmented feedback in motor skill learning. These studies have shown that the use of augmented feedback is most effective when it is provided to learners after their performance or trial. However, there have been some debates about its application. For example, the view that one should "provide KP or KR as soon or as often after performance as possible" has been challenged by many researchers. The findings of Guadagnoli and Kohl (2001) indicate that teachers and coaches should apply the KR when students and athletes are learning a new motor skill, while Thorpe and Valvano (2002) state that the most powerful and effective type of feedback in motor learning is KP, especially for those skills that require high-level movement. From a motor learning perspective, both KR and KP are equally important depending on which stage the teacher or coach is emphasizing.

Feedback can be delivered to students in many ways during or after their motor skill performance and practice. The most common types of feedback are: teachers' verbal comments, augmented feedback (KR/KP from kinesiological analysis), and visual feedback in the form of videotape playbacks. In the normal practice of teaching and coaching, a complete instruction sequence is the teacher's description of a task, demonstration of the performance, and then students' practice. The teacher provides verbal comments or physical instruction (demonstration of correct form, or a mirror image of the student's performance) and feedback on the skill a student is performing (e.g., "Quick!" "Slow down!" or "Great!") or has just completed (both KP and KR). With the development of IT in education today, many teachers and coaches also use videotapes to record students' performances, followed by biomechanical motion analysis of the video playback to allow students to receive "technologically" augmented feedback about their motor skill performance. Figure 9.2 is an example of the electronic device used to show kinesiological analysis of students' running performance.

MAJOR FUNCTIONS AND SOURCES OF AUGMENTED FEEDBACK

The most common ways of providing learners with augmented feedback to facilitate their learning and performance are through verbal description, demonstrations, and physical guidance. From the motor skill learning perspective, augmented feedback serves three major functions: (1) providing learners with information on correct movements and errors to help them establish a correct movement image; (2) providing information on outcome of performance to establish a connection or comparison between the outcome movement and performance process (the connection between the KR and the KP), and at the same time encourage and motivate students' learning; and (3) providing feedback to students while the movement is being performed, or immediately after the performance is completed to assist and facilitate their learning process. Immediate information feedback can play a very important role in error detection and correction. For example, a teacher can confirm a correct basketball shooting skill by using brief verbal cues (e.g., "Good," "Quick," or "Higher") or gestures to indicate the correct or incorrect movements while a student is performing the skill or by giving a physical demonstration of the skill immediately after the movement is completed (demonstrate both correct and incorrect skills or provide the outcome of performance). Using the information from the immediate feedback, the student can determine which modifications to make for the next trial. Augmented feedback is important during skill acquisition because the effectiveness of students' skill learning depends on how the teacher delivers the instruction and feedback. (Figure 9.3 is a schematic of how the learning process is affected by various augmented information.)

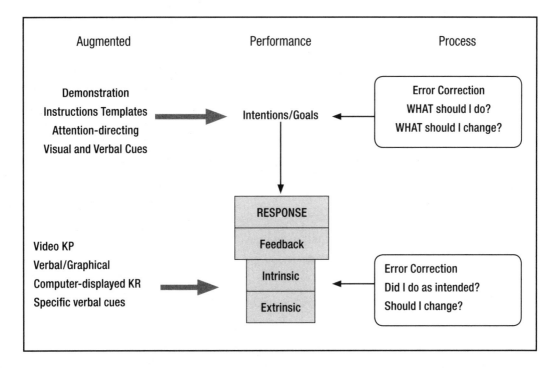

FIGURE 9.3. Schematic diagram to illustrate how the learning process is affected by various augmented information sources. Error-detection and correction processes are informed by augmented information in the form of feedback and pre-practice information. This information influences the intention and goals of the performer and subsequently the movement response.

APPLICATION OF FEEDBACK TO LEARNERS BASED ON CLASSIFICATION OF MOTOR SKILLS

Many research studies on augmented information feedback have recommended that effective feedback to learners should be based on the classification of motor skills. The type of skill is one of the most important variables influencing motor skill learning. Students will learn more slowly if the feedback given neglects to take this into account. Therefore, teachers and coaches providing instruction and feedback should consider the following two types of motor skill: process-outcome versus outcome-oriented motor skills and reaction time (RT) versus non-RT motor skills. Augmented feedback given for a process-oriented motor skill can have a very different effect from that given for an outcome-oriented motor skill, because it is difficult to talk about feedback for the one without discussing feedback for the other. While the feedback has a different focus for each of these motor skills (i.e., process or result), the two kinds of feedback are closely related and equally important in terms of motor skill learning.

Feedback Given for Process-oriented Motor Skills

As defined in the previous chapters, the evaluation of a process-oriented motor skill is based on teachers' and coaches' subjective judgments rather than on the final outcome. For example, referees in gymnastics, figure-skating, and diving competitions make judgments on an athlete's performance based on how the entire program routine is processed. Coaches and referees focus on evaluating how athletes execute their body movements in terms of style, posture, and rhythm, etc. in a competition program. Feedback for the many events that involve process-oriented motor skills should focus on the following; (1) providing constructive and clear instructions to athletes before or after an action; for example, when teaching a young beginner to dribble a basketball, the instructor should provide instruction on the rules related to dribbling such as one-hand dribbling, and not carrying or palming the ball; (2) emphasizing how to do the actions, focusing on the kinematics of format of actions, for example the correct way to move the arms, hands, and feet in bas-

ketball, and on shooting arm positions; (3) teaching motor skills from simple to complex with emphasis on kinematic progress, for example, by using a big ball first, followed by gradually smaller-sized balls, or by focusing only on one set of skills at first, such as those required when using one hand, and bringing in the other hand later on; (4) using visual tools such as video-clips, movie and live demonstrations to compare errors in skill executions, for example, using the video replay function to compare a beginner with a skillful performer; and (5) emphasizing mental imagery training to formalize kinematic elements of technical structures, for example, having all students close their eyes and mentally rehearse dribbling the ball from one end of the court to the other. In general, without appropriate external instructions from coaches or instructors, athletes cannot make improvements in these types of motor skills.

Feedback Given for Outcome-oriented Motor Skills

For outcome-oriented motor skills, referees can make an objective judgment to determine the outcome of competition based on the end result. For example, in events such as the 100-meter-dash, high jumping, long jumping, soccer, basketball, volleyball, and swimming, the decision as to who is the winner is made according to the time, height, distance, or score. The feedback given for these outcome-oriented motor skills will focus on how to achieve the maximum distance, the fastest speed, and the most points in the competition. For example, basketball players' shooting style and technique can vary as long as they have a good shooting percentage; likewise the style or technique of 100-meter dash athletes or high jumpers can vary as long as it can maximize their capacity. Thus, training for outcome-oriented motor skills needs to have various emphases but it should incorporate the shared principles. When designing training programs, coaches, teachers, or instructors should understand the key characteristics of the particular skill structures required for the sport and match the athletes' individual characteristics with the specific outcomes of the motor skills. Any variables that can contribute to the outcome should be considered for training emphasis, so it is important to be creative when designing training regimens.

Feedback Given for RT and Non-RT (Open and Closed) Motor Skills

The strategies for giving augmented feedback on RT and on non-RT motor skills are very different, as is the effectiveness of the feedback. RT motor skills are performed in an unpredictable and changing environment. Athletes are required to respond immediately to an opponent in a game situation; any delay could lead to failure or less efficiency in the game. For example, a baseball player may have a delayed RT when hitting a baseball or a boxer may fail to avoid a punch from his opponent. Picture the consequence if there is a 0.1 second delay in a boxer's RT against his opponent's punch—he might be knocked out and lose the fight. Since it is impossible, for example, for baseball hitters to prepare in advance when facing an oncoming baseball, or for volleyball players to plan their next action in a competition, athletes have to be trained to quickly respond to their opponents' unpredictable actions and to make the right move against an opponent in these types of sports. Teachers and coaches should therefore select a good training model (real game situations and environment) and strategies to provide opportunities for athletes to train their intrinsic (sense) feedback to react to opponents' movements.

There are many ways to train athletes to develop their intrinsic feedback, which is a critical determinant of success in competitions involving RT-based motor skills. One of the major obstacles all athletes who play sports involving RT-based motor skills have to face is that they do not know what is coming next. These kinds of sports need players with fast RT as well as swift movements so that they can quickly respond to an opponent's moves and take action. The training for RT-based motor skills should include real game situations to simulate the challenge of competition intensity. Athletes should have opportunities to practice specific skill movements in challenging and difficult situations, such as encountering multiple defenders (e.g., when shooting a basketball, or in handball), or passing a ball in a very limited space (e.g., soccer passing drills), in order to develop their ability to execute the skills in competitions. However, when teaching a new RT-based motor skill, or if the athletes are young, it may be better to start with a non-RT based motor skill training approach. This approach is particularly useful when teaching complex motor skills. For example, T-ball can be used for new baseball players to practice their batting skills, and tennis players can practice swinging the racquet by hitting balls from a serving machine. Once the athletes' skills start to improve, RT-based motor skills can then be introduced to meet real game situations; the baseball player will hit baseballs pitched by a pitcher, and the tennis player will hit balls served by the coach or opponent.

COURTESY OF U.S. AIR FORCE

In contrast, non-RT based motor skills are defined as predictable and the environment in which they are performed is unchanging. Non-RT based motor skills, such as shooting at a static target, diving, dance, gymnastics, high jump, etc., require athletes to complete a predetermined and practiced routine in competition. The structures of the motor skills executed during practice and in a competition are also exactly the same. Because they do not have to face any unpredictable stimuli, the athletes can decide in advance what they are going to do in a competition. Augmented feedback given during training for non-RT based motor skills is important and varies based on age, experience, cognitive level, etc. This type of motor skill can be perfected through sufficient practice with appropriate feedback. For example, the basketball free throw needs to be practiced over and over again until the player has established his/her own stable shooting pattern and style. This will allow the player to contribute a higher successful shooting percentage in a game situation.

FEEDBACK GIVEN AT THREE STAGES OF LEARNING

Despite the fact that many different motor learning theories concerning a better approach to motor skill acquisition have been discussed in the literature, the three-stage motor skill learning model which Fitts and Posner (1967) proposed is still frequently used to describe the nature of the learning process. Anyone who has ever learned a new motor skill will have gone through this three-stage skill acquisition model. The feedback provided by teachers and coaches at each of the three stages has a different emphasis and plays a different role with different effects. The three-stage model is described in the following sections.

Feedback Given at the Cognitive Stage

In the *cognitive stage,* the athlete is introduced to a new sports skill, attempts to understand the nature of the skill, and develops a general mental image of the movement being taught through different intrinsic and extrinsic feedback sources. For example, athletes receive the information from listening to teachers' or coaches' verbal introductions and physical demonstrations. They get feedback information from intrinsic sources (vision, hearing, proprioception, and touch) and augmented feedback (KP and KR) during practice. At this stage, athletes will encounter a lot of confusion, make errors, and have uncoordinated body postures with each trial. They might be attempting to focus on one thing while ignoring others. They will have many questions in relation to performance. Teachers and coaches, at this stage, use verbal instructions and physical demonstrations to help novice athletes to establish a movement image and pattern. They try to facilitate understanding by having students/athletes use all their senses (vision, hearing, proprioception, and touch), by having them observe the movement patterns of more experienced performers, by mental rehearsal, and by practicing comparison between visual image and physical execution. The feedback provided by teachers and coaches should focus appropriately on important movement techniques or routines and leave those less important details for later correction. For example, when teaching a Tai Chi program, we initially focus on the steps of the routine without correcting exact arm positions and body posture. Too much feedback on details (e.g., forms plus kinesthetics) at the cognitive stage might overwhelm students and slow down their learning process. Once the cognitive stage is completed, teachers and coaches can focus more on kinematic movement techniques and practice the kinesthetic forms of the motor skill being taught.

Feedback Given at Motor Stage

The *motor stage,* also called the *associative stage,* is the intermediate stage of acquiring a motor skill, which comes after athletes have established a general movement image and pattern from the first stage. Athletes and students at this stage are beginning to understand how to coordinate the different components of the body in the skill performance. They physically practice repeatedly and try to refine the skill and movement patterns by modifying and coordinating movement components. With practice, they find they gradually need to think less and less about the skill in order to perform it perfectly. Using the above example, the learning of a Tai Chi program at this stage will focus less on the routine, and more on kinematic movement techniques and kinesthetic forms with emphasis on exact arm positions and body posture. At the motor stage, teachers and coaches use trial-and-error feedback during training to facilitate students' practice, to reduce the frequency of errors and improve the movement consistency. Students' attention will focus less on the visual sense and rely more on proprioception, which they will use to detect their body posture and coordinate their movement positions.

Feedback Given at Autonomous Stage

The *autonomous stage* is the final stage of the Fitts and Posner learning stage model when athletes have the highest level of movement proficiency. In the *autonomous stage,* athletes are able to control their body posture and coordinate their movement positions automatically; they can perform the motor skills without any conscious effort or input from intrinsic and extrinsic feedback sources. For example, Tai Chi students can direct their attention to other aspects of the performance, such as breathing and relaxation, which can be refined in coordination with the Tai Chi movements. They do not need to pay as much attention to the Tai Chi routine and arm/leg movements; they can even perform multiple tasks at the same time (e.g., breathing, meditating, listening to music, and performing Tai Chi movements with the correct routine).

Key Terms to Remember

- The *neuro-stimulation and memory perspective* for establishing proper cognitive image memory theory has been integrated into the cognitive neuroscience and cognitive psychology areas, and the two fields became an interdisciplinary theory a number of decades ago (Baars & Gage, 2012; Banich & Compton, 2010).

- *Brain imaging* involves analyzing activity within the brain while various cognitive tasks are performed.

- *Memory theory* plays an integral role in terms of motor skill learning. According to Van Dijk (2006), motor skill learning processes interact with cognitive and sensory processes, and this best summarizes the neurological nature of a human's learning.

- *Cognitive psychology* approaches is the branch of psychology that studies mental processes including how people think, perceive, remember, and learn. (Cherry, n.d.)

- *Proper cognitive image* is the premise for building a correct neuromuscular movement or motor skill performance. And learning and establishing a correct motor skill depends on proper motor programs that include correct instruction and feedback, and repeated practice (Haskell et al., 1977; Thomas et al., 1988).

- *Feedback* refers to information from the sensory system that indicates the status of a movement to the central nervous system. In a closed-loop system, feedback is used to make corrections to an ongoing movement (Magill, 2011).

- *Temporary effects of feedback* occur when instructors are interacting with and instructing students with large amounts of feedback, there are many temporary effects of feedback that will influence performance. However, when the feedback is removed during the retention phase when students perform independently, their performance deteriorates.

- *Intrinsic feedback,* also called sensory feedback, comes directly through the senses (including visual, auditory, proprioceptive, and tactile) of the person who is performing the skill.

- *Multi-Store Model* refers to the three "stores" of human memory: the sensory memory store, the short-term memory store (limited capacity, short duration), and the long-term memory store (potentially unlimited capacity and duration). Each store has a certain function in terms of our memory and storing and recalling information. (Atkinson & Shiffrin, 1968)

- *Extrinsic feedback,* also called augmented feedback, comes from the outside environment and external sources.

- *Knowledge of result* is a category of augmented feedback that gives information about the outcome of performing a skill or about achieving the goal of the performance (Magill, 2011).

- *Augmented Feedback* is a generic term used to describe information about performing a skill that is added to sensory feedback and comes from a source external to the person performing the skill (Magill, 2011).

Student Assignments for Connecting Theory to Practice

- Explain what feedback is.
- Explain why feedback is crucial during motor learning process.
- What types of feedback are available that instructors or coaches can use?
- Can athletes learn motor skills without feedback from others? Explain why or why not.
- In order to be effective, how should coaches properly give feedback to learners?
- In the three different stages of learning process, explain how an instructor should effectively provide feedback to their students.
- Without feedback, can a diver learn diving skills based on video-tapes, pictures, and other media tools?
- Can a basketball player effectively improve motor skills without coaches' feedback?
- List the characteristics of effective feedback based on three stages of motor learning.
- List what types of feedback are available.

REFERENCES

Anderson, D. I., Magill, R. A., Sekiya, H., & Ryan, G. (2005). Support for an explanation of the guidance effect in motor skill learning. *Journal of Motor Behavior, 37,* 231–238.

Atkinson, R. C., & Shiffrin, R. M. (1968). Chapter: Human memory: A proposed system and its control processes. In K. W. Spence & J. T. Spence (Eds.), *The psychology of learning and motivation* (Volume 2; pp. 89–195) New York, NY: Academic Press.

Baars, B., & Gage, N. M. (2012). *Fundamentals of cognitive neuroscience: The conscious brain.* Oxford, UK: Elsevier Science Publishing Co. Inc.

Banich, M. T., & Compton, R. J. (2010). Cognitive neuroscience. Belmont, CA: Wadsworth.

Brookhart, S. M. (2008). *How to give effective feedback to your students.* Alexandria, VA: Association for Supervision and Curriculum Development.

Cherry, K. (n.d.). What is cognitive psychology? Retrieved from: http://psychology.about.com/od/cognitivepsychology/f/cogpsych.htm

Chen, D. D., Kaufman, D., & Chung, M. W. (2001). Emergent patterns of feedback strategies in performing a closed motor skill. *Perceptual and Motor Skills, 93,* 197–204.

Edwards, W. (2010). *Motor learning and control: From theory to practice.* Belmont, CA: Wadsworth Cengage Learning.

Feinstein, S. G. (2009). *Secrets of the teenage brain: Research-based strategies for reaching and teaching today's adolescents.* Thousand Oaks, CA: Corwin Press.

Foster, J. K. (2008). *Memory: A very short introduction.* New York, NY: Oxford University Press.

Guadagnoli, M. A., & Kohl, R. M. (2001). Utilization of knowledge of results for motor learning. *Journal of Motor Behavior, 33,* 217–224.

Haskell, S. H., Barrett, E. K., & Taylor, H. (1977). *The education of motor and neurologically handicapped children.* London, UK: Croom Helm.

Kirk, D., MacDonald, D., & O'Sullivan, M. (2006). *The handbook of physical education.* London, UK: SAGE Publications.

Magill, R. A. (2011) *Motor learning and control* (9th ed). New York, NY: McGraw-Hill.

Magnussen, S., & Helstrup, T. (Eds). (2007). *Everyday memory.* Hove, UK: Psychology Press.

Plotnik, R., & Kouyoumdjian, H. (2010). *Introduction to psychology.* Belmont, CA: Wadsworth Cengage Learning.

Shea, C. H., Shebilske, W., & Worchel, S. (1993). *Motor learning and control.* Upper Saddle River, NJ: Prentice Hall.

Sherwood, L. (2011). *Fundamentals of human physiology.* Belmont, CA: Brooks/Cole, Cengage Learning.

Sternberg, R. J. (2000). *Psychology: In search of the human mind.* San Diego, CA: Harcourt College Publishers.

Sullivan, K. J., Kantak, S. S., & Burtner, P. A. (2008). Motor learning in children: Feedback effects on skill acquisition. *Physical Therapy, 88,* 720–732.

Thomas, J. R., Lee, A. M., & Thomas, K. T. (1988). *Physical education for children: Concepts into practice.* Champaign, IL: Human Kinetics.

Thomas, K. T., Lee, A. M., & Thomas, J. R. (2008). *Physical education methods for elementary teachers.* Champaign, IL: Human Kinetics.

Thorpe, D. E., & Valvano, J. (2002). The effects of knowledge of performance and cognitive strategies on motor skill learning in children with cerebral palsy. *Pediatric Physical Therapy, 14,* 2–15.

Van Dijk, H. (2006). *Motor skill learning: Age and augmented feedback.* PhD thesis, University of Twente, Enschede, Netherlands.

Walsh, C. M., Ling, S. C., Wang, C. S., & Carnahan, H. (2009). Concurrent versus terminal feedback: It may be better to wait. *Academic Medicine, 84,* S54–S57.

Weinberg, R. S., & Gould, D. (2010). *Foundations of sport and exercise psychology.* Champaign, IL: Human Kinetics.

Application of Psychological Principles to Motor Learning Process

OBJECTIVES

- Understand the role of attention in motor skill learning
- Understand various attention styles
- Understand relationship between arousal and attention focus
- Understand various motivation strategies of teaching motor skills
- Understand the goal setting strategies
- Understand how anxiety can affect motor learning process and introduce strategies to properly deal with anxiety
- Understand proper communication strategies to connect with students while teaching motor skills
- Understand how mental imagery can play a positive role in motor learning process and the way of engaging in mental imagery

INTRODUCTION

Teaching motor skills is an integrated process which involves psycho/muscular activities. From the psychological perspective, motivation of learning, control of anxiety, proper use of attention, goal setting, visualization, confidence-building, and other psychological factors play important roles contributing to the success of motor skill learning. At the muscular level, ultimately, the goal of an athlete who is learning a motor skill is to execute the coordinated movements with precise timing and rhythms. To do this the learner must make the appropriate decisions and send the signals to the relevant muscle groups for the action to be taken. Needless to say, properly applying psychological principles to the motor skill learning process is a vital part of any skill training regimen. For example, if a learner has excellent genetic abilities, but lacks the motivation to learn, his/her learning outcome will probably be compromised. This chapter provides a brief introduction to the essential psychological principles practitioners should know, which will directly contribute to the success of motor skill learning.

THE ROLE OF ATTENTION IN MOTOR SKILL LEARNING

Motor learning is an internal process that happens in an individual's brain. During the process of learning, attention needs to be given to the relevant stimuli in order to help the brain remember the rules, procedures, regulations, and interaction process between the learner and the environment. Thus, if one does not pay proper attention to relevant stimuli and transfer these rules of learning to the long-term memory, no learning will occur. Therefore, attention is a critical factor contributing to the learning process (Jeannerod, 1994; Wulf, 2007; Wulf, Shea, & Lewthwaite, 2010). Firstly, let us discuss the structure of attention so that learners can effectively use attention span and attention focus in their learning process. The first rule of attention control is to understand that human attention is limited, which means that at any given time our attention is limited, depending on what we are doing (Taylor & Thoroughman, 2007). For example, if an individual is driving a car in downtown New York while doing the mental math calculation 43 x 12, he/she is trying to accomplish two tasks simultaneously. This could cause the driver to have a car accident because driving a car on the busy streets of New York City requires a great deal of attention, and so does the math calculation. As doing these two distinctive tasks simultaneously demands a great deal of attention, the driver is unable to execute either task effectively as the human attention span is limited. As a result, crashing the car is very possible in this situation. This example illustrates that sufficient attention span is essential for engaging in certain types of activities. Conversely, an individual can eat lunch, listen to music, and chat with a friend at the same time without any problem since these three activities require minimal attention. From these two illustrations, it is clear that every task requires a different amount of attention based on its nature. With this thought in mind, a practitioner should know how much attention is needed for a student to learn a particular motor skill so that appropriate teaching strategies can be applied to accomplish the designated goals.

In order to learn a new motor skill, the athlete should grasp the key elements of the skill structure so that the particular skill can be learned properly. For example, when hitting a home run in baseball, the hitting power is the most crucial factor contributing to the distance the ball will travel. Even though many technical elements can be taught, such as correct grip, stance, hip movement, swing movement, transfer of force, head position, upper body position, etc., the instructor should know which factors contribute to hitting the ball the maximum distance for a home run. From a biomechanical perspective, the distance the ball travels is determined by (1) angular velocity; (2) radius of rotation of arm swing motion; and (3) weight of swing arm and baseball bat (Hall, 2011; Hamill & Knutzen, 2009). Ultimately, these three factors will determine how far an athlete can hit the ball. When teaching baseball players how to hit a home run, the concepts of all three technical elements should be taught and the learner's attention should be focused on using the correct way to manipulate these factors in order to hit the ball a long distance. Since human attention is limited, proper attention must be paid to certain elements and principles at any given time for the best performance. Understanding and grasping the key elements of the motor skill structure is essential so that the learner's attention can be directed to these relevant and critical elements of learning.

There are four types of attention focus people use in practical settings, each of which has its own unique and specific purpose. Based on the particular requirements of the motor learning stage and the skill being learned, students should choose the correct attention technique for achieving their learning goal. These four types of attention focus are summarized as follows.

1) *Internal attention* occurs when one internally visualizes or imagines something in one's mind without relying on external information. For example, a person can sit on a chair and imagine that he/she is shooting a basketball without actually doing or seeing anything.

2) *External attention* implies that an individual focuses on external stimuli such as watching a teammate shoot the ball into the goal (Wulf, Shea, & Park, 2001).

3) *Narrow attention* indicates that an individual concentrates on a focal point such as watching where the ball is traveling or where a bird is flying.

4) *Broad attention* means that an individual pays attention to a broad range of stimuli at a given time (Weinberg & Gould, 2011; Wulf & Prinz, 2001). For example, before passing the ball to a teammate, a soccer player pays attention to the whole range of teammates' and opponents' movements in order to make the best decision for the pass.

Based on the perspectives of internal vs. external and narrow vs. broad attention, the following four categories of attention styles are commonly used in practical settings:

1) *Narrow and internal attention,* when a learner visualizes that he/she is shooting basketball without using external visual cues.

2) *Broad and internal attention,* when a football passer visualizes that he is observing which of his teammates is in the best position for a pass.

3) *Narrow and external attention,* in which a visual cue is used to see where the baseball is traveling in order to catch it.

4) *Broad and external attention,* when a player uses the positions of teammates as visual cues in order to choose to whom to pass the ball.

With a good understanding of each of these four categories, a learner should choose the correct attention style to use in order to achieve his/her goal based on the immediate situation.

RELATIONSHIP BETWEEN AROUSAL AND ATTENTION FOCUS

Arousal is a degree of activation of the physiological process from a state of deep sleep to the most excited moment. According to Lander, Wang, and Courtet (1985), there is a very close relationship between arousal levels and attention focus (see Figure 10.1). For example, let us arbitrarily divide arousal into three different categories: low, intermediate, and high arousal levels. At the low arousal level, an individual's attentional focus tends to be broad, meaning that he/she will pay attention not only to competition-related stimuli, such as opponents, teammates, ball, basket, game flow, etc., but also to those stimuli that are not directly related to game situations such as audience, friends, referees, coaches' shouts, and opponents' accusations. Conversely, if a soccer player is dribbling with a high arousal level, his/her attention will be narrow, focusing only on the ball without noticing any nearby team members. Lastly, at the intermediate arousal level, an individual's attention focus is at an optimal level, meaning that the athlete only pays attention to those stimuli relevant to game situations, and disregards any other stimuli. With these concepts in mind, learners must adjust their arousal to the optimum level according to the characteristics of their own attention styles in order to accomplish different goals.

MOTIVATION STRATEGIES OF TEACHING MOTOR SKILLS

According to Weinberg and Gould (2011), motivation has two basic elements, direction and intensity. Direction refers to whether or not an individual wants to do something, for example either play basketball or go shopping on a particular afternoon. Intensity refers to how much effort an individual puts into doing something. A basketball player could spend one hour of training with a high degree of intensity, or spend an hour loafing around trying to kill time without putting in much effort. The critical question is why motivation is such an important contributory factor in motor learning outcomes. There are five major reasons why a high level of motivation promotes motor learning outcomes: (1) it intensifies an individual's efforts to learn; (2) it promotes the required attention for motor

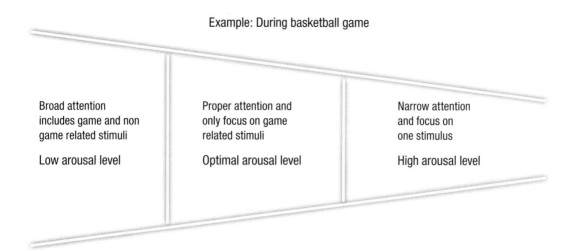

Example: During basketball game

| Broad attention includes game and non game related stimuli | Proper attention and only focus on game related stimuli | Narrow attention and focus on one stimulus |

Low arousal level / Optimal arousal level / High arousal level

FIGURE 10.1. Relationship between arousal level and attention focus.

skill learning; (3) it promotes an individual's creativity of learning; (4) it stimulates long-term memories of learning; and (5) it provides the sustained energy required for the learning process (Edwards, 2010). From the above, we can see that motivation is crucial to the outcome when learning a skill.

Through many years of research, various motivation theories of learning have been developed, two of which are widely used and have proved to be effective. One is the so-called competence motivation theory (Harter, 1982; Harter, 1988), which states that an individual's motivation level largely depends on this person's perception of how competent he/she is in a particular task. If individuals perceive themselves to be good at playing football, their motivation to play football is very high. Likewise, if athletes perceive that their competence level at gymnastics is high, they will be strongly motivated to practice. Thus, athletes' perception of their competence is a critical factor contributing to their level of motivation regardless of their actual ability. With this concept in mind, the way in which a coach, teacher, or practitioner cultivates learners' perception of competence should be a major strategy for enhancing their motivation level. The *need for achievement theory* is another motivation theory that receives a great

> **Influence of high motivation on motor learning outcomes**
>
> 1. **It intensifies an individual's efforts to learn.**
> 2. **It promotes the required attention for motor skill learning.**
> 3. **It promotes an individual's creativity of learning.**
> 4. **It stimulates long-term memories of learning.**
> 5. **It provides the sustained energy required for the learning process.**

attention from practitioners. This theory focuses on an interactional view that considers personal and situational factors to be predictors of human behaviors (Atkinson, 1974; McCleland, 1961). According to this theory, personal factor refers to the concept that some people's motive is to achieve success while others' motive is to avoid failure in competitive situations. Thus, if a person's motive is to achieve success, his/her main focus while engaging in certain activities is to direct all his/her effort to facing the challenge for success. Conversely, if an individual's motive is to avoid the failure of doing something, he/she would tend to focus on negative aspects of the engagement, so his/her anxiety level will be high and motivation of engagement will be low. In addition, situation factors of this theory reflect on the possibility of success in the certain situation or task, and incentive value of success. For example, in sports competition situations, in general, there are three possibilities for the outcome of competition: (1) most likely lose, (2) 50/50 chance to win or lose, and (3) most likely win. A low achiever of motivation would like to face the first or third of the above situations, but would like to avoid the competition with a 50/50 situation. A high achiever would like to face the competition with a 50/50 chance to win or lose. According to the need to achieve motivation theory, both personal and situation factors influence individual motivation. Personal factors refer to personality traits and situational factors that indicate specific learning environments. Since motor learning

> **Perceived competence motivation theory**
>
> **A student's motivation of learning relies on his/her own perception of how competent he/she is for what he/she is doing.**

is an internal process, a learner's intrinsic motivation is a critical factor in the effectiveness of the motor learning process. The following motivation strategies can be used to elevate learners' interest in learning.

MAKE MOTOR LEARNING AN ENJOYABLE AND ENTERTAINING PROCESS

Making motor learning fun and entertaining is an essential strategy for enhancing learners' motivation. The methods practitioners use to make practice sessions enjoyable depend on the learners' age, gender, and skill level. For example, to teach motor skills to children, the learning environment could be set up with games or competitive situations so that they will enjoy the thrill of winning or beating opponents without worrying about whom they compete with. Also, innovative or fun-related learning activities are good learning approaches for elevating young children' motivation to learn since they have a short attention span and easily get bored with rigid or dry practice. In addition, cooperative learning is another effective strategy as children like to play or learn things together with their friends. When teaching motor skills to young adults, practitioners could focus on the development of the learners' independent decision-making and problem-solving abilities. For example, an instructor could demonstrate a new motor skill, and then ask the learners to capture the key elements of the structure of this particular skill. Thus, the learners must not only observe the demonstration carefully, but they also need to engage in the cognitive process of figuring out the elements of the motor skill. Making the learning process fun and entertaining could greatly enhance learners' interest in the learning process. Practitioners should be creative and use student-centered approaches to teaching.

INDIVIDUALIZED GOAL-SETTING

Since every learner has unique characteristics of age, skill level, personality type, motivation structure, physical genetic make-up, physical conditioning, etc., it is essential to set goals that are specific to each individual based on his/her characteristics rather than setting a group motor learning goal. Various goals can be set, for example, short-term, long-term, process, outcome or performance goals. A short-term goal is a goal that can be reached within a short period of time, such as one week, one month, or three months. Conversely, long-term goals take a relatively long time to achieve, maybe six months, one year, or more. Process goals deal with the techniques required to perform a motor skill instead of looking at the end result. For example, the process goal of hitting a baseball focuses on learning all the different elements required to execute the hitting action, such as stance, grip, swing motion, speed of action, and hip movement rather than being concerned with whether the athlete actually hits the ball. In contrast, the outcome goal refers to the result of the learner's action. Lastly, performance goals monitor the progress of a learner's performance over time to see how much it has improved. In sum, the goals set should be challenging but achievable for the best outcome. If the goals set are too high or too low, learners' motivation could be compromised. Research studies revealed that once the goal setting is properly implemented, it works extremely well in sports and motor learning settings (Burton & Weiss, 2008; Locke & Latham, 1990).

STRATEGIES TO CONTROL ANXIETY IN MOTOR LEARNING PROCESS

Lazarus (2000) defined that anxiety as "facing uncertain, existing threat," and it is a negative emotional state that may have a substantial impact upon how an athlete performs when facing an uncertain, existing threat. Anxiety in motor learning process should be addressed because many learning environments are in a group setting. A number of elements could trigger anxiety during the learning process. For example, learners may be scared of demonstrating in front of a group, embarrassed about making mistakes when performing motor skills, fearful of being injured when trying out a new risky movement, nervous about competing with an opponent who has better skills, afraid that they will be unable to reach teachers' expectations, or feel uncomfortable playing against a strange team, etc. In reality, there are many reasons why learners might be anxious during the motor learning process, so instructors should know how to help them eliminate their anxiety. There are many psychological strategies available to help learners and instructors develop insight into each learner's characteristics of learning so that appropriate anxiety control strategies can be used to remedy the problems.

Confidence is an imperative psychological characteristic that has a positive relationship with motor learning and sport performance, whereas a lack of confidence is associated with anxiety, depression, and dissatisfaction (Vealey, 1988; Vealey, Hayashi, Garner-Holman, & Giacobbi, 1998).

Such an undesirable belief could negatively affect learning outcomes, especially for beginners. Therefore, confidence building is an effective psychological strategy to eliminate anxiety and allow the learner to maintain concentration. An instructor could use positive reinforcement by reminding the learner about an earlier fine performance or praising any positive performance. The feeling of pleasure when hearing the instructor's positive reinforcement can be a powerful resource for building the learner's self-confidence. Setting challenging but achievable goals is also an effective strategy. Obviously, repeated successes provide learners with the valuable information that they are competent to perform the skill. Another effective psychological strategy for confidence-building is the use of positive self-talk, which can help learners to eliminate anxiety and maintain concentration. The main purpose of self-talk is to help learners focus their attention on their strengths in order to accomplish their desired goal. Learners should list the negative thoughts that crop up regularly on the left side of a piece of paper, and then write positive self-talk on the right side to replace the negative self-talk. Whenever negative self-talk arises, the learner should immediately replace it with positive self-talk. By repeatedly practicing positive self-talk, learners will eventually be able to switch from negative to positive self-talk quite freely. Positive attention focus or beliefs produce positive learning outcomes. Confidence-building is a gradual process; with the correct use of the aforementioned strategies learners' confidence level will be enhanced effectively.

Strategies of enhancing self-confidence

- **Positive self-talk**
- **Understand every self-strength**
- **Focus on opponents' weakness**
- **Remind past successful experience**
- **Remember coaches' positive comments**
- **Visualize the winning situation**

MENTAL IMAGERY

Mental imagery is actually a form of mental stimulation without requiring external stimuli. Carpenter (1894) proposed the ideomotor principle of imagery, which indicates that when an individual engages in mental imagery, that person's neuromuscular activity pattern is activated so that such a process facilitates motor learning. According to this theory, when a learner visualizes performing a motor skill routine, the brain actually sends electrical impulses to the related muscle groups and the pathway of the neuromuscular activities is exactly the same as if the learner is performing the activity in reality. The research findings show that mental imagery has a variety of effects on motor skill learning: it can improve learning outcomes, correct wrong skill movements, strengthen motor programs, and perfect the desired skill structure. The findings of the research studies prove that skill practice combined with mental imagery produces maximum learning outcomes.

To receive positive learning outcomes, the vividness and controllability of the mental imagery should be developed. The vividness of mental imagery refers to the clarity of the visualization process, and controllability denotes that an individual can freely control whatever he/she wishes to visualize without interference from other irrelevant stimuli. For example, a learner could engage in the mental imagery process without being distracted by a huge audience with uncontrollable noises. Imagery can be practiced through internal or external mental imagery. Internal mental imagery occurs when learners visualize an action from their own vantage point. For example, a soccer player can visualize shooting a penalty by paying attention to the intrinsic feedback such as the muscular force used, the direction of the kick, the movement of the swing, the feeling of contact with the ball, and body positions. By repeatedly practicing internal mental imagery, the learner can strengthen the blueprints of the desired skill routines in the brain in order to perform the skill correctly. External mental imagery occurs when a learner visualizes someone else performing a motor skill; he/she is an observer instead of a doer (Taylor & Wilson, 2005). Mental imagery is particularly useful when an athlete is learning a new or challenging motor skill because the imagery process helps him/her to correct faulty skill movements, and to strengthen the proper kinematic movements. In order to cognitively establish a correct image of how to perform the desired motor skill, external mental imagery is an ideal approach because the learner can first observe an elite athlete's demonstration and then engage in

Mental imagery process of learning motor skills

- **Use either internal or external visualization**
- **Visualize proper motor skill**
- **Visualize proper strategies**
- **Visualize proper tactics**
- **Visualize self-successful experience**
- **Visualize all the strengths the student has**
- **Combine technical training with mental imagery**

technical practice. Since muscles can only do two things, develop tension or relax, all human movements (motor skills) are commanded by the brain, so the use of mental imagery, if done properly, should be deemed as an effective way of contributing to the motor skill learning process for maximizing learning outcomes.

COMMUNICATING EFFECTIVELY WITH LEARNERS

Motor skill learning is a feedback-based process and the instructor's feedback plays a significant role in contributing to students' learning outcomes. The effectiveness of the instructor's communication can be very broad such as motivating students, giving technical instruction, correcting improper movements, evaluating progress, problem solving, engaging in team management, or analyzing skill movements. The instructor's communication can help students to learn motor skills effectively in order to achieve the designated training objectives, or vice versa. Ultimately, the instructor's communication skills play a significant role in contributing to the effectiveness of students' learning of motor skills.

Communication can be verbal or nonverbal. Verbal communication takes place through language, while nonverbal communication occurs through facial expressions, body language, or gestures. Effective verbal communication includes the following characteristics. (1) Communication should occur at the right time. For example, feedback should be provided as soon as a trial is completed so that the learner still has a fresh impression of the neuro-muscular trace in his/her brain. Thus, the feedback received by the learner is more effective. (2) The content of the communication should be well organized and appropriate. Some teachers like to blame or criticize learners by focusing on their weaknesses, some use positive reinforcement as their main communication approach, and some spend a great deal of time explaining the mechanics of the techniques. (3) The method of communication should be appropriate.

The way a practitioner delivers the information is an important factor contributing to the effectiveness of communication, for example, a practitioner's voice, tempo, rhythm, and speed, along with body language, can indicate different meanings. The content and the method of communication are two different things: a practitioner can praise a learner verbally, but have a sarcastic facial expression which sends the message that he/she is not happy with what the learner is doing. Thus, verbal communication relies to a great extent on the timing, content, and method of communications. Instructors should learn how to communicate with learners for effective teaching of motor skills.

Furthermore, in the teaching environment, instructors need to know what they should and should not say to students. The following are brief guidelines for instructors on how to speak to students:

- Provide positive feedback and emphasize learners' strengths.
- Emphasize what learners should do instead of what they should not do.
- Emphasize how to perform certain motor skills instead of punishing learners if they cannot do them.
- Focus on the learning process and strategies of learning, rather than the results.
- Emphasize the weaknesses of the opponents.
- Provide key elements of skill structures instead of giving too much instructional information.
- Do not criticize any student who is not doing well in front of the class.
- Do not over-emphasize the difficulty level of the motor skill which is being taught.
- Provide precautions and injury prevention strategies for any motor skill with physical or psychological risks involved.
- Do not yell at students in practice or scrimmage learning environments.

The second major type of communication is nonverbal, in which the practitioner or teacher communicates with learners by using body language, facial expressions, or gestures to convey the intended information. For example, a teacher might smile warmly at a learner following a trial, clearly indicating that he/she is quite happy with the performance. Or, if an athlete played well during practice, the coach might pat the athlete's back to signify that he/she is pleased. In contrast, if a coach scowls at an athlete, this reflects displeasure. According to research (Weinberg & Gould, 2011), nonverbal communication sends more meaningful and more accurate information to others when compared to verbal communication. Therefore, instructors should learn how to effectively communicate with students by using verbal and nonverbal approaches based on the situation and the students' characteristics. Since motor learning is a psycho/muscular learning process, psychological consideration of the learning process plays a vital role contributing to learning outcomes.

This chapter briefly introduces a number of psychological principles that can be integrated into the learning process. Since each learner has a unique learning style, the teacher should engage in teaching activities based on the learner's characteristics. For example, some learners like to learn through demonstrations, video-clips, or films while others prefer to listen to the instructor's verbal explanations. Other students may like to learn through a combination of visual and audio approaches. In addition, there are many differences between learners reflected in their age, experience, motivation, physical characteristics, intelligence, coachability, etc. Thus, motor learning is a multi-faceted process that requires teachers with comprehensive knowledge and skills to accomplish the goals.

Key Terms to Remember

- *Attention* is the taking possession in mind (James, 1890).
- *Internal attention* occurs when one internally visualizes or imagines something in one's mind without relying on external information.
- *External attention* implies that an individual focuses on external stimuli such as watching a teammate shoot the ball into the goal.
- *Narrow attention* indicates that an individual concentrates on a focal point such as watching where the ball is traveling or where a bird is flying.
- *Broad attention* means that an individual pays attention to a broad range of stimuli at a given time.
- *Arousal* is a degree of activation of the physiological process from a state of deep sleep to the most excited moment.
- *Perceived* competence motivation theory states that an individual's motivation level largely depends on this person's perception of how competent he/she is in a particular task.
- *Intrinsic motivation* refers to an individual engaging in something for his/her own interest, pleasure, or enjoyment without needing extrinsic rewarding.
- *Extrinsic motivation* refers to an individual doing something for the extrinsic reasons such as obtaining rewards, scholarship, materials, pleasing someone, etc.
- *Goal-setting* refers to an individual setting an expectation that he/she tries to reach.
- A *short-term goal* is a goal that one tries to achieve within a short period of time.
- A *long-term goal* is a goal that one tries to achieve within a long period of time.

- *Anxiety* is a negative emotional state characterized by nervousness, worry, and apprehension and associated with activation or arousal of the body (Weinberg & Gould, 2011).

- *Self-confidence* is a self-belief an individual can successfully accomplish the designated goal.

- *Mental imagery* is actually a form of mental stimulation without requiring external stimuli.

- *Interpersonal communication* involves at least two people and meaningful exchange (Weinberg & Gould, 2011).

- *Nonverbal communication* refers to communication occurring between at least two people with the exchange using means other than the verbal approach.

Student Assignments for Connecting Theory to Practice

- Please explain the role of application of psychological principles to motor learning process.

- Which psychological principles are important to motor learning process?

- What is attention and what types of attention are used during motor learning process?

- Give examples of particular attention used at a particular time in a sports setting.

- What is anxiety and why does competitive anxiety affect motor performance?

- Distinguish the difference between anxiety and arousal.

- How does one enhance intrinsic motivation?

- How does one enhance extrinsic motivation?

- Explain why confidence is important in relation to motor performance?

- How can coaches help learners build confidence?

- Explain the purpose of mental imagery.

- How and when should mental imagery be used?

- What are the obstacles of communication?

- How can proper communication contribute to the motor learning process?

REFERENCES

Atkinson, J. W. (1974). The mainstream of achievement-oriented activity. In J.W. Atkinson & J. O. Raynor (Eds.), *Motivation and achievement* (pp. 13–41). New York, NY: Halstead.

Burton, D., & Weiss, C. (2008). The fundamental goal concept: Investigating the goal concept: The path to process and performance success. In T. Horn (Ed.), *Advances in sport psychology* (3rd ed., pp. 339–375). Champaign, IL: Human Kinetics.

Carpenter, W. B. (1894). *Principles of mental physiology.* New York, NY: Appleton.

Edwards, W. (2010). *Motor learning and control: From theory to practice.* Independence, KY: Cengage Learning.

Hall, S. J. (2011). *Basic biomechanics.* Boston, MA: McGraw-Hill.

Hamill, J., & Knutzen, K. M. (2009). *Biomechanical basis of human movement.* Philadelphia, PA: Lippincott Williams & Wilkins.

Harter, S. (1982). The perceived competence scale for children. *Child Development, 53,* 87–97.

Harter, S. (1988). Causes, correlates, and functional role of global self-worth: A life-span perspective. In J. Kolligan & R. Sternberg (Eds.), *Perceptions of competence across the life-span.* New Haven, CT: Yale University Press.

James, W. (1890). *The principles of psychology.* New York, NY: Dover Publisher.

Jeannerod, M. (1994). The representing brain: Neural correlates of motor intention and imagery. *Behavioral and Brain Sciences, 17,* 326–338.

Joseph, H., & Knutzen, K. M. (2009). *Biomechanical basis of human movement.* Philadelphia, PA: Lippincott Williams & Wilkins.

Lander, D. M., Wang, M. Q., & Courtet, P. (1985). Peripheral narrowing among experienced and inexperienced rife shooters under low- and high-stress conditions. *Research Quarterly, 56,* 122–130.

Lazarus, R. S. (2000). How emotions influence performance in competitive sports. *The Sport Psychologist, 14,* 229–252.

Locke, E. A., & Latham, G. P. (1990). *A theory of goal setting and task performance.* Englewood Cliffs, NJ: Prentice Hall.

McCleland, D. (1961). *The achieving society.* New York, NY: Free Press.

Schmidt, R. A., & Wrisberg, C. A. (2008). *Motor learning and performance: A situation-based learning approach.* Champaign, IL: Human Kinetics.

Taylor, J. A., & Thoroughman, K. A. (2007). Divided attention impairs human motor adaptation but not feedback control. *Journal of Neurophysiology, 98,* 317–326.

Taylor, J., & Wilson, G. S. (2005). *Applying sport psychology: Four perspectives.* Champaign, IL: Human Kinetics.

Vealey, R. S. (1988). Sport-confidence and competitive orientation: An addendum on scoring procedures and gender differences. *Journal of Sport and Exercise Psychology, 10,* 471–478.

Vealey, R. S., Hayashi, S. W., Garner-Holman, M., & Giacobbi, P. (1998). Sources of sport confidence: Conceptualization and instrument development. *Journal of Sport & Exercise Psychology, 20,* 54–80.

Weinberg, R. S., & Gould, D. (2011). *Foundations of sport and exercise psychology.* Champaign, IL: Human Kinetics.

Wulf, G. (2007). *Attention and motor skill learning.* Champaign, IL: Human Kinetics.

Wulf, G., Shea, C., & Lewthwaite, R. (2010). Motor skill learning and performance: A review of influential factors. *Medical Education, 44,* 75–84.

Wulf G., Shea, C., & Park, J. H. (2001). Attention and motor performance: Preferences for and advantages of an external focus. *Research Quarterly of Exercise and Sport, 72,* 335–344.

Wulf, G., & Prinz, W. (2001). Directing attention to movement effects enhances learning: A review. *Psychonomic Bulletin & Review, 8,* 648–660.

Transfer of Learning: The Key Principle of Motor Skill Training Implementation

OBJECTIVES

- Understand each stage of learning has the specific goals to accomplish and gradually shape to the designed ultimate goal of learning

- Understand two different motor learning processes: (1) organized motor learning process, and (2) implicit motor learning process. Understand why the organized learning process is highly recommended for maximizing motor learning outcomes.

- Understand the concept of transfer of learning and its impact on motor skill learning

- Understand the gap and reasons between practice and competition performance

- Understand the concepts of positive and negative transfer

- Understand the concepts of practice condition and competition condition

- Understand various ways of practice

- Discuss how to effectively design training and learned skills in practice that can be positively transferred to competition

- Understand why competition performance is commonly poorer than practice performance

- Understand the main flaws of training and know how to remedy them

- Understand the concepts of target skill and target environment in order to purposefully design training

INTRODUCTION

Practitioners use various methods of engaging in sport skill training to help learners to achieve their goals of learning. Some learners are beginners while others are elite athletes; learners at different levels have varied learning objectives. From the scientific perspective, practitioners' ultimate goal of sport skill training should maximize learning outcomes that can be applied to the designated target contexts. Learning and performance are two different elements, and they are easily confused by many practitioners. For example, during practice, practitioners often artificially manipulate the learners' performance by making training easy or difficult. As the difficulty level of the training greatly affects learners' practice performance, a good practice performance does not necessarily indicate that a learner has learned more during the training session, or vice versa. Clearly, practitioners' major focus in sport skill training should not be the learners' practice performance, but to design a training program that maximizes the learning outcomes of learners based on their skill level. To accomplish this, practitioners should have a good understanding of the principle of transfer of learning and implement it effectively in practice settings. This chapter will focus on the concepts of transfer of learning, principles of organizing practice, how to manipulate practice conditions to achieve the goal of practice, and how to maximize learning outcomes in training. Once practitioners have a clear understanding of the difference between practice performance and learning, the motor skill learning process can be implemented for the purpose of achieving maximum learning outcomes. First, two types of learning processes will be introduced in the following sections.

ORGANIZED AND IMPLICIT LEARNING PROCESSES

Motor performance can be achieved through two different motor learning processes, and one of motor learning processes is called the *organized motor learning process*, which has clear objectives with well-designed processes of training, and practice conditions. The practice conditions are manipulated by coaches or practitioners, based on scientific principles, for achieving training objectives. The following are some of the many advantages of the organized motor skill learning process:

- Training includes clear learning objectives.
- Training is scientifically designed.
- Training is based on the learners' characteristics.
- Teacher provides necessary feedback to learners.
- Evaluation and assessment of learning progress and effectiveness are properly implemented.

- Training methods are periodically modified based on the needs of learning progress.
- Learning is effective.

Through the above-mentioned advantages, individuals can learn much faster and more effectively achieve their training objectives. The goals of motor learning processes vary according to the different professions or occupations of the learners. For example, at the elite level competitive sports such as the Olympic Games and professional or collegiate competitions are becoming more and more challenging for athletes. Not only do they need to be physically talented, they also need to use every possible avenue to gain a competitive edge, such as the latest equipment, cutting-edge technology, proper nutrition, and psychological training to maintain the optimal psychological state for competition. Many countries around the world invest a great deal of capital for hiring sports scientists to work with athletes so that they can achieve peak performance. These scientists include exercise physiologists, biomechanical experts, sport psychologists, nutrition experts, medical doctors, massage specialists, and physical training experts. In most cases, these professional experts provide exceptional services to the athletes who receive the great benefit of enhancing their talents through the varied aspects of training. All these processes contribute to the benefits of the organized training regimens that are designed to maximize learning outcomes. For example, by applying biomechanical principles to motor learning, athletes can focus on the key mechanical aspects of motor skill training and thus learning becomes much more effective (Kreighbaum & Barthels, 1996). Based on exercise physiology principles, practitioners know how athletes' bodies respond to each exercise according to their individual differences (Bowers & Fox, 1992). These practitioners will then manipulate the factors such as frequency, mode, intensity, and volume of training based on the athletes' physiological characteristics, because both over- or under-training could compromise the outcome of the training. Likewise, to properly prepare athletes' energetic physical states for training, nutritional considerations should be emphasized, so that the body is fueled to meet the physical demands made of it (Fox, Bowers, & Foss, 1993). Furthermore, coaches should also understand how to motivate the athletes, how to help them manage their competitive anxiety, how to effectively communicate with them, and how to develop teamwork strategies, etc., all of which can be resolved through psychological methods. In sum, the integration of sports science principles with the motor skill learning processes has become an integral part of organized training. Needless to say, sports science and technology are playing more important roles than ever before in the motor learning process.

The second process, the *implicit learning process,* is a way of learning without pre-determined goals, training procedures, and assessment of learning. It is a trial-and-error procedure of learning based on observations of other people's actions and without instructions or assistance from trained professionals. Due to financial or personal reasons, learners may choose to learn motor skills on their own instead of having organized training. As there are no professional experts to provide instructions and feedback, the implicit-motor learning process has many limitations for the learner. For example, in a sports arena that involves process-oriented motor skill learning, such as gymnastics, diving, ice-skating, or freestyle skiing, learning outcomes cannot be effectively achieved through implicit learning process because learners cannot observe their own practice routines during the execution of the motor skills. Ultimately, they need to rely on external feedback from instructors in order to make corrections for the next movement. Thus the implicit motor learning process is ineffective in these sports. Implicit motor learning has the following characteristics:

- Motor learning takes place by observing other people's demonstrations or actions.
- Learning takes place through the self-practice approach.
- No instructions and feedback are provided.
- Learning is based on trial-and-error approaches.
- No formal evaluation and assessment are implemented.
- Time and environment of learning are flexible.
- Learning progress is relatively slow and ineffective.

In contrast, the implicit motor learning process could be possibly practiced with certain progress by learners for outcome-oriented motor skills such as soccer, basketball, volleyball, tennis, etc. With a long period of practice, athletes involved in these sports might be able to improve their motor skills since they can see the results of their own performance. For example, a basketball player knows whether or not his/her own shots scored in practice or competition, and likewise a tennis player knows whether or not his/her forehand stroke was successful. In addition, a basketball player could reach certain skill levels through the implicit motor learning by observing other players' actions and then imitating them. For outcome-oriented motor skills, implicit motor learning could bring the learners to a certain level of play. But, generally speaking, the effectiveness of the implicit motor learning process is unpredictable and is usually less fruitful because it largely relies on learners' cognitive talents, physical make-up, learning environment, and motivation. Some learners could form bad habits without knowing it while others may never be successful because of the following limitations of this type learning process:

- Learner has difficulty figuring out the key elements of the motor skill.
- It is very possible for learners to form bad habits during the learning process.
- Learner may never reach his/her athletic potential without a competent instructor's feedback.

- Implicit learning can only be implemented for outcome-oriented motor skill learning.

- The problems and weaknesses in learning are usually masked.

- The desired learning progress is difficult to achieve.

Even though the implicit motor learning process has numerous weaknesses, there are certain obvious advantages, such as no cost or low cost of learning, flexible times of training, convenient learning environments, and learning based on self-interest and self-style, etc. In sum, the implicit motor learning process has many disadvantages compared to the organized motor learning process. For this reason, this chapter introduces the principles involved in the organized motor learning processes so that relevant professionals can teach motor skills efficiently and correctly for achieving the designated goals of learning.

TRANSFER OF LEARNING

People engage in motor learning activities for a number of reasons: athletes participate in the motor skill learning process to achieve peak performance in competition, soldiers learn motor skills for combating the enemy, students for health and fitness and to cultivate life-long skills for participating in sports, those who participate for recreation are seeking health, fitness, and enjoyment, and so on. Therefore, practitioners should understand the goals of their students in order to purposefully design training methods. The importance of transfer of learning has been well documented by Magill and Anderson (2013), Teixeira (2000), and Krakauer, Mazzoni, Ghazizadeh, Ravindran, and Shadmehr (2006).

In the athletic arena, a practical problem is the huge gap that exists between athletes' practice and competition performances, and many coaches try very hard to figure out the underlying reasons for such a gap (Wang, 2010). In other words, why can't these athletes transfer the motor skills learned in practice to competition settings? Also, some athletes might learn a new motor skill, but later on the learned motor skill might negatively affect the learning of other new skills; this is referred to as *negative transfer*. Conversely, for some athletes there may be a positive impact in that learning one skill contributes to learning another new skill; this is referred to as *positive transfer*. Clearly, one of the imperative goals of the motor learning process is to discover how practitioners, coaches, or teachers can structure the motor learning process in such a way that the learned skills will be transferred to other new skills effectively, practice performance can be transferred to competition performance, and the learned skills exhibited in training contexts will be transferred to the target contexts. The following section will introduce several concepts related to the transfer of learning with which practitioners can become familiar so that appropriate training can be structured based on these concepts.

Transfer of Learning From One Skill to Another Skill

According to Schimdt and Wrisberg (2008), transfer of learning is the gain or the loss of a person's proficiency in one task as a result of previous practice or experience in another task. More specifically, transfer of learning basically deals with three different issues: (1) how a learned motor skill can positively or negatively affect learning a new skill; (2) how learning a simplified motor skill can positively contribute to learning the entire skill; and (3) what an individual learns during practice sessions can be transferred to the target context (Example: competition settings, war zone in military combat, etc.). In fact, an essential element of practicing motor skills is the manipulation of practice conditions in order to accomplish the designated goals of learning (Wang, 2010). Therefore, the principle of transfer of learning is critical for the motor learning process.

Obviously, transfer of learning can be positive or negative (Magill & Anderson, 2013). Positive transfer refers to a situation where learning one skill will have a positive impact on learning another skill. For example, mastering soccer skills could possibly have a positive impact on learning martial arts skills. (Figure 11.1). Conversely, negative transfer of learning occurs when the skills learned interfere with learning another skill. For example, mastering golf skills might have a negative influence on learning volleyball. Golf is a non-reaction time (NRT) based sport, and volleyball is a reaction time (RT) based sport; therefore, the motor control systems for performing these two types of skills are quite different. (Figure 11.2)

Learned soccer skills may be positively transferred to learning martial arts skills

FIGURE 11.1. Positive transfer of learning.

Learned golf skills may be negatively transferred to volleyball tennis.

FIGURE 11.2. Negative transfer of learning.

The examples in Figures 11.1 and 11.2 illustrate positive and negative transfer of a particular skill in relation to another skill. But transfer of learning can be also applied to the performance perspective. The question is, can practice performance be effectively transferred to competition performance? Can practice performance be transferred to a variety of different target contexts such as military, physical therapy, or recreational settings, etc.?

During the motor learning process, practitioners should focus on positive transfer to maximize the learning outcome and also be aware of potential negative transfer that needs to be prevented or against which precautions need to be taken. While there are some causes leading to negative transfer, obviously the design of training plays an important role in the process (Bardy, 2011; Holt, Ward, & Wallhead, 2006).

PROPER WAYS OF STRUCTURING TRAINING BASED ON THE PRINCIPLES OF TRANSFER OF LEARNING

Transfer of learning is an imperative concept of motor learning, practitioners can use a variety of training methods to assist learners in mastering motor skills, especially if the skills are difficult (Meijer & Roth, 1988; Seidler, 2010). These methods are based on years of research and practice. *Part practice* involves breaking down a difficult motor skill into two or more parts to be practiced one by one using a progressive approach. For example, a soccer shooting skill can be broken down into five different parts, namely the approach phase, placement of support foot, swing motion of the kicking foot, the foot contacting the ball, and follow-through (Wang & Griffin 1997; Wang & Weise-Bjornstal, 1994). Since teaching all the components together is a great challenge, dividing the entire skill into five parts is a much easier approach. Once each part has been learned satisfactorily, the learner can combine all these five parts together to learn and execute the complete skill; this is referred to as *whole practice*. Both part and whole practice have been well introduced by Martens (2012), Magill and Anderson (2013) and Schmidt and Wrisberg (2008); also, many studies have been done to verify the usefulness of these practices.

When practicing baseball batting or gymnastic floor movements, the procedure or routine could be broken down into separate discrete skills first which are later combined once each skill segment can be performed well.

Another practice method is *slow-motion practice* in which the speed of execution of the motor skill is slowed down. This is a very effective and useful technique because it allows the learner sufficient time to receive external feedback, to analyze it, and to make corrections while learning (Ernest, 2011). Also, according to the speed/accuracy trade-off theory (Fitts, 1954; Fitts & Posner, 1967), when the speed of action is slow, the accuracy of the movement systemically increases. For example, in basketball it is much easier to learn how to execute faking movements when they are practiced in slow motion because the body's sensory systems can sense intrinsic kinematic feedback and external stimuli such as ball, opponents or teammates, etc., and respond to them accordingly in an accurate and timely manner. Many difficult skills can be practiced slowly in order to develop the correct forms and movements, and the speed can gradually be increased once the learned skills have been processed. Obviously, manipulation of the speed of practicing motor skills is an imperative factor during the motor learning process.

TRANSFER OF LEARNING FROM PRACTICE CONDITIONS TO COMPETITION CONDITIONS

In the athletic arena, coaches use various ways of engaging in sport skill training to help athletes achieve peak performance in competition. From the scientific perspective, the ultimate goal of sport skill training is to design a training program that maximizes athletes' learning outcomes which can eventually be transferred to competition settings. Unfortunately, many coaches pay great attention to athletes' practice performance because coaches could mistakenly perceive practice performance as truly reflecting competition performance. In fact, learning and performance are two different elements and they are easily confused by some coaches. For example, during practice, practitioners can easily manipulate the practice performance of athletes by making the training easy or difficult. A good practice performance does not indicate that the athletes have learned more during the training session, or vice versa. The difficulty level of training greatly affects athletes' practice performance so the major focus of sport skill training should not be a good practice performance, but rather maximizing athletes' learning outcomes based on their skill level. Fitts and Posner (1967) introduced the classic motor learning stage models, and they proposed that motor learning can be divided into three stages: (1) cognitive, (2) associate (motor), and (3) autonomous. Practitioners should manipulate practice conditions based on the characteristics of each stage of learning. For example, at the lower level of training, for beginners, practice conditions should be structured in such a way that they are easier than competition conditions, and conversely, at the elite level they should be much harsher and more difficult than in competition.

As we can see in Figure 11.3, novice athletes have not reached the expectation level of competition, so their motor skill training should be easy, simplified, and less pressured, in an environment that is appropriate for learning rather than focusing on competition. Over a prolonged period of training, the learned motor skills can be transferred to competition

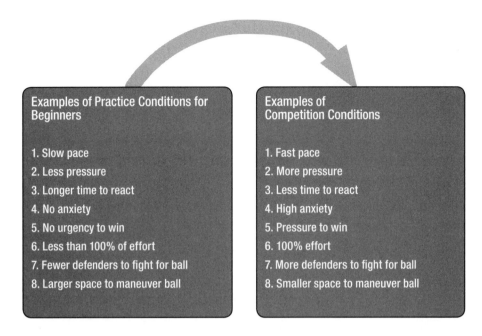

FIGURE 11.3. Practice conditions versus competition conditions.

conditions and then gradually from low-level to high-level competition conditions. This is a relatively long process but eventually, with proper training, the learned motor skills can be effectively transferred to competition conditions.

In contrast, at the elite level of training, practice conditions should be harsher and more difficult than competition conditions. In this case, athletes' practice performance may not be very good but they learn more because performance and learning are two different concepts; learning is an internal process that cannot be directly measured while motor performance is a physical process that can be observed. The ultimate goal of practice is to promote learning, not to improve practice performance. If motor performance is manipulated in practice, such as by setting easy goals, playing in a more relaxed setting with a more specialized field size, having weaker opponents, having a slower speed of play, and so on, obviously the athletes will perform very well, giving the coach the false impression that they are doing a fine job. In fact, with this kind of training, athletes learn very little so they do not do well in real competitions where the conditions are much tougher because the motor skills learned in practice cannot be effectively transferred to competition conditions (Wang, 2010). Therefore, at the elite level coaches should design training programs with extremely harsh and challenging practice conditions such as playing soccer at very fast speeds, with severe, intense scrimmages, very little space to pass the ball, more defenders around, very slippery grass, and competing with high level, very aggressive opponents, etc. Needless to say, when training in such severe practice conditions, the athletes' practice performance will be low, but they learn more. When competing in real competitions, these athletes can effectively transfer their learned motor skills to competition conditions extraordinarily well. Figure 11.4 illustrates the practice conditions of high-level training and competition conditions.

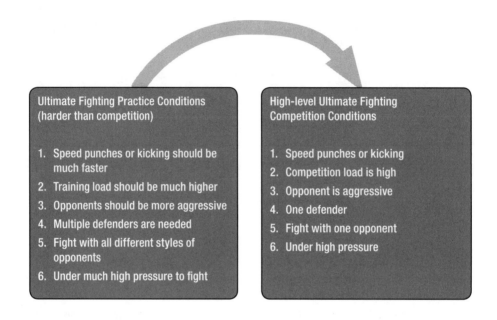

FIGURE 11.4. Comparison of practice and competition conditions.

More importantly, practitioners should be well aware that a practice performance is only temporary and short lived, so it is not important whether an athlete's performance is good or bad because the learning outcome is the ultimate goal of practice. With this concept in mind, many different practice conditions should be planned that are more challenging, more difficult, and much harsher than in competition so that positive transfer will occur later to competition conditions.

In sum, for novice learners, simplified methods of practice should be provided to make learning easy, interesting, and entertaining and in which progress is apparent. When learners feel that they are making progress, their confidence level and enthusiastic motivation will increase. The learned knowledge can also be gradually transferred to the long-term memory in order to achieve a permanent learning outcome (Hikosaka et al., 2002; Kalat, 2009). Conversely, at the elite level, practice conditions should be set up that should be more difficult or more challenging for the learners. The goal of motor learning is to promote long-term changes in skill movements for designated forms or structures.

Examples of Manipulation of Practice Conditions for Soccer Skills

Manipulation of:

1. Ball possession time
2. Friction of object surface and floor or ground surface
3. Pressure or size of the soccer ball
4. Numbers of opponents
5. Size of play field
6. Speed of play
7. Aggression of play
8. Level of opponents
9. Practice time
10. Resting interval
11. Intensity of practice
12. Allowed touches
13. Allowed attacking direction
14. Fatigue training
15. Length of practice
16. Practice under different weather
17. Equipment of sports, etc.

Examples of Manipulation of Practice Conditions for Baseball Skills

Manipulation of:

1. Size of baseball
2. Color of baseball
3. Distance between pitcher to batter
4. Speed of pitching
5. Weight of the bat
6. Size of the bat
7. Directions of the incoming ball to catch
8. Speed of the incoming ball to catch
9. Difficulty levels of the incoming ball to catch
10. Level of the opponents
11. Different weathers
12. Different sizes of pitching targets
13. Speed of pitching
14. Fatigue training
15. Length of practice, etc.
16. Equipment of sports

Block vs. Random Practices

For the purpose of obtaining positive transfer of learning, some other practice approaches will be also introduced, described as follows: blocked practice and random practice. *Blocked practice* involves consistently repeating the same motor skill again and again (Lee, 1988). In general, novice learners should use this type of practice to develop proper movement patterns and basic motor skills. For example, a novice tennis player should spend a block of time practicing the forehand stroke again and again for a certain period of time in a practice session to develop the proper movement pattern for this stroke. Once the forehand stroke practice has been done, the player can spend a block of time practicing the backhand stroke, and so on. The blocked practice method is widely used at the cognitive stage or motor stage of learning.

In *random practice,* the learner practices several motor skills together, performing each motor skill only once and then switching to another skill (Guadagnoli & Lee, 2004). For example, a soccer player practices heading, shooting, and trapping altogether, executing each skill once and then moving on to the next skill. Random practice is usually implemented at the higher level of skill training. The pattern of random practice is very similar to competition conditions in which athletes do not execute the same motor skill twice consecutively and usually all the actions are different from each other. Therefore random practice is similar to real game situations and thus can be well applied to competition contexts.

Conversely, blocked practice, which involves repetition of the same motor movements, is quite different from competition conditions and therefore this type of practice is generally used in early practice settings by novice or intermediate level athletes. Obviously, a table-tennis player who can engage in the forehand stroke three hundred times in practice without losing the ball may not necessarily be a good player because this practice condition is very different from competition conditions in which every action is different. Hence, practitioners should design training programs that are appropriate for the specific level of athletes.

In random practice, it is important that adjacent motor skills are as different from each other as possible so that the learner must come up with a new solution for executing a skill every single time. The generation of these distinctive solutions by the brain during random practice sharply promotes learning as a more meaningful impression will be left on the brain with every practice trial. For example, in basketball, a random practice sequence of passing, dribbling, beating the opponent, and shooting would be a good practice arrangement because each motor skill sharply differs from the next one so the player must quickly engage in an entirely different skill every single time. This type of practice simulates the competition conditions closely, which significantly promotes athletes' learning in a target context situation.

Constant practice and varied practice are different ways of structuring practice within one task (one skill) which have been studied extensively for different uses in motor learning processes. *Constant practice* refers to situations in which a learner practices a specific version of a particular task. An example of this would be a basketball player practicing basketball free-shooting from a designated position repeatedly for a block of time (constant practice). Alternatively, a basketball player can also practice free-shooting, but from different positions one by one. This is referred to as *varied practice* since the player shoots the ball from a variety of positions. In other words, one skill is practiced but from different positions. Practitioners can manipulate many different variables to engage in practice, such as distance, direction, speed, with or without a defender, stationary or in motion, etc.

Research studies have shown that both random and varied practice are recommended for sports skill training as well; these kinds of practice are relatively more challenging to engage in and promote long-term learning outcomes as well. Practitioners should design appropriate training programs according to the athletes' specific situations (Figure 11.5).

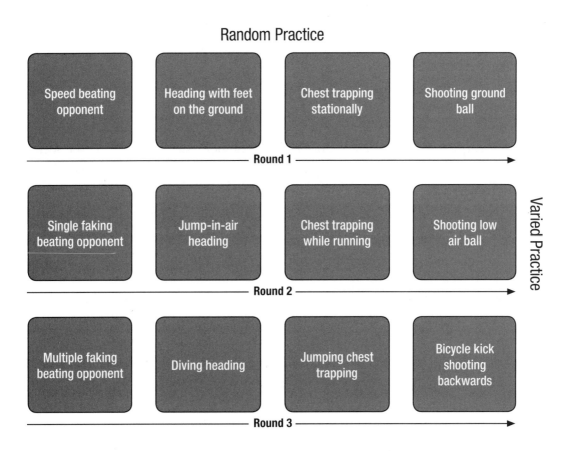

FIGURE 11.5. Random and varied practice arrangement of soccer training.

Random & Varied Practice

Finally, practitioners can structure motor skill training by combining random and varied practice to maximize learning outcomes at the upper level of training (Schmidt & Wrisberg, 2008). Even though initially this type of training sounds somewhat confusing, with consistent and determined efforts, practitioners can become accustomed to such a practice arrangement. The term *random* and *varied practice* refers to two different practices combined into one. Figure 11.5 illustrates the details of such a practice arrangement in soccer. In the figure, the horizontal practice arrangement is the random practice and the vertical arrangement is varied practice. The athlete first practices beating an opponent, and second practices heading the ball with feet on the ground, then chest trapping the ball while stationary, and finally shooting a ground ball. This makes a perfect random practice arrangement. The second and third rounds are based on the above illustrations. If we look at the first column, all three skills are for beating opponents, but the skills are different so this arrangement is referred to as varied practice. The second, third, and fourth columns are also similarly called varied practice based on the column arrangements. Combining both random and varied practice is a very good way of practicing, with real-world skill training implications. Practitioners should creatively design training and practice methods that are logical and efficient for the purpose of enhancing athletes' abilities when they subsequently play in competitions.

Training Implications

Based on the above analysis of the different approaches to training for positive transfer of motor learning, the manipulation of practice conditions should be the central focus of training. Simpler or more difficult practice conditions than the target context should depend on the levels of learners or athletes. For training open motor skills (reaction time-based motor skills), which are executed in unpredictable environments, practitioners should focus on shortening reaction time in response to external stimuli, having quick movement times, setting up a competitive environment of play, competing against strong opponents with limited space, etc.

However, coaches or practitioners should have a very different mind-set when designing practice conditions for closed motor skills (non-reaction time based motor skills) because these skills are performed under competition conditions that are stable and predictable. The goal of practicing these types of motor skills is to perform a designated motor skill with maximum consistency, reaching the process criteria without needing to worry about changes of movement structures based on the environment. Thus, the training for closed motor skills should focus on the process, kinematics, format, techniques, and how to do things with the proper form and maximum consistency.

To be effective in training more difficult motor skills, practitioners need to break down a difficult motor skill into several parts which should be practiced separately and then later combined together to practice the entire skill. The key issue is how to break a whole skill into separate parts, more specifically at which points should the skill be broken down so that later on the entire motor skill can be reconnected together without negative consequences. Attention should also be given to the fact that there could be a relationship between any two adjacent parts of a motor skill. For example, in a gymnastic floor movement, in order to perform a 180 degree airborne rotation, the athlete must develop reasonable horizontal linear momentum and then transfer this to vertical momentum in order to have a sufficient airborne time. Thus, the athlete's ability to successfully complete this difficult skill largely depends on how high he/she can jump into the air, which in turn depends on the speed of linear momentum before jumping. If it is too fast, the linear inertia will push the athlete's body to continuously move forward and, as a result, he/she will unable to properly and suddenly jump into a vertical direction. But if the approach is too slow, the athlete cannot jump high enough from the horizontal to vertical direction so the athlete is unable to complete a 180-degree rotation due to lack of both height and sufficient airborne time. From this example, we can see that although the approach run and the airborne phase are two separate parts that can be practiced individually, they are also interconnected because the quality of the approach run determines how high the jump will be. Without sufficient jump height, the athlete simply cannot perform the airborne rotation and execute the summersault properly. This example clearly demonstrates how each part of a skill can positively or negatively affect the adjacent part. Hence, practitioners should have a clear understanding of biomechanical principles related to each part of a motor skill and then practice the different parts scientifically and logically.

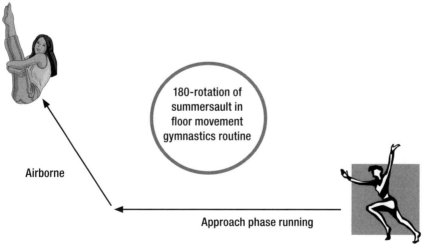

FIGURE 11.6. Gymnastic practice routine.

Eventually, all these separate parts are combined together to be one entire skill. During the process of practice, practitioners could use different kinds of equipment, slow motion, and simplified practice methods to accomplish the designated goals of training. Practitioners should be creative and aware of the relationships between the adjacent parts of the skills. In sum, training closed motor skills is truly different from training open motor skills. The above introduction just illustrates a few examples for each category of skill practices so that practitioners can base training programs on their learners' practical situations such as skill level, age, type of sport, experience, etc.

Perceptual Elements Elements

1. **Football player is seeing his teammates.**

COURTESY OF BIGSTOCKPHOTO.COM

2. **Rugby player is watching opponent to determine what to do next.**

COURTESY OF BIGSTOCKPHOTO.COM

3. **Runner is hearing how far away his opponents are.**

COURTESY OF GEEK PHILOSOPHER PHOTOS

Conceptual Elements

Example 1.	Understand soccer offside rule.
Example 2.	Understand basketball carry rule.
Example 3.	Understand volleyball game rules.
Example 4.	Understand the meaning of soccer counterattack.
Example 5.	Understand tennis serving rule.
Example 6.	Understand gymnastic judging criteria.
Example 7.	Understand basketball substitute rule, etc.

In order to maximize learning outcomes through transfer of learning, in addition to controlling practice conditions as described above, practitioners should also encourage learners to pay attention to conceptual and perceptual factors during the motor learning process because they are an integral part of the whole learning process. *Perceptual factors* are those stimuli to which attention is paid through human exterioceptual senses such as vision, audition, cutaneous sensations, and smell. In other words, the learner must pay attention to external stimuli by using his/her exteriosensory organs; this is a crucial part of an overall learning process. A basketball player must have a sense of the whereabouts of his/her teammates and opponents at every moment in competition. Likewise, a martial arts master should not only always be alert for the opponents in front of him/her, but also through audition be aware of those behind. The proper use of the human senses, integrated with motor learning, should be deemed as one of the most imperative factors to control in the learning process.

In addition, learners should have a good understanding of the *conceptual factors* that include rules, strategies, tactics, game plans, formations, etc. By understanding these concepts, athletes can use such knowledge to gain advantages in competition, avoid faults, and play by the rules. For example, soccer players should understand the meaning of the offsides rule, intentional and unintentional faults, etc. and as well know other rules and regulations of the game. Each sport has its own unique rules, regulations and play concepts that should be considered as an integral part of motor learning process.

In conclusion, motor learning is a manipulated process based on the specific characteristics of the sport, physical activities, or physical exercise being learned. Also, motor learning training process should be designed to take into account the learners' experience, skill level, gender, personality, psychological well-being and many other factors. Once practitioners understand the key principles of the motor learning process, they can creatively design motor skill practice for maximizing learning outcomes without worrying about the practice performance that can be artificially boosted or downgraded temporarily. The key issue is how practitioners can achieve the maximum positive transfer of learning for long-term learning outcomes.

Key Terms to Remember

- *Transfer of learning* is the gain or the loss of a person's proficiency in one task as a result of previous practice or experience in another task.
- *Part practice* involves breaking down a difficult motor skill into two or more parts to be practiced one-by-one using a progressive approach.
- *Whole practice* refers to the learner combining all different parts of a skill together to learn and execute the complete skill.

- *Slow-motion* practice refers to slowing down the speed of execution of the motor skill during the learning process.

- *Blocked practice* involves consistently repeating the same motor skill again and again.

- *Random practice* involves the learner practicing several motor skills together, performing each motor skill only once and then switching to another skill.

- *Constant practice* refers to situations in which a learner practices a specific version of a particular task.

- *Varied practice* refers to a learner practicing the same skill at different positions, directions, or with other variables.

- *Perceptual factor* refers to those stimuli to which attention is paid through human exterioceptual senses such as vision, audition, cutaneous sensations, and smell.

- *Conceptual factors* include rules, strategies, tactics, game plans, formations, etc.

Student Assignments for Connecting Theory to Practice

- Explain the main principles of designing motor skill training based on the theory of transfer of learning.

- Explain the main rationales of designing motor skill training for high-level athletes and explain why.

- Explain the main rationales of designing motor skill training for novice athletes and explain why.

- When training novice learners, which practice strategies would you like to use? Explain why.

- When training elite athletes, which practice strategies would you like to use? Explain why.

- Which factors would you like to manipulate when you design motor skill training? Explain why.

- What are the common problems for designing motor skill training? Explain why?

- Explain the importance of transfer of learning concept in motor learning process.

REFERENCES

Bardy, B. G. (2011). Learning new skills in Multimodal Enactive Environments. *BIO Web of Conferences, 1,* 4.

Bowers, R. W., & Fox, E. L. (1992). *Sports physiology.* Dubuque, IA: Wm. C. Brown Publishers.

Ernest, B. (2011). *Slow practice will get you there faster* (2nd ed.). Ljubljana: Ben Hogan.

Fitts, P. M. (1954). The information capacity of the human motor system in controlling the amplitude of movement. *Journal of Experimental Psychology, 47,* 381–391.

Fitts, P. M., & Posner, M. I. (1967). Human performance. Belmont, CA: Brooks/Cole.

Fox, E., Bowers, R., & Foss, M. (1993). *The physiological basis for exercise and sport.* Dubuque, IA: Brown & Benchmark.

Guadagnoli M. A., & Lee, T. D. (2004). Challenge point: A framework for conceptualizing the effects of various practice conditions in motor learning. *Journal of Motor Behavior, 36,* 212–224.

Hikosaka, O., Rand, M. K., Nakamura, K., Miyachi, S., Kitaguchi, K., Sakai, K., . . . Shimo, Y. (2002). Long-term retention of motor skill in macaque monkeys and human. *Experimental Brain Research, 147,* 494–504.

Holt, J. E., Ward, P., & Wallhead, T. L. (2006). The transfer of learning from play practices to game play in young adult soccer players. *Journal of Physical Education and Sport Pedagogy, 11,* 101–118.

Kreighbaum, E., & Barthels, K. M. (1996). *Biomechanics: A qualitative approach for studying human movement.* Boston, MA: Ally and Bacon.

Lee, T. D. (1988). Transfer-appropriate processing: A framework for conceptualizing practice effect in motor learning. In O. G. Meijer & K. Roth (Eds.), *Advances in psychology: Complex movement behavior – The motor-action controversy.* New York, NY: Elservier nScience Publishing Company.

Magill, R. A., & Anderson, D. (2013). *Motor learning and control: Concepts and applications.* Boston, MA: McGraw Hill.

Martens, R. (2012). *Successful coaching.* Champion, IL: Human Kinetics

Meijer, O. G., & Roth, K. (1988). *Advances in psychology: Complex movement behavior – The motor-action controversy.* New York, NY: Elservier nScience Publishing Company.

Kalat, J. W. (2009). *Biological psychology* (10th ed.). Belmont, CA: Wadsworth.

Krakauer, J. W., Mazzoni, P., Ghazizadeh, A., Ravindran, R., & Shadmehr, R. (2006). Generalization of motor learning depends on the history of prior action. *Journal of Plos Biology, 4,* e316–371.

Schmidt, R. A., & Wrisberg, C. A. (2008). *Motor learning and performance: A situation-based learning approach.* Champaign, IL: Human Kinetics.

Seidler, R. D. (2010). Neural correlates of motor learning, transfer of learning, and learning to learn. *Exercise Sport Science Review, 38,* 3–9.

Teixeira, L. A. (2000). Timing and force components in bilateral transfer of learning. *Brain and Cognition, 44,* 455–469.

Tous-Ral, J. M., Muiños, R., Liutsko, L., & Forero, C. G. (2012). Effects of sensory information, movement direction, and hand use on fine motor precision. *Journal of Perceptual Motor Skills, 115,* 261–272.

Wang, J. (2010). Strategies for filling a gap between practice and competition performances. *Journal of Physical Education, Recreation and Dance, 81,* 26–32.

Wang, J., & Griffin, M. (1997). Kinematical analysis of the soccer curve ball kick. *The Professional Journal of the National Strength and Conditioning, 19,* 54–58.

Wang, J., & Wiese Bjornstal, D. (1994). Mechanical and anatomical analysis of the soccer instep shot. *The Professional Journal of the National Strength and Conditioning, 16,* 34–38.

Index

About the Authors

JIN WANG

Jin Wang, PhD, is a tenured professor in health and physical education at Kennesaw State University in Kennesaw, Georgia, USA. He teaches motor learning, motor development and sport psychology. Dr. Wang graduated from the University of Minnesota with a PhD in kinesiology. He has published more than 60 peer-reviewed articles and made more than 130 presentations at conferences, congresses, and symposiums. Dr. Wang is a certified sport psychology consultant for the Association of Applied Sport Psychology; a registered sport psychology consultant for the United States Olympic Committee Registry; a research consortium fellow of the American Alliance for Health, Physical Education, Recreation and Dance (AAHPERD); and a member of the Scientific-Technical Committee of Football in Spain. Dr. Wang was the Chair of the Sport Psychology Academy of AAHPERD, and the Director of Sport Psychology at the International Council for Health, Physical  Education, Recreation and Dance. Dr. Wang was a recipient of the distinguished scholarship award at the Southern District of AAHPERD and the College of Health and Human Service at Kennesaw State University. He also received the R. Tait McKenzie Award from the American Alliance for Health, Physical Education, Recreation and Dance. Dr. Wang has been invited to many different countries as a technical and sport psychology consultant to provide his consultations to world-class, Olympic, professional athletes and coaches. He is an invited speaker and consultant of many sports organizations and countries.

SHIHUI CHEN

Shihui Chen, PhD, an associate professor at the Health and Physical Education Department at the Hong Kong Institute of Education, earned an MS in Adapted Physical Education from the University of Wisconsin, LaCrosse, and a PhD in Adapted Kinesiology from the University of New Mexico, USA. He is the current director (HK) of the Asian Society of Adapted Physical Education, as well as the Secretary General of Asian Council of Exercise and Sports Science (ACESS). Dr. Chen was a tenured associate professor at the University of Texas Pan American, and had taught motor learning and development, motor development of children with disabilities, and adapted physical education for undergraduate and graduate programs. Dr. Chen is also the program leader of the sports science program, and the MEd and EdD program coordinator at HKIEd. Dr. Chen is the APE section editor for APCESS journals (AJESS). He is a certified Adapted Physical Educator (CAPE). Dr. Chen was the Research Fellow of the Research Consortium under AAHPERD; he has successfully received more than 20 research, teaching development, and knowledge grants, and has conducted many public seminar and workshops for HK school teachers. Dr. Chen has published approximately 60 research articles in referred journals.